HEAVEN

HEAVEN

The Logic of Eternal Joy

Jerry L. Walls

OXFORD
UNIVERSITY PRESS

2002

OXFORD
UNIVERSITY PRESS

Oxford   New York
Auckland   Bangkok   Buenos Aires   Cape Town   Chennai
Dar es Salaam   Delhi   Hong Kong   Istanbul   Karachi   Kolkata
Kuala Lumpur   Madrid   Melbourne   Mexico City   Mumbai   Nairobi
São Paulo   Shanghai   Singapore   Taipei   Tokyo   Toronto

and an associated company in Berlin

Copyright © 2002 by Jerry L. Walls

Published by Oxford University Press, Inc.
198 Madison Avenue, New York, New York 10016

www.oup.com

Library of Congress Cataloging-in-Publication Data
Walls, Jerry L.
Heaven : the logic of eternal Joy / Jerry L. Walls.
p. cm
Includes bibliographical references and index.
ISBN 0-19-511302-0
1. Heaven.   I. Title.
BT846.2 .W35 2002
236'.24—dc21   2001036294

2 4 6 8 9 7 5 3 1

Printed in the United States of America
on acid-free paper

To Yukie
In appreciation for your anticipation

and

To Angela Rose
(Death, having lost its sting, will no
longer raise questions I
cannot answer to your satisfaction)

and

Jonathan Levi
(Yes, Cokes are free in Heaven and
that's only the beginning,
and no it will never get boring)

I also dedicated *Hell* to you two,
but this is the one you want!

ACKNOWLEDGMENTS

Several people deserve thanks for help in producing this book. Among those who read parts of it in various stages and offered critical comment are: Avery Dulles, Yukie Hirose, Toddy Holeman, Curt Lee, Jim Lyons, Ed Madden, Terry Muck, Richard John Neuhaus, Sue Nicholson, Jim Thobaben, and Külli Toñiste. I also benefited much from the summer discussion group organized by Brian Marshall, which discussed earlier versions of several chapters over dinner at the Lexington City Brewery. Detailed comments on several chapters by Paul Griffiths and Mike Peterson were very useful in helping me clarify and strengthen my arguments. Pat Wilson and I have been arguing about the issues of the last chapter of this book ever since our days in graduate school together at Notre Dame. This discussion as well as his criticism of earlier versions of the chapter have been invaluable, though he remains unconvinced that life has the sort of meaning I affirm. In the same vein, thanks to my students at Asbury Theological Seminary for stimulating discussion of the issues addressed in this book over several years. Thanks also to Phil Tallon for research on the cover art. And to Billy, Collins, and Strawn for moral support. Finally, I want to express gratitude to the administration of Asbury Theological Seminary for sabbatical leaves that allowed me to concentrate on writing this book for extended periods of time.

CONTENTS

HEAVEN

INTRODUCTION

I

In one of the most intriguing passages in Augustine's *Confessions*, he relates a remarkable experience he had with his mother, Monica, just a few days before she died. At the time, he was a recently baptized Christian whose conversion was due in no small part to the persistence, prayers, and tears of his mother. They had been on a long and tiring journey and were refreshing themselves before a sea voyage they had planned. He reports that they were alone and were leaning from a window that overlooked the garden of the house in which they were staying. Their conversation, which Augustine described as "serene and wonderful," turned to pondering the question of what life in heaven for the saints must be like. As they sought for insight into this great mystery, they were led to the conclusion "that no bodily pleasure, however great it might be and whatever earthly light might shed lustre upon it, was worthy of comparison, or even mention, beside the happiness of the life of the saints." Then something extraordinary occurred. While their discussion about heaven continued and they were "longing for it and straining for it with all the strength of our hearts," Augustine claims that "for one fleeting instant we reached out and touched it."[1]

Shortly after this ecstatic, mystical experience in which the pair momentarily tasted heaven, Monica said that she was ready to die. Her only reason for wanting to stay in this world had been to see her son converted to Christianity. "God has granted my wish and more besides, for I now see you as his servant, spurning such happiness as the world can give. What is left for me to do in this world?"

About five days after this, Monica was in bed with a fever. Earlier she had expressed a desire to die in her own country and be buried at her husband's side. Now she asks only of Augustine that after her death, "wherever you may be, you should remember me at the altar of the Lord." As he carried out this wish a few days later, Augustine prayed to God that those who read his book would remember both his father and his mother. In particular, it was his prayer that they "will be my fellow citizens in the eternal Jerusalem for which your people sigh throughout their pilgrimage, from the time when they set out until the time when they return to you."[2]

Now let us "fast forward" to the twenty-first century. It is most instructive to compare Augustine's longing for heaven with all his heart and his conviction that Christians sigh for it "throughout their pilgrimage" with the attitude of some contemporary Christian spokesmen. Consider, for instance, the place heaven occupies in Harvard theologian Gordon Kaufman's systematic theology. A few pages after expressing the view that we have no reason to believe life continues beyond the grave, he writes, "We are now in a position to dispose rather quickly of such symbols as the 'last judgment,' 'heaven,' and 'hell.'"[3]

Augustine and Kaufman are vastly separated by far more than mere time. Indeed, it would be hard to overstate the difference between the perspective of one who believes heaven is a glorious reality to be longed for throughout one's life and that of one who sees heaven as nothing more than a symbol to be disposed of "rather quickly."

Or compare Monica's spurning of the happiness of this world and her anticipation of heaven with the views of contemporary feminist theologian Rosemary Radford Ruether. Ruether wonders whether the whole notion of life after death is even a concern for women. Following Charlotte Perkins Gilman, Ruether suggests that male religion has focused on death and how to escape it, while for women the pivotal experience has been birth, and the primary concern has been to nurture ongoing life on this earth. Accordingly, Ruether sees the cosmic matrix of matter and energy, rather than individual persons, as the thing that is everlasting. "Acceptance of death, then, is acceptance of the finitude of our individuated centers of being, but also our identification with the larger matrix as our total self that contains us all."[4] In light of this, Ruether has a very different conception of our calling in life and how this affects our wishes for our children. "It is not our calling to be concerned about the eternal meaning of our lives, and religion should not make this the focus of its message. Our responsibility is to use our temporal life span to create a just and good community for our generation and for our children."[5]

Again, there is a gaping chasm between the aspirations Monica had for Augustine and those Reuther says we should have for our children. While a just and good community is hardly a thing to be lightly regarded or devalued, no such temporal good could even begin to compare with the eternal community of perfect joy that Monica desired for her son to experience.

It may be tempting for contemporary persons to dismiss Augustine and Monica's preoccupation with heaven as part and parcel of a precritical, even premedieval, mindset that is no longer tenable for those who have lived through the Enlightenment and beyond. The fact is, however, that heaven has been a pervasive element in Christian thinking through the ages, and contemporary indifference to the hereafter is the exception to the norm. Consider, for instance, the comments of the great Leibniz on another author he was reviewing. Leibniz noted that the author observed that frequently we are poor judges of real happiness, and that often there is more happiness in a contented poor man than in the palace of a great man. While this is a commonplace observation in every age, the author went on to claim that "the greatest felicity here on earth lies in the hope of future happiness," a view that Leibniz went on to endorse as completely agreeing with his own.[6] Now this latter view is not a commonplace of every age, and certainly it is rather foreign to many persons in our age, even many who profess to believe in heaven.

A fuller statement of the sort of perspective Leibniz represents is spelled out by John Wesley in the eighteenth century in the preface to his sermons.

> To candid, reasonable men I am not afraid to lay open what have been the inmost thoughts of my heart. I have thought, I am creature of a day, passing through life as an arrow through the air. I am a spirit come from God and returning to God; just hovering over the great gulf, till a few moments hence I am no more seen—I drop into an unchangeable eternity! I want to know one thing, the way to heaven—how to land safe on that happy shore. God himself has condescended to teach the way: for this very end he came from heaven. He hath written it down in a book. O give me that book! At any price give me the Book of God! I have it. Here is knowledge enough for me. Let me be *homo unius libri*.[7]

Wesley's nod toward "candid, reasonable men" reminds us that he lived and wrote during the height of the Enlightenment, when reason was increasingly recognized as the guide to life. It was Wesley's conviction that the only truly reasonable way to live is with the goal of heaven in clear sight.

Of course, part of what makes a belief or way of life reasonable is the larger web of beliefs to which it is connected. Notice how Wesley situates heaven in such a larger web. First, he describes himself as a "creature of a day" whose life in this world amounts to only "a few moments" in comparison to eternity. The context of eternity charges this life with enormous significance and magnifies the importance of choices that might seem trivial in a smaller domain.

Next, consider what he viewed as the central event of history, and how it is intimately related to this account of the human drama: "God himself has condescended to teach the way: for this very end he came down from heaven." The point of the incarnation was to achieve human salvation, a salvation that eventuates in a perfected relationship with God. Heaven is another name for this perfected relationship. Furthermore, this framework of beliefs determines what is truly important for human beings to know, namely, the way to achieve this relationship. This explains why Wesley calls himself *homo unius libri*, a man of one book. This is certainly not a literal description of his reading habits, given that he read widely in all areas of learning. But it is a serious statement of the relative importance of what can be known. The one thing that is absolutely essential for us to know is the way to heaven.

But for traditional Christianity, knowledge of the way to heaven is not only important for heaven's sake, it is also crucial for this life to be truly meaningful. Indeed, the strong version of this claim maintains that life here is meaningless unless there is a hereafter. A closely related claim is that morality, an essential component of a meaningful life, requires heaven. Without an afterlife, so the argument goes, there are no convincing moral sanctions. One of the most forthright versions of this thesis was advanced by Wesley's earlier compatriot, John Locke.

> The philosophers, indeed, shewed the beauty of virtue: they set her off so as drew men's eyes and approbation to her; but leaving her unendowed, very few were willing to espouse her. . . . But now there being put into the scales, on her side, "an exceeding and immortal weight of glory," interest is come about to her; and virtue now is visibly the most enriching purchase, and by much the best bargain. . . . The view of heaven and hell will cast a slight upon the short pleasures and pains of this present state, and give attractions and encouragements to virtue, which reason and interest, and the care of ourselves, cannot but allow and prefer. Upon this foundation, and upon this only, morality stands firm, and may defy all competition.[8]

Locke's account of the connection between heaven (and hell) and morality has struck some as a rather repugnant version of Christian hedonism.[9] Evaluations aside, however, it is clear that for Locke morality needs not merely God but the more specific doctrines of heaven and hell if it is to be firmly established.

It is important to understand that it is this broad framework of beliefs about eternity, incarnation, morality, meaning, and revelation that makes sense of the traditional Christian emphasis on heaven. Heaven is an integral part of this majestic and sweeping vision of life. Isolated from this framework, it is hard to understand the passionate interest previous generations of believers have had in it. But when viewed in its proper context, it is not at all surprising that heaven has had remarkable resilience and staying power, even in the face of modern criticism of the larger framework of beliefs that give it life.

In view of this context, it is no great wonder that fascination with heaven survived the Enlightenment and continued strong into the nineteenth century, despite the rising tide of secularism. One measure of this fascination is the fact that over fifty books on heaven were published in the United States alone between 1830 and 1875. A novel on heaven, *The Gates Ajar*, published in 1868 by Elizabeth Stuart Phelps, was, next only to *Uncle Tom's Cabin*, the most popular book of its period.[10] And deep into the twentieth century, belief in heaven remained prevalent, at least in the United States. A Gallup poll published in *Newsweek* during Easter season 1989 indicated that 94% of Americans believe in God and 77% believe in heaven. Of those who believe, 76% rated their prospects of making it there good or excellent.[11] A poll from 1994 suggested that belief in heaven is becoming even more widespread. Of those polled, 93% affirmed belief in heaven, while 69% of these thought they had a good or excellent chance of going there.[12]

II

These figures notwithstanding, the *Newsweek* article raises doubts about the continuing viability of belief in heaven. These doubts are connected with the well-documented decline of belief in heaven's ever shady counterpart, namely, hell. Such was the trend as long ago as the seventeenth century, and by the nineteenth century, fear of damnation was largely a thing of the past. Thus, Kenneth L. Woodward raises the obvious question: "If hell has, for all of its old intents and purposes, disappeared from modern consciousness, can heaven be far behind?" The aforementioned Harvard theologian is quoted, not surprisingly, in support of this projection. Citing what he sees as "irreversible changes," he declares, "I don't think there can be any future for heaven and hell."[13] Historical data might also be adduced in support of this claim. Colleen McDannell and Bernhard Lang, who have traced the variations in heavenly belief from the first century through the late twentieth, agree that heaven does not have near the significance in Christian thought that it previously had. Those who have rejected the symbolic view of heaven and insisted on its reality are still left, for a number of reasons, "with an equally meager picture of heaven."[14] Even the most conservative are not exempt from this situation, according to McDannell and Lang. "Although fundamentalists would discard the suggestion that heaven no longer is an active part of their belief system, eternal life has become an unknown place or a state of vague identity."[15]

While heaven has been conceived in a variety of pictures and images in the history of Christian thought, it has consistently been understood as a definite reality with identifiable features. Two basically different accounts of heaven have recurred down the ages, according to McDannell and Lang. On one end of the spectrum is the theocentric view of heaven. In its most extreme version, heaven is a timeless experience of contemplating the infinitely fascinating reality of God in all of his aspects. Eternal joy on this account consists entirely of the beatific vision, requiring no dimension of human fellowship to be complete. On the other end of the spectrum is the anthropocentric view of heaven. There the emphasis is upon being reunited with family and friends. In its most fully developed version, heaven is essentially like this life, without, of course, the evil and suffering that mar our present happiness. Heaven thus construed would include poetry, pianos, puppies, poppies, and sex, all at their best.

Given the variety of views along this spectrum, it is not easy to identify *the* orthodox or traditional view of heaven. If we consult historic standards of orthodoxy such as creeds and confessions, we receive precious little help on this question. In Luther's Large Catechism, for instance, he barely mentions "the life everlasting" in his commentary on the Apostles' Creed. The Westminster Confession is hardly more articulate on the nature of heaven. In its chapter on the last judgment, we are informed that after the judgment "shall the righteous go into everlasting life, and receive the fullness of joy and refreshing which shall come from the presence of the Lord."[16] No further description of heaven is forthcoming. This reserve is particularly striking in view of the overall length of this document and its relatively detailed discussion of matters such as providence, liberty of conscience, the sabbath, and the civil magistrate. The Thirty-Nine Articles of the Anglican Church are even more reticent on the subject of the hereafter. While there is an article repudiating purgatory, no article is devoted to heaven or everlasting life. The Anglican Catechism does, however, have a section on the Christian hope. There, heaven is defined as "eternal life in our enjoyment of God." A few questions later, everlasting life is described as "a new existence, in which we are united with all the people of God, in the joy of fully knowing and loving God and each other."[17]

As modest as these descriptions are, they indicate that a theocentric view of heaven has been the dominant model of orthodox theology. This is not to say that an extreme version of that model was accepted as normative, but that the theocentric dimension was emphasized as the essence of heaven. Augustine's developed view of heaven is instructive in this connection. While he held a rather ascetic view of heaven in his earlier thinking, his picture of heaven was more human in his mature thought, without losing its theocentric shape. Augustine's mature account of heaven in its broad features was dominant throughout the period of medieval theology. And while the Renaissance was characterized by predominantly anthropocentric visions of the afterlife, the reformers, both Protestant and Catholic, recovered an essentially theocentric conception of heaven at the end of this period. After surveying a number of such reformers on both sides of the divide, McDannell and Lang observed, "If we eliminate the diverse and unique elements which mark the heaven of Luther, Calvin, Polti, de Sales, Nicole, and Baxter, and concentrate on what they share in common, a theocentric model emerges."[18] This general consensus is reflected in the rather concise remarks on heaven we find in the classical confessions.

It is noteworthy that the nineteenth century witnessed a resurgence of anthropocentric, and sometimes sentimental, visions of heaven. Indeed, as noted earlier, that period was characterized by fascination with heaven, and not surprisingly, earlier anthropocentric accounts of the afterlife were developed in even more imaginative detail. It is worth pondering whether contemporary agnosticism about heaven is at least partly a backlash against such earlier excesses, somewhat like the reformers' reaction against overly elaborate Renaissance speculations.

No doubt this reaction is a factor in the current reserve about heaven, but there is surely more involved. The restraint in the classical confessions does not reflect any of the ambivalence about heaven that characterizes the contemporary mindset. Believers such as Baxter and Wesley who would readily assent to these confessions as articulating the doctrinal substance of their faith were hardly lukewarm about heaven. So the reserve about heaven in classical confessions still has lying behind it profound belief and warm desire. Indeed, the modesty of the confessions may be read as allowing considerable room for speculation within certain bounds. That is, perhaps they intended to leave significant space for a certain variety of opinions about the details of the life everlasting. They may also reflect the fact that heaven has not been a matter of formal controversy in the same way that Christology and soteriology have, matters that receive more detailed comment in official confessions. Apart from the issue about purgatory, heaven has not been a subject of much formal theological controversy.

To reiterate, then, heaven has been a subject of hearty and substantive belief in Christian culture since the first century, even while official statements of faith maintained reserve about the details of the afterlife. And while many still profess belief in heaven, that belief seems to be more vague and ambivalent now than it has ever been. The question is, Why is this the case?

III

I do not think there is a simple answer to this question. Surely a number of factors are involved. Some, no doubt, are simply at a loss when they try to think seriously about the matter. Kenneth Grayston has recently suggested that Protestants refrain from talking about heaven "less perhaps from loss of belief in life after death as from an embarrassed lack of imagery for speaking of the subject."[19] Part of the remedy for this, Grayston believes, is a fresh understanding of biblical imagery, particularly that of the book of Revelation and its contemporary significance. The book of Revelation has been given to fanciful as well as fanatical interpretation, and a recovery of its imagery that avoids these extremes is surely crucial for a substantive belief in heaven.

But going beyond imagery, others, no doubt, simply find the idea of heaven incredible or even unintelligible. Even believers are likely to find the notion baffling in certain respects. Worries about these can undermine a meaningful belief in heaven. Consider in this light the following autobiographical musings from eminent American philosopher W. V. Quine.

> I may have been nine when I began to worry about the absurdity of heaven and eternal life, and about the jeopardy that I was incurring by those evil doubts. Presently I recognized that the jeopardy was illusory if the doubts were right. My somber conclusion was nonetheless disappointing, but I rested with it. I said nothing of this to my parents, but I did harangue one or another of my little friends, and I vaguely remember a parental repercussion. Such, then, was the dim beginning of my philosophical concern. Perhaps the same is true of the majority of philosophers.[20]

Unfortunately, Quine does not specify the nature of his worries about the absurdity of eternal life and heaven. From the standpoint of the stark naturalism of his later philosophical views, heaven would obviously seem absurd, but presumably he was not a full-blown naturalist at age nine. Rather, he implies that disbelief in heaven was one of the things that first led him to his eventual naturalism. Indeed, it was instrumental in awaking him from his "dogmatic slumbers" into a life of philosophical reflection, as he suggests may be true for the majority of philosophers.

If so, then the notion of heaven is, to say the least, a potent source of philosophical stimulation. I believe Quine is quite right about this. His claim that heaven is absurd is another matter, and certainly requires more than dogmatic assertion. If pressed, no doubt Quine would offer more, for the idea of heaven does raise genuine perplexities, as already noted. For instance, there are problems surrounding the issue of personal identity. This is a difficult question in its own right, but it is exacerbated when we think of persons taking on immortality. There are also questions about the whole idea of eternal joy. It has been argued that such a notion is not even internally coherent. And beyond this, there are questions about the relation between salvation and belief in Jesus. How can one's eternal fate depend upon one's beliefs about a specific historical person, particularly if one lives in a culture where Christian teaching is not readily available, if at all? These are some of the issues I will tackle.

There is no doubt that some have given up belief in heaven because they have been troubled by questions such as these. I am inclined to think that the number of persons in this category is relatively few, however. Most who are indifferent about heaven could not formulate the problem of personal identity and say why it poses a difficulty for the Christian doctrine of everlasting life.

In addition to internal problems in the notion of heaven, belief in the doctrine has also been adversely affected by broad cultural and intellectual trends. The naturalistic mindset of the radical Enlightenment has certainly taken its toll on conviction about heaven's reality. Where miracles are ruled out as impossible, the distinctly Christian basis for belief in heaven is undermined. In particular, if Jesus' resurrection is denied, believers can no longer hold faith in the New Testament promise that they will be raised to life in the same manner as Jesus was. Gordon Kaufman is quite explicit about this connection. In step with his fellow radical theologians, Kaufman rejects the claim that Jesus was actually raised from the dead and construes the "appearances" of Jesus accordingly. The consequence is obvious: "If, however, the man Jesus was not restored to life as traditionally believed, 'the appearances' being events of quite another order, then the special basis on which the Christian hope for immortality was founded is completely gone."[21]

Surely some of those who have given up belief in heaven have done so because they have consciously and reflectively come to believe in a naturalistic worldview. And many others have only a vague belief in heaven, or none at all, because they have unconsciously been steeped in the spirit of the age with its implicit, if not always spoken, naturalism. Where it is tacitly assumed that science and religion are at odds and that a truly rational person cannot believe in a real supernatural God, a meaningful belief in heaven will inevitably dissipate, even if it does not overtly disappear.

But there is more involved in the decline in hearty belief in heaven than the implicit assumption that science and religion are incompatible and the background hubris of naturalism. To see what more may be involved, reflect for a moment on Charles Taylor's analysis of modern unbelief: "Secularization doesn't just arise because people get a lot more educated, and science progresses. This has some effect, but it isn't decisive. What matters is that masses of people can sense moral sources of a quite different kind, ones that don't necessarily suppose a God."[22] By contrast, "An 'age of belief' is one in which all credible moral sources involve God."[23] In such an age, there is no way to make sense of the spiritual dimension of our lives without a serious belief in God.

If Taylor's analysis of the springs of secularism is correct, I think it has obvious implications for the hope of heaven as well. In short, substantive belief in heaven has declined largely because many modern people think they can make moral and spiritual sense of their lives without it.

One likely source of this attitude is no doubt Kant's moral philosophy. It is well known that Kant believed we needed belief in God, freedom, and immortality as "postulates of practical reason" in order to make sense of morality. But while morality leads to religion, morality must be kept pure from religious considerations. Kant issued the following warning in this regard: "But here again everything remains disinterested and based only on duty, without being based on fear or hope as incentives, which, if they become principles, would destroy the entire moral worth of actions."[24] Ironically, the hope of heaven cannot have a place in moral motivation, even though immortality must be postulated to make sense of morality. Indeed, this view may be more than ironic; it may be incoherent. But whether Kant's position is coherent or not, his suspicion of heaven as a legitimate moral motivation lingers with us to this very day.

Another important taproot of the modern rejection of heaven as a moral source is the combined effect of the work of Marx, Feuerbach, and Freud. Take the following words of Feuerbach as typical in this regard: "God is the existence corresponding to my wishes and feelings: he is the just one, the good, who fulfills my wishes. Nature, this world, is an existence which contradicts my wishes, my feelings. . . . But heaven is the existence adequate to my wishes, my longing; thus there is no distinction between God and heaven."[25] And in the same vein, consider these lines from Freud: "We shall tell ourselves that it would be very nice if there were a God who created the world and was a benevolent Providence, and if there were a moral order in the universe and an afterlife; but it is a very striking fact that all this is exactly as we are bound to wish it to be."[26]

Our age is very sensitive to the voice of suspicion warning us of deceptive self-interest disguised in the most lofty of moral and religious dress. It would be nice indeed if heaven existed, but the fact that we feel this way is for our postmodern age a strong indication that it must not.

Taken together, these sources depict belief in heaven as a positively pernicious moral influence. Whereas Locke saw heaven as necessary to underwrite virtue, for these modern voices heaven undermines virtue. While traditionally belief in heaven has been seen as essential for giving meaning to this life, these writers see it as a belief that compromises and corrupts this life. To hope for heaven is to be dishonest, self-deceived, self-absorbed, and emotionally immature. Moreover, the hope of heaven can be, and has been, used to exploit and manipulate the economically disadvantaged by urging them to sacrifice their earthly happiness in return for a mansion above. With all this ringing in modern and postmodern ears, it is no wonder that substantive hope for heaven has been muted at best. Nor is it surprising that those who are indifferent toward heaven, or even hostile, can claim a mantle of moral superiority.

Recall that Ruether depicts concern for heaven as driven by a masculine individualism that refuses to accept our finitude and identify with "the larger matrix as our total self that contains us all." Indifference toward heaven, by contrast, is a selfless stance in favor of nurturing continuing life on this earth. Not to care about heaven is thus a morally courageous position over against the morally, spiritually, and emotionally inferior position of those whose thirst for immortality reflects a dishonest accounting of our place in the total scheme of things.

Kaufman sounds the same note in challenging those who are interested in personal survival after death.

> To insist, for example, that God will surely grant man some sort of self-aware life in "heaven" after his death on earth is to demand an assurance which finite man can never have and about which, if he truly trusted God, he would not concern himself. . . . Men's unwillingness fully to trust God unless they know what he will do with them is an expression of the lingering desire to establish and preserve themselves, to be their own masters; it is a manifestation of unfaith.[27]

Kaufman is not singling out the masculine gender in this critique but is using the phrase "finite man" generically. For Kaufman, to be concerned with personal survival after death is at the heart of human sinfulness, for male and female alike. In the spirit of existentialist theologians for whom radical faith precludes objective evidence or assurances of any kind, Kaufman characterizes the heaven-bent as guilty of "unfaith." Their hearty desire for heaven is not an indication of mature faith but rather the opposite. It amounts to a childish and unrealistic unwillingness to trust God fully with our lives.

This transmutation of belief in heaven from a vitally positive spiritual and moral source into a decidedly negative one represents a religious and cultural shift of cosmic proportions. It is hard to exaggerate the consequences this shift has not only for how we conceive of salvation but also for how we conceive of ourselves and the very purpose and meaning of our lives.

IV

In view of this point alone, it is arguable that the doctrine of heaven is ripe for serious reconsideration. Moreover, there are abundant signs that Kaufman was dead wrong when he pronounced that there is no future for heaven and hell.

Consider the pervasive spiritual hunger in our culture as expressed in fascination with everything from angels to Zen. Closer to the center of the alphabet, as well as to our concerns, near-death experiences have generated enormous interest ever since they were brought to popular attention in the seventies. Even the decline of serious consideration of hell, which the *Newsweek* article noted, may be a thing of the past. In just the five years since that article appeared, three major university presses published books about hell, two of which defended it against philosophical challenges.[28] If hell is making a comeback, can heaven be far behind?

In what follows, I will show that the doctrine of heaven is far from absurd and can be defended against common objections raised against it. More positively, I will argue that the doctrine of heaven is essential to any version of Christianity worth believing, and furthermore that it is an extremely valuable concept for addressing difficult philosophical issues, not the least of which are pressing questions about theodicy, morality, and the meaning of this life. I will also argue that the phenomenon of near-death experiences can plausibly be read as supporting the Christian doctrine of heaven.

Advancing these claims will require engaging a cluster of questions that range across theology, metaphysics, epistemology, and moral philosophy. I will operate primarily as a philosopher of religion in addressing these issues, but at points I will be concerned with points of scriptural exegesis and historical theology. These are essential sources for a distinctly Christian view of heaven, which will be my main focus. I am less concerned with professional boundaries and more with engaging the full range of issues necessary to give my subject adequate treatment. Thus, I will not worry if I stray into systematic theology or related disciplines from time to time. However we approach the matter, it is clear that heaven involves a host of questions that are intellectually fascinating as well as existentially galvanizing.

HEAVEN AND GOD'S GOODNESS

I

A short time before David Hume died, James Boswell conducted an interview with the great philosopher. He described Hume as peaceful, even cheerful, and fully aware that he was approaching his end. As they talked, Boswell reports that he "contrived" to introduce the subject of immortality into the conversation: "I had a strong curiosity to be satisfied if he persisted in disbelieving in a future state even when he had death before his eyes. I was persuaded from what he now said, and from his manner of saying it, that he did persist."[1]

The details of this conversation are fascinating. Hume assured Boswell that the prospect of annihilation did not make him uneasy, and in a manner fitting such a claim, carried on the interview with humor and wit. Boswell admits that the experience temporarily unnerved him. "I was like a man in sudden danger eagerly seeking his defensive arms; and I could not but be assailed by momentary doubts while I had actually before me a man of such strong abilities and extensive enquiry dying in the persuasion of being annihilated. But I maintained my faith."

Boswell continued to probe, however, seeking a vulnerable spot in Hume's position. At one point in the account, he recalls an earlier conversation on the same topic.

He had once said to me on a forenoon, while the sun was shining bright, that he did not wish to be immortal. This was a most wonderful thought. The reason he gave was that he was very well in this state of being, and that the chances were very much against his being so well in another state; and he would rather not be more than be worse.[2]

This is a most interesting reason to reject immortality. Hume apparently saw no reason to believe heaven could be better than this life, or even as good. So it was not worth desiring or hoping for. Boswell put forward the prospect of seeing again his departed friends and asked if that held any attraction for him. Hume allowed that it did, but pointed out that they did not believe in immortality either. By all accounts, Hume maintained these convictions, along with his cheerful spirit, until his death a few weeks later.

While Hume's easy embrace of extinction may be disconcerting to believers, there is nevertheless something admirable about it. By his own account, he "never suffered a moment's abatement of [his] spirits" during his final illness.[3] He was untroubled by the implications of his philosophy and did not flinch from them in the face of death. On this point, Hume provides his critics no material to forge a charge of inconsistency between his espoused views and his own existential reactions in the crucible of life.

I want to argue, however, that Hume's philosophical case against heaven is another matter altogether. That case rests finally upon his views about God, particularly as expressed in his posthumously published *Dialogues Concerning Natural Religion*. As Hume's discussion makes clear, the most important religious issue is not merely whether God exists but what he is like. His position on this question leaves him vulnerable indeed.

II

Hume's philosophy is notoriously naturalistic. It is an attempt to give a fully satisfactory account of man and his world relying only on evidence that can be gleaned from sense observation and introspection. Whatever can be inferred from this evidence is a proper philosophical conclusion. What cannot be so inferred is philosophically out of bounds.

In view of Hume's well-known naturalism, it may come as something of a surprise that he did not urge an atheistic conclusion in his *Dialogues*. Quite to the contrary. In fact, none of the characters in the *Dialogues* is an atheist. Indeed, there is a general consensus throughout all the twists and turns of the debate on the fact of God's *being*. What is at issue is the apparently secondary matter of God's nature. It is noteworthy that Philo, the character in the *Dialogues* who is generally regarded as closest to Hume's actual views, is the one who insists that God's existence is virtually self-evident. He puts this point in the form of a question: "Supposing there were a God, who did not discover himself immediately to our senses; were it possible for him to give stronger proofs of his existence, than what appear on the face of nature?"[4]

Despite Hume's apparently staunch theism, believers should be fairly warned against embracing him as an intellectual or spiritual ally. His version of theism is so qualified that few, if any, believers would recognize it as a satisfactory account of their convictions. This, of course, would come as no surprise to Hume, for he made it clear that the sort of belief in God he affirmed had no religious significance whatsoever. Moreover, the *Dialogues* are laced throughout with irony, and all theistic affirmations must be read in this light.

The minimal content of Hume's theism is evident at the very end of the *Dialogues* where Philo sums up what he has argued throughout.

> If the whole of natural theology, as some people seem to maintain, resolves itself into one simple, though somewhat ambiguous, at least undefined proposition, *that the cause or causes of order in the universe probably bear some remote analogy to human intelligence*: If this proposition be not capable of extension, variation, or more particular explication: If it afford no inference that affects human life, or can be the source of action or forbearance: And if the analogy, imperfect as it is, can be carried no farther than to the human intelligence; and cannot be transferred, with any appearance of probability, to the other qualities of the mind: If this really be the case, what can the most inquisitive, contemplative, and religious man do more than give a plain, philosophical assent to the proposition, as often as it occurs; and believe that the arguments, on which it is established, exceed the objections which lie against it?[5]

By "plain philosophical assent," Hume means something very different from religious belief. This is apparent from the manner in which he empties his proposition of all religious value.

In the first place, Hume emphasized, the proposition is extremely modest. It is "not capable of extension, variation, or more particular explication." Hume has made this point in a vivid way a few pages earlier when he argues that the difference between atheism and theism is really just a verbal dispute. The theist will admit that the intelligence who designed the world is "very different from human reason," while the atheist will concede that the "original principle of order bears some remote analogy to it."[6] If theism contains no more distinct content than this, it is pointless for theists to quarrel with atheists.

Second, the proposition has no practical consequences. It affords "no inference that affects human life, or can be the source of any action of forbearance."[7] This points up as clearly as anything the wide gulf between Hume's philosophical assent to a minimal sort of theism and genuinely religious belief in God, for religious believers typically think that belief in God has practical implications that pervade all aspects of life.

But Hume's proposition lacks religious significance in another respect that is even more fundamental: The analogy on which it rests entails nothing about God's moral nature. Hume makes this point when he says the analogy "cannot be transferred, with any appearance of probability, to the other [i.e., moral] qualities of the mind."

Bluntly put, Hume's claim is that there is no good reason to infer that the designer of the universe is a morally good being. Rather, as we shall see, he maintained that the more probable conclusion is that God is neither good nor evil. This is a deeply important claim in its own right, but it should be noted that it underlies our two previous points as well. Hume's proposition of natural theology is modest in content largely because it says nothing about God's moral nature. Moreover, one of the main reasons the proposition is devoid of practical import is because it has no moral substance. Belief in divine goodness is one of the primary warrants for the notion that God should be obeyed, worshiped, and so on.

Indeed, most religious believers would probably sooner compromise their belief in God's omnipotence, if pressed, than their belief in his perfect goodness. This is suggested by the popular appeal of some recent religious books that scale back claims about God's power while strongly emphasizing his compassion and empathy with our suffering. Of course, most believers would probably prefer to retain strong claims about God's power as well. But it is a significant fact about religious sensibilities that convictions about divine goodness are held with such tenacity.

Obviously then, Hume struck a vital religious nerve when he turned his guns on God's goodness. This will be the focus of our concern in this chapter. First, I will spell out Hume's arguments aimed at undermining belief in divine goodness. Then I will turn to argue that Hume's view that God is amoral must be rejected, not only on intuitive grounds but on Hume's own principles as well. Finally, I will show that these conclusions have important implications for the doctrine of heaven.

III

Hume delivered a number of shrewd blows in his assault on the notion of divine goodness. The heart of his attack, of course, centers on the fact of evil in our world. In making his case, he develops three closely related, but distinct, arguments. The first of these I will call the inductive argument, the second I will call the a priori argument, and the third I will call the probability argument. The first of these I will spell out in more detail since it is especially relevant to my later argument.

The inductive argument is based on empirical evidence that our world is filled with distress. Hume establishes this point by reciting a long litany of human and animal suffering. Human suffering of all varieties is especially described with great eloquence. As an instance, consider the following as put forward by Demea, the orthodox believer in the *Dialogues*.

> The miseries of life, the unhappiness of man, the general corruptions of our nature, the unsatisfactory enjoyment of pleasures, riches, honours; these phrases have become almost proverbial in all languages. And who can doubt of what all men declare from their own immediate feeling and experience?[8]

While Cleanthes, the advocate of natural religion, contests this claim, it is accepted and elaborated by Philo. As it is further developed, Hume takes it as beyond dispute that neither man nor animals are happy in our world and that the course of nature does not tend toward such ends.

With these premises established on inductive grounds, Hume turns to introduce some important theological premises into the discussion and to draw some significant conclusions from them: "His power we allow is infinite: Whatever he wills is executed: But neither man nor any other animal are happy: Therefore he does not will their happiness. His wisdom is infinite: He is never mistaken in choosing the means to any end: But the course of nature tends not to human or animal felicity: Therefore it is not established for that purpose."[9] Notice that God's power and wisdom are fully granted and even insisted upon. It is precisely these that generate the difficulty in light of the inductively supported claims that neither man nor animals are happy. For if God is infinitely powerful as well as wise, and therefore always implements the appropriate means to achieve his desired ends, then it follows from the observed facts that he does not desire happiness for man or animals.

It is apparent where Hume's argument is headed. But to make fully explicit his intended conclusion, we need one more premise. This premise sets forth a stipulation that must be met if God is to be called good in the ordinary sense of the term. For God to be good in the ordinary sense of the term means simply that his goodness must be of essentially the same nature as human goodness. The stipulation then is this: For God to be good in the ordinary sense of the term, he must desire happiness for men and animals. And with this premise in place, the really crucial conclusion that follows is that God is not good in the ordinary sense of the term.

Of course, for all this argument shows, God could still be good in some manner that is incomprehensible to us. Hume, however, would not be much impressed by such a claim. For if God's goodness is not similar to human moral goodness at least to the minimal extent that he desires human happiness, then we are at a loss to understand what it means for God to be good.

It is at just this point that heaven comes into the discussion. Demea, the orthodox believer, appeals to eternity and the hereafter to overturn the negative conclusion about God's goodness: "This world is but a point in comparison of the universe: This life but a moment in comparison of eternity. The present evil phenomena, therefore, are rectified in other regions, and in some future period of existence."[10]

This suggestion, however, is rejected out of hand by Cleanthes: "These arbitrary suppositions can never be admitted, contrary to matter of fact, visible and uncontroverted. Whence can any cause be known but from its known effects? Whence can any hypothesis be proved but from the apparent phenomena?" For our natural theologian, the notion of heaven is pure speculation, an "arbitrary supposition." It has nothing to do with the world of sober fact, "visible and uncontroverted." He goes on to insist that the goodness of God must be vindicated exclusively in terms of the evidence of this world.

Notice the logic of the dispute. Demea, the orthodox believer, and Philo, the philosophical skeptic, agree over against Cleanthes that the world is full of pain and suffering. On the other hand, Demea and Cleanthes agree against Philo

HUME'S PHILOSOPHICAL POSITIONS ON RELIGION

	World full of suffering	God is good	Afterlife
Demea—orthodox believer	Yes	Yes	Yes
Philo—philosophical skeptic	Yes	No	No
Cleanthes—natural theologian	No	Yes	No

that God is good. Demea's belief in divine goodness leads him to a belief in an afterlife as the place where God's goodness will be fully vindicated. Cleanthes, in rejecting the afterlife, is compelled to argue that evil and misery are not as pervasive as his opponents claim it is. Philo, affirming the evil of this world and denying an afterlife, accordingly rejects divine goodness. We can chart these positions as in the table.

The principle that is crucial to Hume's whole line of argument here is that a cause can be known only from its known effects. Hume develops this in more detail in his argument against a future state in *An Inquiry Concerning Human Understanding*. This particular section of the *Inquiry* is also written in dialogue form. Here is his answer to the notion that we ought to expect reward or punishment for our behavior beyond the ordinary course of events in this life.

> You persist in imagining, that, if we grant the divine existence, for which you so earnestly contend, you may safely infer consequences from it, and add something to the experienced order of nature, by arguing from the attributes which you ascribe to your gods. You seem not to remember, that all your reasonings on this subject can only be drawn from effects to causes; and that every argument, deduced from causes to effects, must of necessity be a gross sophism; since it is impossible for you to know anything of the cause, but what you have antecedently, not inferred, but discovered to the full, in the effect.[11]

His spokesman never tires of repeating this point and insists over and again that careful reasoning always proceeds from effects to causes and never the other way around.

Hume raises, however, a challenge to this principle by means of an analogy. Suppose, he says, we saw a half-finished house surrounded by piles of bricks, mortar, and masonry tools. Surely we would rightly infer not only that the house was designed thus far but also that more would be added to it, that it would be improved, perfected, and so on.

> Why then do you refuse to admit the same method of reasoning with regard to the order of nature? Consider the world and the present life only as an imperfect building, from which you can infer a superior intelligence; and arguing from that superior intelligence, which can leave nothing imperfect; why may you not infer a more finished scheme or plan, which will receive its completion in some distant point of space or time?[12]

This analogy seems appropriate and persuasive as well as clever, but it does not carry the day in Hume's discussion.

The reason given is that there is an infinite difference between the subjects of the analogy. While we can correctly reason this way about human productions, we cannot do so when dealing with the divine. The difference is "that man is a being, whom we know by experience, whose motives and designs we are acquainted with, and whose projects and inclinations have a certain connexion and coherence, according to the laws which nature has established for the government of such a creature."[13] None of this holds with regard to God, Hume claims, so the analogy breaks down.

We are back then to the principle that a cause can only be known by its known effects, and in Hume's view the visible facts of the world are the only known effects from which we may know anything about the invisible cause of the world. As the preceding argument made clear, he thought the facts of our world offer no support at all for the notion that God is good. Rather, they undermine this claim in a rather savage way. And if there are no other relevant facts, as Hume insists, then the prospects for defending divine goodness appear bleak.

Let us turn now to Hume's a priori argument. This argument is directed, at least initially, to those who may be unconvinced by the inductive argument. Some may object to the argument by denying its inductively derived premises. In the *Dialogues*, its target is Cleanthes, who denies that the world is as full of unhappiness as Philo claims it is and argues that the amount of happiness in our world actually outweighs the amount of misery.

In response to this objection, Philo invites Cleanthes to engage in a simple thought experiment. The question he poses for consideration is the following: "Is the world considered in general, and as it appears to us in this life, different from what a man or such a limited being would, *beforehand*, expect from a very powerful, wise, and benevolent Deity?"[14] So then, the challenge is to imagine what sort of world we, or some other being of limited understanding, would expect a very powerful, wise, and benevolent Deity to create. Hume is confident that the honest person will surely admit that our world is not the sort of world we would expect such a deity to create, even if we disagree with his judgment about the proportion of misery in our world. Notice also that this argument forbids consideration of an afterlife. The question is whether this world "as it appears in this life" is what we would expect from a perfect Deity. If it is not, Hume thinks we should not infer the existence of such a Deity.

Hume makes no claim that his argument is absolutely conclusive. He readily grants that if one were antecedently convinced of God's goodness by some good argument, he might retain this belief in the face of the evil phenomena of our world. If God's goodness "could be established on any tolerable reasons *a priori*, these phenomena, however untoward, would not be sufficient to subvert that principle."[15] It is possible that there are good explanations for all the evil in our world.

But, of course, Hume does not think we have any good a priori reason for believing in God's goodness. As in his first argument, he insists that our beliefs

Whatever God's ultimate aim in creating us as he did, it is clear, if Hume is right, that he has in fact made us in such a way that we feel approval for actions that promote human happiness and feel disapproval for and judge as vicious those that cause human misery. And if God always implements appropriate means to achieve his desired ends, it is clear that he desires us to feel as we do with respect to the causes of human happiness and misery.

Our next premise is a strengthened version of another of Hume's claims noted earlier. While it goes beyond what Hume explicitly says, it is warranted because of his view that our world is full of misery.

3. God made this world in such a way that it is evident that he did not intend to promote human happiness through it, but rather, misery.

Since we have no reason, according to Hume, to believe in an afterlife, we have no reason to believe God ultimately desires our happiness or will secure it. This is bad enough, but there is another conclusion to be drawn from the preceding premises. Given the notion that our world was intended to promote misery, and the notion that God designed us to feel disapproval for actions that cause misery, it follows that:

4. God desires us to feel disapproval toward him for creating this world as he did, or even judge him vicious.

The notion that God wants us to judge him vicious surely comes as something of a surprise, but it seems warranted for those who accept Hume's claims.

Some may object to this conclusion that our natural disapproval for actions that cause human misery does not properly extend to the action of the Creator in structuring the world as he did but only to particular actions within the world. However, this objection will not hold if we recall a point made earlier, namely, that if moral attributes are meaningfully to be applied to God, they must retain the ordinary meaning they have when applied to men. Hume insisted that God's goodness must be similar to human goodness in the sense that he desires happiness for his creatures. And if this is so, our judgment about God's goodness will naturally be based on considerations that are similar to those relevant to judging human goodness.

God's action in structuring the world is a highly relevant consideration, for it is among the most important evidence we have for making judgments about God's concern for human happiness. According to Hume, the only way we can know anything about God's moral nature is by making inferences from known effects. And the structure of the world is surely a known effect of great significance in this regard. Indeed, this assumption underlies Hume's inductive argument that I have sketched.

This point is strengthened, moreover, when we recall Hume's probability argument in which he maintained that much, if not all, of the evil in the world could be eliminated if God had structured the world differently in four respects. God's failure to do this must, from Hume's perspective, require a negative moral judgment on God's intentions.

It may be objected further that perhaps God is indifferent to whether or not we infer that he is vicious, even if that inference is reasonable. But this objection is unconvincing for much the same reason as the previous one. If goodness means essentially the same thing when applied to God as it does when applied to men, there is reason to think we will naturally make judgments about God's moral nature when confronted by relevant considerations. It is as reasonable to assume God intends us to make these judgments as it is to think he designed us to make certain moral judgments about human actions. So the foregoing inference that God wants us to judge him vicious seems entirely justified on Hume's principles.

There is, moreover, no easy way to avoid the conclusion that God must actually be evil, once we have come this far with Hume. The fourth premise leads to something of a dilemma: Is it the case that God really is vicious and wants it to be known by those who think about the matter? Or is it the case that he is not vicious but wants the conclusion to be drawn nevertheless? Is God amused by leading us to absurd and frightening conclusions? Either way, we have a God who is perverse, at best.

V

At any rate, Hume's conclusion that God is amoral seems highly implausible when we take into account our own moral nature. It is an important part of the very empirical realm that is so central to Hume's philosophy, and he should have considered it far more carefully than he did in drawing inferences about the unseen cause of our world. As I have already suggested, the reasonable conclusion to draw if we believe that God has purposely created us in such a way that we value happiness is that he must also value human happiness. This is surely a legitimate application of Hume's principle that "like effects have like causes." And if God does value human happiness, then he is good in the same sense that we are good.

Notice that this conclusion also has implications not only for Hume's inductive argument but also for his a priori and probability arguments as well. Each of these depends heavily on the principle relating like effects to like causes. If we can infer that God is good using this principle, the force of the latter two arguments is blunted along with the inductive argument. Recall that Hume admitted these arguments were not conclusive but were open to rebuttal if one had good reason to believe God was good. If one has such a reason, one might persist in believing in God's goodness, even in the face of evil.

On the other hand, if our moral intuitions do not give us reason to believe God values human happiness, then, as I have argued, he must be evil. Either way, I want to emphasize, God is decidedly not amoral.

If the claim that God is amoral cannot be sustained, an important consequence follows, namely, that belief in God has deep practical implications. As we recall from our earlier discussion, it is central to Hume's whole case that the proposition of natural theology does not in any way affect human life or action. The belief that God is good or evil does, however, clearly affect human life.

There is a long tradition maintaining that belief in a good God who provides moral order in the universe is a powerful reinforcement for moral behavior. It has not so often been recognized however, that an equally strong argument can be given to support the notion that belief in an evil God would undermine moral commitment. This argument has been developed by Robert Adams.

> We are to think of a being who understands human life much better than we do—understands it well enough to create and control it. Among other things, He must surely understand our moral ideas and feelings. . . . And now we are to suppose that that being does not care to support with His will the moral principles that we believe are true. . . . I submit that if we really believed there is a God like that, who understands so much and yet disregards some or all of our moral principles, it would be extremely difficult for us to continue to regard these principles with the respect that we believe is due them.[21]

As Adams puts it a bit earlier, belief in such a God would be "morally intolerable." It would not only be thoroughly demoralizing but even unthinkable. We could not, without deep distress, seriously entertain the belief that the all-powerful Creator of our universe stands opposed to what we value most. It would be morally devastating to think the highest power in existence does not wish human happiness. Indeed, there is no thought more terrible than that the God of the universe is evil.

The same difficulty, Adams goes on to argue, attends the suggestion that God might be morally slack. While this thought is perhaps not quite as disturbing as the notion that God is out-and-out evil, it also serves to weaken moral resolve. If God himself is morally ambivalent, it is hard to see how lesser beings can hope to do better.

So it seems that the only kind of God we can plausibly believe in is a perfectly good God. It is not only the case that our natural intuitive belief is that if there is a God, he must be good; we are revolted by the thought that there might be an evil God or a God of mixed character.

But is it still not possible, for all I have argued, that there might exist an evil or a morally imperfect God? This scenario has been sketched in a vivid way in an interesting article by Steven M. Cahn entitled "Cacodaemony." Cahn argues that there is a problem of goodness that is exactly parallel to the traditional problem of evil faced by theists. Moreover, "classic arguments in defense of the view that every evil in the world makes possible a world containing even greater goods can be exactly paralleled by arguments in defense of the view that every good in the world makes possible a world containing even greater evils."[22] Cahn defends this claim by spelling out a "soul-breaking" cacodaemony that corresponds in its main points with Hick's soul-making theodicy.

Cahn does not specifically comment on our moral intuitions in his cacodaemony, but we can easily imagine what role they might have. Perhaps they were instilled as a necessary backdrop to evil character formation. That is, an evil character can only be meaningful if it is freely chosen, and this can best be accomplished if persons achieve it by systematically quenching their moral intuitions through consistently making evil choices. Another possibility might be that the evil God gave us our moral intuitions merely to toy with us, as suggested earlier. On this account, his intention might be to punish us forever in the end for being so foolish as to take our moral feelings so seriously.

Is this a credible possibility? In response to this, I am inclined to say this is conceivable in roughly the same sense it is conceivable that I am a brain in a vat or that all my experiences are caused by an evil demon manipulating my mind. Insofar as these are live options, the belief that God might be evil is a live option. It cannot be conclusively refuted, but, on the other hand, it is not the sort of claim anyone really takes seriously or should take seriously. Indeed, Cahn does not take his cacodaemony suggestion seriously, pronouncing it in the end "highly unlikely." So what is his point? According to Cahn, his argument shows that it is no more reasonable to believe in the good God of traditional theism than in the evil demon of his scenario. "Thus, although the problem of goodness and the problem of evil do not show either demonism or theism to be impossible views, they show them both to be highly improbable. . . . [T]he reasonable conclusion is that neither the Demon nor God exists."[23]

While Cahn's claim that theodicy is not better off than his alternative from a purely theoretical standpoint is quite dubious, it is also worth stressing that his conclusion is a badly truncated account of what is reasonable to believe in the face of substantive moral and religious options. This point was made with both force and flair by John King-Farlow in a response to Cahn's article. As he emphasizes, Cahn ignores completely the practical considerations stressed by Pascal and William James, considerations that rightly come into play in religious and moral commitments.

> The cerebral purity of philosophers who eschew thoughts of appropriate utilities in favour of probability alone, when discussing religious and other deeply practical issues, is the purity of a spotlessly gleaming and perfect mirage. The rational man who searches for living water in the desert will prefer an imperfect, dusty, and otherwise untidy oasis. A risky wager to Maximize Expected Utilities of ethically promising kinds (in the face of radical uncertainty) can at least be part of a realistic strategy. Even if Cahn were right about the relevant probabilities, his conclusion would be a bizarre place for putting an end to concerned reasoning about a religious enigma.[24]

When such practical considerations are given due weight, it is clear that the only kind of God it is reasonable to believe in is a perfectly good one.

Returning to Hume, it appears he should have affirmed either outright atheism or a more full-blooded theism. Both our moral intuitions and Hume's principles lead us to the conclusion that if the Creator who gave us our moral nature is not good, then he must be evil. Since the idea of an evil deity is morally and practically intolerable, Hume should either have denied God's existence or accepted his goodness. His alternative proposal that the Creator of our universe is amoral is deeply incoherent.

Before exploring the implications of this conclusion for the doctrine of heaven, let us consider briefly a contemporary version of a position on God's relation to the world that is practically in the same boat as Hume's view. I have in mind what we might broadly call contemporary deism. Particularly interesting here are the writings of some scientists who see religious significance in what we have recently learned from physics and cosmology, but who, like Hume, stop rather short of affirming full-blooded theism. Consider as an example Paul Davies, the 1995 recipient of the Templeton Prize for Progress in Religion.

In his Templeton Prize address, entitled "Physics and the Mind of God," Davies provides an eloquent statement of the religious significance of certain aspects of scientific belief. He finds that the nature of the universe points to meaning and significance for our lives, particularly in its lawfulness that "permits complex order to emerge from chaos, life to emerge from inanimate matter, and consciousness to emerge from life, without the need for the occasional supernatural prod; a lawfulness that produces beings who not only ask great questions of existence, but who, through science and other methods of inquiry, are even beginning to find answers."[25]

Davies notes that our age is one in which men and women are yearning for a deeper meaning to their lives. Such meaning has been undermined by the picture of us living out our existence "on a remote planet wandering amid the vastness of an uncaring cosmos." Some have recoiled from this by turning to "ancient wisdom and revered texts that place mankind at the pinnacle of creation and the center of the universe." Others have embraced New Age mysticism or bizarre cults. Davies wants to propose an alternative to all of these options.

> We have to find a framework of ideas that provides ordinary people with some broader context to their lives than just the daily round, a framework that links them to each other, to nature, and to the wider universe in a meaningful way, that yields a common set of principles around which peoples of all cultures can make ethical decisions yet remain honest in the face of scientific knowledge; indeed, that celebrates that knowledge alongside other human insights and inspirations. The scientific enterprise as I have presented it may not return human beings to the center of the universe, it may reject the notion of miracles other than the miracle of nature itself, but it does not make human beings irrelevant either. A universe in which the emergence of life and consciousness is seen, not as a freak set of events, but fundamental to its lawlike workings, is a universe that can truly be called our home.[26]

Davies's call for a meaningful life is certainly welcome, and his account surely includes many essential components of any worthy conception of such a life.

Nevertheless, it is worth asking what is distinctively religious about his vision. Does it offer anything for which a sober naturalist could not hope?

In particular, Davies's statement is conspicuously lacking in any direct reference to our relationship to God. A meaningful life is one that links us to each other, to nature, and to the wider universe, but there is no hint that we can be so linked to God himself in a meaningful way. These relations with each other and so on are expected to yield principles for making ethical decisions, but there is no indication how this is supposed to occur. Certainly there is no intimation that God might directly provide such moral guidance, especially since Davies puts little stock in "ancient wisdom and revered texts." Indeed, Davies is reticent to suggest that God really cares for us in any personal sense. Human beings are not the "center of the universe" on whose behalf God has performed miracles.

The same sort of reticence is evident in Davies's earlier work, *God and the New Physics*. His discussion of miracles includes an "inconclusive dialogue" that shows little sympathy for their place in a meaningful vision of religious life.[27] His discussion of the end of the universe sketches various scenarios for the demise of the universe as we know it but offers little comment on anything beyond. He concludes, "Only a truly supernatural God could wind it up again."[28] Whether Davies believes in such a supernatural God is entirely unclear. Moreover, he has little sense of what we are entitled to believe God would do in terms of winding things up again. In the same vein, he affirms that we can "make scientific sense out of immortality" and that the survival of the personality must be left open as a possibility. But again, nothing is said to indicate this is a probability, either religiously or scientifically.[29]

VI

From a religious standpoint, it is clear that Davies's position is not much of an advance over Hume's minimal theism. To be sure, it is elaborated with impressive scientific data and illustrations that surpass anything that could have been imagined in the eighteenth century. But while Davies does not deny the religious and practical implications of his scientific/theistic speculations as Hume did—indeed, quite the contrary—his positive statements in this regard are rather modest. As indicated earlier, they include little, if anything, that a naturalist in a generous mood would feel compelled to deny.

But Davies's position is not only religiously inadequate, it is also philosophically unstable, if not incoherent, in much the same way Hume's is. If God is responsible in any meaningful sense for the creation of our world and its structure, including the existence of human consciousness, then, again, it is reasonable to believe in a strong account of God's goodness, for moral concerns are at the heart of the human consciousness and reflection Davies celebrates. If we desire a meaningful life for ourselves and others, and if this is at the heart of our ethical convictions, then is it not reasonable to believe the God who is ultimately responsible for our consciousness and moral reflection shares these concerns? And if he shares these concerns, is it not reasonable to believe he supports them in substantive ways? Indeed, is there not reason to hope that even our highest aspiration, to know God himself and to be rightly related to him, can be met?

Here then is the connection between God's goodness and heaven. If God is perfectly good as well as supremely powerful, then he surely has both the ability and the desire not only to make himself known to us but also to preserve and perfect his relationship with us, if we are willing. A good God would not create us with the kind of aspirations we have and then leave those aspirations unsatisfied. If immortality is possible, as Davies affirms, then it should also be judged to be probable, if God is good.

Let us return to Hume and his illustration of the unfinished house. Recall that Hume argued that this is not a good analogy because in the case of men we can understand their "motives and designs" but in the case of God we cannot. This judgment depends heavily on Hume's claim that God is amoral. But if God is perfectly good in something like the ordinary sense of the term, then we are in a position to make some tentative judgments about how he will behave toward us. Heaven, in this case, is not an "arbitrary supposition" but a reasonable inference from God's perfect goodness and power and from the present state of humanity and the world. In short, Demea's fundamental logic, as sketched earlier, is right on target.

Had Hume believed in God's goodness, his deathbed musings about heaven could have been entirely different. Instead of rejecting heaven as unworthy of hope, he might have hoped for a deeper level of relationship not only with his departed friends but most of all with God, the author of all his deepest desires for meaning and satisfaction. The partial happiness of this life, mixed as it often is with misery, might have been viewed as a pointer to and a preparation for perfect joy in a flawlessly finished house.

Such reasoning is surely plausible if one has grounds for believing in God's goodness. It also suggests the important role the notion of heaven plays in any satisfactory theodicy. I will develop this idea more fully in a later chapter. For now, I want to emphasize that it is central to Christianity that we are not left to our own inferences and best guesses on these matters, as likely as these may be at a general level. At the heart of the Christian faith is the claim that God has distinctively revealed himself and that his revelation addresses these concerns quite directly.

To see this, let us consider Richard Swinburne's recent philosophical defense of revelation. What I want to underline is that the notion of heaven is integral to the whole project. In particular, it is crucial in Swinburne's account of a priori considerations that lead us to expect revelation. After spelling out the nature of human beings and their capacities, along with certain features of the divine nature, Swinburne puts the nub of the argument as follows: "If there is a God who wills men's eternal well-being and chooses to allow men the choice of whether to seek it or not, there is reason to expect that he will take steps to ensure that they acquire information as to how to attain that well-being. . . . So there is a priori reason to suppose that God will reveal to us those things needed for our salvation."[30]

As Swinburne has argued on several occasions, these a priori considerations are quite relevant when making historical judgments about alleged instances of revelation. If we have no a priori reason to believe God would reveal himself, then we will require any purported revelation to meet very stringent historical tests. However, if we judge it likely that God has reasons to reveal himself, then our historical demands will be less severe.[31] For instance, if I have good reason to believe there are no blue-tailed, red-beak finches in our area, I will be rightly skeptical of your claim to have seen one on your morning walk. But if there is new evidence that suggests they may be migrating into the area, I will be much less doubtful of your claim.

Distinctively Christian doctrine about God has developed out of claims that God has "been in the area," with the express purpose of making himself known to us. Let us briefly reflect on how integral the notion of heaven is to those doctrines that are most distinctively Christian, namely, the doctrines of the Trinity, incarnation, atonement, resurrection, and the second coming of Christ.

The doctrine of the Trinity is essential to Christianity and sets it apart not only from generic versions of philosophical theism but also from other historic religions that affirm theism, such as Judaism and Islam. Although it is the most basic of the doctrines just mentioned from a logical point of view, it was last in order of epistemic and theological development. To put it another way, the order of being and the order of knowing diverge on these matters.

While all of these doctrines are logically interrelated, the Resurrection has priority in the order of knowing. It was the resurrection, above all, that dramatically forced the question of Jesus' identity and led the early Christians to believe in his divinity. The doctrine of incarnation, then, follows resurrection in the epistemic order. The doctrine of atonement was likewise understood only with reflection on the meaning of Jesus' life and death in retrospect of the resurrection. Finally, the doctrine of the Trinity was formulated to make theological sense out of the fact that Jesus is divine, yet distinct in some sense from the Father and from the Holy Spirit, who was poured out on the church at Pentecost. In short, it was the impact of the resurrection that required the early believers to reformulate their conception of God. It was the working out of the implications of this event that gave Christian doctrine its unique shape.[32]

Recall from the introduction that the resurrection is the ground of the specifically Christian hope for eternal life. Because Jesus was raised from the dead, we hope to be also, in a body like his resurrected body. If the resurrection is denied, the basis of this hope is undercut. There is, then, a tight connection between the defining event of Christian doctrine and the notion of heaven.

But this is true not only of the resurrection but also of the other central Christian doctrines I have mentioned. Incarnation and atonement were part and parcel of God's saving activity, which culminated in resurrection and ascension. These events achieve human salvation, a salvation fully accomplished at the second coming of Christ, when believers anticipate a perfected relationship with God and other believers. This perfected relationship involves being taken up, in some sense, into the very life of the Trinity. John Wesley articulated this remarkable Christian hope in the following words: "And to crown all, there will be a deep, an intimate, an uninterrupted union with God; a constant communion with the Father and his Son Jesus Christ, through the Spirit; a continual enjoyment of the Three-One God, and of all creatures in him!"[33]

As this sketch makes clear, the notion of heaven is not a mere appendage on the main body of Christian doctrine. Rather, it pervades it through and through. To deny or downplay heaven is to distort the very foundational doctrines of the faith. If this denial and trivialization is consistently followed through, it will twist that faith into an unrecognizable shape. The main thrust of this chapter has been to show that any meaningful account of God's goodness implies some notion of heaven. We have now seen that this conclusion holds even more strongly for those who have passed beyond this generic claim to faith in the Christian God.

2

HEAVEN, THE NATURE OF SALVATION,
AND PURGATORY

I

As we saw in the introduction, Christians have disagreed about what heaven will be like. As fascinating as this dispute is, it has never occupied center stage in Christian polemics. What has been seriously contested, however, is how to get to heaven. Surely this is a more important question than any dispute about the finer particulars of what heaven is like. Calvin made this point vividly in dismissing what he considered superfluous questions about the afterlife: "For few out of a multitude care how they are to get to heaven, but all long to know beforehand what takes place there. Almost all are lazy and loath to do battle, while already picturing to themselves imaginary victories."[1]

While the issue of how to get to heaven has been front and center in the history of theology, this is not to say that it has always been overtly framed in those terms. Rather, the issue has typically, and appropriately, been viewed through the lens of soteriology rather than eschatology. What has been hotly and famously debated down the centuries of church history is the question of how we are saved, or how we are restored to a right relationship with God. Some have emphasized God's sovereign choice to save whomever he will, while others have emphasized the need for human cooperation with grace. Some have emphasized the importance of moral transformation and good works, while others have stressed that salvation is by faith alone. The notable disputants in these controversies include Augustine and Pelagius, Luther and the Roman

Church, Molina and the Thomists, Wesley and Whitefield. Very recently, the fragile unity of American evangelicalism has been tested by another variation of this debate under the name of the "Lordship Controversy."[2]

The connection between these controversies and heaven is not hard to see. Heaven represents the telos and the climax of salvation. Salvation is about being saved *for* something as well as being saved *from* something. Heaven is that goal toward which salvation aims. Thus, soteriological debates are, in the end, debates about how to get to heaven. But there is another important connection here as well, for one's views about how to get to heaven may have implications about the very nature of heaven. In other words, how one construes salvation will naturally affect how one understands the end of salvation, namely, heaven. There is then, a relation between these famous debates about soteriology and the less controversial disputes about what heaven is like. While we should appreciate Calvin's point about the relative importance of being clear about how to get to heaven, we should not overlook the fact that our answer to this question will naturally have implications for our view of what heaven is like. I want to explore these connections more fully in this chapter.

Among orthodox Christians, there would be general agreement that salvation is by faith. This broad agreement would, however, come under strain as adherents of various traditions spelled out their understanding of saving faith. While the precise nature of this faith is a matter of controversy within Christian circles, the whole notion that faith can justify one or get one to heaven has been morally offensive to many thinkers outside the fellowship of orthodox belief.

One of the most notable of these is Kant, whose "religion within the limits of reason alone" was of the strictly moralistic variety. He saw orthodox believers as creating a God who was easy to please, a God who would accept various religious practices as substitutes for genuine moral transformation. Indeed, the more morally useless such practices are, the more holy they are considered to be by many believers. Kant viewed all such religion as illusion. Among such prominent illusions are the notions that God is pleased by our worship and our profession of articles of faith.

> The illusion of being able to accomplish anything in the way of justifying ourselves before God through religious acts of worship is religious superstition. . . . It is a superstitious illusion to wish to become well-pleasing to God through actions which anyone can perform without even needing to be a good man (for example, through profession of statuatory articles of faith, through conformity to churchly observance and discipline, etc.).[3]

Although Kant does not specify which articles of faith he had in mind in this passage, it is a safe guess that he was thinking of orthodox staples such as Jesus' deity, resurrection, and atoning death. Kant was critical of such "historical" doctrines not only because he believed they encouraged superstitious illusion but also because they could not be known by reason alone and thus were not universally accessible.

The notion that certain beliefs are required for salvation, particularly certain beliefs about Jesus, is, however, firmly rooted in the Christian tradition. A particularly striking example of this notion comes in one of the classic Christian confessions of faith, namely, the Athanasian Creed, which is introduced with these solemn words: "Whoever will be saved, before all things it is necessary that he hold the Catholic Faith. Which Faith except everyone do keep whole and undefiled, without doubt he shall perish everlastingly." What follows after this introduction is a rather detailed explication of the central doctrines of the Trinity and the incarnation. The creed concludes with words reminiscent of the introduction: "This is the Catholic Faith, which except a man believe faithfully, he cannot be saved."

Holding the catholic faith cannot be reduced to believing certain doctrinal propositions, no matter how precisely they are defined. Faith is more than a matter of intellectual assent, as the following discussion will show. Yet it is clear that the Christian tradition has insisted that belief in its central doctrines is an integral component of saving faith. Assent to these doctrines requires a certain level of understanding, of course, so the necessity of assent has been appropriately qualified to take such factors into account. But this qualification only underlines the fact that full-blooded faith in its normative shape includes a significant measure of doctrinal belief.

Moreover, and significantly, the notion that one must believe certain things about Jesus in order to be saved can be traced to words attributed to Jesus himself. In the Gospel of John, for instance, he is reported as saying, "[I]f you do not believe that I am the one I claim to be, you will indeed die in your sins."[4] Some critics of Christianity have not hesitated to ascribe moral blame to Jesus himself because of such teaching. Richard Robinson expresses this conviction pointedly as follows.

> It is most important to reject the view that it is a sin not to believe in Jesus; for the view that a belief can be sinful is very harmful and wrong. It destroys the whole ideal of knowledge and reason, and prevents man from achieving the knowledge in which much of his dignity and much of his safety lie. No belief is as such morally wrong; but it is morally wrong to form one's beliefs in view of something other than truth and probability; and Jesus demanded this moral wrong.[5]

Robinson goes on to claim that many people have, as a result of Jesus' teaching on the need for faith, tried to "hypnotize" themselves into believing things their honest judgment could not support. This component of Jesus' preaching constitutes nothing short of a "blasphemy against reason."

These are serious charges, and if they hold up, the Christian doctrine of salvation by faith is morally defective. I want to show, however, that such charges are wide of the mark, that the dominant account of faith supports our best moral sensibilities. Crucial to my argument is the natural connection between heaven and the nature of salvation. This is what I want to explore in the next few pages.

II

To begin to see this connection, let us reflect on this passage from Augustine, in which he describes the eternal felicity of the city of God: "He shall be the end of our desires who shall be seen without end, loved without cloy, praised without weariness."[6] Notice that the very essence of heaven as envisioned here is a relationship with God characterized from the human perspective by endless fascination, love, and gratitude. Clearly such a relationship with God could only be experienced by one who had certain attitudes, desires, and beliefs. For instance, it would be ruled out for one who did not believe God was worthy of praise or who felt no desire to be united to him.

This point is very significant when we recall that, according to traditional Christian belief, human beings in their fallen condition are not disposed to love and worship God. Indeed, their more natural inclination is to self-centeredness, ingratitude, and disobedience. It is this inclination which severs a meaningful relationship with God and destroys human happiness. Augustine describes the human condition as one in which we are engaged in an internal war. Our higher selves are in conflict with the vices of our fallen nature. But this war is symptomatic of a deeper conflict, namely, that between fallen human beings and their Creator. There would be no internal turmoil had human nature "continued steadfast in the uprightness in which it was created. But now in its misery it makes war upon itself, because in its blessedness it would not continue at peace with God." Thus, internal peace and true happiness cannot be achieved unless we first experience peace with God.

Fortunately for us, God took the initiative to restore peace. Augustine construes the incarnation as an event in which the Son of God became a partaker of our nature so that we, by participating in his righteousness and immortality, might "lose our own properties of sin and mortality, and preserve whatever good quality He had implanted in our nature, perfected now by sharing in the goodness of His nature." To desire heaven then is essentially to desire the complete fulfillment of the process in which God restores us to peace with himself and thereby creates peace and happiness in our souls. Augustine puts it like this: "We long, indeed, for the cessation of this war, and, kindled by the flame of divine love, we burn for entrance on that well-ordered peace in which whatever is inferior is forever subordinated to what is above it."[7]

He makes the same point in another context while discussing the Christian concept of the supreme good in comparison to the philosophers' account of it. For Christians, the supreme good is eternal life. Again, Augustine construes the supreme good in terms of the spiritual peace that results when vice is destroyed: "But what is it we wish to do when we seek to attain the supreme good, unless that the flesh should cease to lust against the spirit, and that there be no vice in us against which the spirit may lust?" He goes on: "Salvation, such as it shall be in the world to come, shall itself be our final happiness."[8]

This point must be emphasized: Salvation itself is our final happiness. There is a tight, integral connection between moral renewal, salvation, and human fulfillment and happiness. This is not, however, simply a matter of the classical idea that "virtue is its own reward." Salvation is much more than mere morality. It is finally a matter of knowing God as fully as we are capable of knowing him and thereby experiencing the fullness of life. "God Himself, who is the Author of virtue, shall there be its reward; for, as there is nothing greater or better, He has promised Himself."[9] Augustine goes on to explain that this means God shall be our satisfaction, that he shall be for us all that we rightly desire.

The same sort of connection between salvation and heaven is also apparent in Aquinas. He too argues that our ultimate felicity does not come in this life but only in seeing God in his essence. We cannot see God with our natural powers, so this vision is a gift of God's grace. And since this vision is a sharing in the very life of God, it is itself eternal life and happiness. Aquinas puts it thus: "In this vision, of course, we become most like God, and we are partakers of His happiness. . . . And so, may they who enjoy the same felicity whereby God is happy eat and drink at God's table, seeing Him in the way that He sees Himself."[10]

Again, it is evident that sinful human beings are disordered in their desires in such a way that they would not naturally enjoy eating and drinking at God's table, since such eating and drinking involves loving God himself in an intimate way. The solution to this problem, according to Aquinas, is that "man's affections must be chiefly perfected by sanctifying grace, which directs man to his ultimate end."[11] The effect of this sanctifying grace is that man is moved to love God, his final end. Aquinas spells out the relationship between this grace and man's final happiness in terms of man being brought by grace to share a vision of God in his very essence: "So, man cannot be brought to this end unless he be united with God by the conformation of his will. . . . Hence, by sanctifying grace man is established as a lover of God, since man is directed by it to the end that has been shared with him by God."[12] By having his will thus conformed to the divine will, man is united to God in such a way that he comes to love what God loves and to share his purposes.

Earlier, Aquinas pointed out that the intention of the lover is to be loved in turn by the one he loves. This holds with respect to God's love for man. However, in contrast with human love, where love is usually elicited by some good thing that already exists in the beloved, God himself creates the good in his beloved. Thus, the effect of God's sanctifying grace is love for himself, a love that unites him with his beloved.

The purpose of this brief sketch has not been to provide a complete or critical account of Aquinas's view of heaven or the beatific vision. My aim, rather, has been to show, as we saw in the case of Augustine, the close connection between Aquinas's concept of saving grace and his account of heaven. In both instances, we have seen a view of heaven, of ultimate felicity, that requires moral transformation and an account of salvation that is thoroughly integral with this picture. There is no hint here that salvation is a magical thing that substitutes for moral renewal or that man can be justified before God without undergoing a real change in his nature.

This point gains significance in light of the fact that the sort of view represented by Augustine and Aquinas is typical of catholic Christianity in its Reformation variations as well as its Roman ones. Let us consider, more briefly, a few more instances of this. Jonathan Edwards provides a good example in the Calvinist tradition. In a sermon entitled "The Way of Holiness," Edwards argues quite forcefully that the only way to heaven is the way of holiness. He defines holiness as embracing three things: conformity of heart and life to God, conformity to Jesus Christ, and conformity to God's laws and commands. For Edwards, there are several clear reasons why those who are not holy in this sense cannot be on the way to heaven. One of his reasons is that because God is holy, nothing could enjoy being united to God without also being holy.

> It is therefore as impossible for an unholy thing to be admitted unto the happiness of heaven as it is for God not to be, or be turned to nothing. For it is as impossible that God should love sin as it is for him to cease to be, and it is as impossible for him to love a wicked man that has not his sin purified, and it is as impossible for him to enjoy the happiness of heaven except God love him, for the happiness of heaven consists in the enjoyment of God's love.[13]

There is nothing arbitrary about the fact that an unholy man cannot enjoy the presence of God and therefore cannot be admitted to heaven. That is why Edwards uses the strong language of impossibility to make his point. The essence of heaven is loving union with God, so one who does not love God is simply not prepared to enjoy heaven. That is why salvation must involve changing us so that we come to love God as we ought. The aim of salvation is to make us holy, and this is what fits us for heaven.

This conception of salvation was fully developed by Edwards's contemporary John Wesley. Wesley states the relation between salvation and heaven as follows.

> 'Without holiness no man shall see the Lord,' shall see the face of God in glory. . . . No, it cannot be; none shall live with God, but he that now lives to God; none shall enjoy the glory of God in heaven, but he that bears the image of God on earth; none that is not saved from sin here can be saved from hell hereafter; none can see the kingdom of God above, unless the kingdom of God be in him below.[14]

Once again, the point is that there is an essential continuity between salvation and heaven. Salvation forms and transforms us into the kind of persons who can enjoy the presence of God.

Moving ahead to more recent writers, we see the same sort of picture of salvation and its relation to heaven in one of the most widely read religious authors of the twentieth century, C. S. Lewis. Lewis's works are laced with references to heaven, and he repeatedly makes the point that we are being formed into either heavenly creatures or hellish ones. "To be the one kind of creature is heaven: that is, it is joy and peace and knowledge and power."[15] It is the work of salvation to make us into heavenly creatures as we cooperate by our free choices, and to be so made is a taste of heaven itself.

Next, as an example of this train of thought from contemporary evangelical Protestantism, consider these lines from popular author and pastor John MacArthur: "Heaven is the perfect place for people made perfect. Perfection is the goal of God's sanctifying work in us. . . . He is making us fit to dwell in His presence forever. The utter perfection of heaven is the consummation of our salvation."[16]

For a final example, the historian Jeffrey Burton Russell has made much the same point by describing heaven as a community of persons who have been transformed by the love of God. "The union of humans with one another in Christ does not simply 'take place' in heaven; it is heaven itself, heartwhole and fine."[17]

What we have seen in this diverse group of writers is a general agreement that the joy and happiness of heaven is precisely the joy and happiness of salvation. Salvation is essentially a matter of loving God and being rightly related to him. This relationship is the source of our deepest delight and satisfaction. Heaven is not a place that could be enjoyed apart from loving God in the way made possible by salvation. There is no question of "going to" heaven if one is not the sort of person who has the sort of desires and affections for God that heaven satisfies.

The consensus among these authors about the relationship between salvation and heaven reflects a broad agreement about the nature of salvation that has been typical of catholic Christianity. We can underline this point by focusing for a moment on the doctrine of justification. As Alister McGrath has shown in his detailed history of the doctrine, justification was understood throughout the medieval period "as the process by which a man is made righteous, subsuming the concepts of 'sanctification' and 'regeneration.'"[18] There was no thought that one could be rightly related to God without actually being made righteous. Moreover, he maintains that "it will be clear that the medieval period was astonishingly faithful to the teaching of Augustine on the question of the nature of justification, where the Reformers departed from it."[19]

In particular, the Protestant Reformers departed from the catholic consensus in seeing justification as a forensic or legal declaration that the believer is *declared* righteous, rather than as a process whereby he is actually *made* righteous. The cause of justification is the alien righteousness of Christ, which is understood to be imputed to the believer. An explicit distinction, moreover, is drawn between justification so understood and sanctification and regeneration.

While these distinctions have been characteristic of Protestant theology, and while justification has often received more emphasis there, it is important to stress that the classical theologians did not neglect the importance of sanctification. Certainly some of Luther's notoriously intemperate comments may suggest otherwise, but a nuanced interpretation of his theology will certainly recognize the place of sanctification in his soteriology. For instance, Karl Holl interpreted Luther's doctrine to mean that "God's present justification of the sinner is based upon his anticipation of his final sanctification, in that man's present justification takes place on the basis of his foreseen future righteousness."[20] Likewise, Calvin secured the importance of sanctification in his soteriology through his notion that believers are incorporated into Christ. Incorporation into Christ unites believers with him, and the two results of this unity are justification and sanctification. As Calvin saw it, these two consequences are "distinct and inseparable."[21]

Unfortunately, what was inseparable for the great Reformers has not always been kept intact by their followers. Some of these have wanted to claim justification while keeping sanctification optional. They have believed that one can be accepted by God and finally saved without the sort of moral and spiritual transformation that is involved in sanctification. This idea has been the target of the kind of criticism cited at the beginning of this chapter. This picture of faith in Christ seems magical and void of moral and intellectual seriousness.

Before moving on from this point, it is worth noting that a group of evangelical and Catholic leaders have recently produced a document entitled "The Gift of Salvation," which reiterates a more classical view of saving faith, including the close relationship between justification and sanctification. The document denies that faith is mere intellectual assent and asserts that it is "an act of the whole person, involving the mind, the will and the affections, issuing in a changed life." It goes on a few paragraphs later to insist that Christians are bound by their faith and baptism "to live according to the law of love in obedience to Jesus Christ the Lord. Scripture calls this the life of holiness or sanctification."[22]

III

In what follows, I want to argue that true Christian faith is morally and spiritually transforming. In particular, I want to show this with respect to the central Christian belief that Jesus is the Son of God incarnate who died to atone for our sins. I will proceed by first focusing on the atonement, and then I will turn more briefly to the claim that Jesus is God the Son incarnate.

Fortunately for our purposes, the doctrine of atonement has recently received a good deal of attention from Christian philosophers. Among those who have written about it are Marilyn Adams, Colin Gunton, John Hare, Philip Quinn, Eleonore Stump, and Richard Swinburne. While there are important differences in their theories and models of the atonement, there is striking agreement that it is intended to sanctify those who claim it through faith in Christ. Consider in this light the words of Philip Quinn, who has developed a model of the atonement in a critical article on Swinburne's account of the doctrine. While Quinn emphasizes the retrospective aspect of forgiveness of sins in this particular article, he concludes as follows:

> I think a full account of the doctrine of the Atonement would also have a prospective dimension. It would stress the idea that divine love, made manifest throughout the life of Christ but especially in his suffering and dying, has the power to transform human sinners, with their cooperation, in ways that

fit them for everlasting life in intimate union with God. As Swinburne puts the point, 'Christ's atoning death must be the supreme means of human sanctification' (p. 171). About this, he and I are in full agreement.[23]

Notice again that sanctification is what fits us for eternal life with God. The question we want to pursue is how the atonement achieves this.

It is, of course, well-known that no single model of the atonement has been officially sanctioned as the orthodox position of the church. Several models have been proposed in the history of theology, so the current diversity on this matter is very much in keeping with what has been the case in the past. My aim in examining some of the contemporary accounts of the atonement is not to defend one model at the exclusion of others but to show how the theme of sanctification and transformation is common to all of them.

Let us begin with some reflections of Marilyn Adams on redemptive suffering as the solution to the problem of evil. Adams notes that from the Christian perspective, sin is the primary evil and notes that sin is what stands in the way of God's objective that we enter into loving relationships with both him and other persons. Since God is perfectly good, he deals with the problem of sin from the standpoint of righteous love. This means he must judge sin but with the purpose of restoring his relationship with us. In particular, Adams observes that since God is righteous, he "has a right to make us face the truth about who we are, who he is, who Christ is, and his rightful claims over us."[24] Indeed, this is necessary if we are to be genuinely reconciled to God, for a profoundly loving relationship cannot be based on deception, dishonesty, or false pretenses.

Consider now that sin is essentially deceptive and dishonest. Sin involves a false picture of both God and ourselves. The story of the fall brings this into focus. Notice that the heart of the serpent's temptation is the suggestion that God is not really good. The serpent asserts that God is withholding something of value from Eve and that it would benefit her to disobey God's command. God does not really have our best interest at heart and his motives cannot be fully trusted. Thus, sin involves a badly distorted conception of God. It implies either that God is not wise enough to know what is best for us or that he knows it but does not want it for us. To act on this premise is to render judgment on God and to pronounce ourselves superior to him.

The theme of sin's deceptiveness is also prominent in the New Testament. Romans 1 describes human depravity as a refusal to acknowledge God with proper gratitude and a consequent darkening of understanding. Sinful actions of all kinds flow from faulty attitudes toward God. Ingratitude toward God is a profound failure to recognize his love and goodness toward us and his desire for our happiness and well-being.

So long as such attitudes prevail, it is obvious that we cannot be united to God in a loving relationship. We cannot trust or obey him in this state of mind. Even if he were to forgive us, we would still be separated from him because of our attitude toward him. What is needed is for us to come to trust God again and to desire to obey him. Then our relationship with him could be genuinely restored.

The question is, how can atonement enable us to see and acknowledge the truth about God and ourselves that will break the deception of sin? Consider Adams's account of what Jesus did as his climactic act of love to those who had rejected him.

> Finally, he bears the cost of divine judgment upon them by accepting martyrdom at their hands. In allowing himself to be crucified, he permits their sinful attitudes to be carried into action and externalized in his own flesh. Because he is a truly innocent victim, his body is the canvas on which the portrait of their sins can be most clearly drawn. In their great jealousy and mistrustfulness toward God, they had subjected his Messiah to a ritually accursed death. Unable to hear divine judgment through other media, there was at least a chance that they would be moved by the love of such a martyr and accept the painful revelation.[25]

As Adams explains, Jesus' death on the cross makes vividly clear for any who are willing to see both the depth of divine love and human corruption. Jesus' pierced and beaten flesh gave unforgettably concrete expression to the often hidden and abstract attitudes of human sinfulness. It showed with inescapable force and realism the true colors of our attitude toward God. On the other hand, Christ's willingness to submit to such a death also shows the splendor and power of his everlasting love. That Christ was fully innocent and unworthy of any sort of punishment brings both truths into the sharpest possible focus.

Of course, the atonement was the climax of a life perfectly lived, and it must be understood in that larger context to be properly appreciated. As Quinn notes, divine love was manifested in the entire life of Christ. In view of this, consider the following lines of Pascal.

> Knowing God without knowing our own wretchedness makes for pride.
> Knowing our own wretchedness without knowing God makes for despair.
> Knowing Jesus Christ strikes the balance because he shows us both God and our own wretchedness.[26]

Returning to Adams's point, we need to know the truth about God and ourselves. The power of the incarnation is that it can teach us both of these truths at once in such a way that we do not lose sight of the other. Pascal's point is that knowledge of either one of these truths alone will produce either pride or despair and thereby only drive us farther from God. The knowledge of both, however, leads to repentance and redemption. Elsewhere, Pascal puts the same point like this: "Jesus is a God whom we can approach without pride and before whom we can humble ourselves without despair."[27] Humility charged with hope draws us back to God and initiates the process of transformation. The life and death of Christ both humbles us and gives us hope that God will forgive us and restore us to a loving relationship with himself.

This has also been an important theme in Eleonore Stump's writings on the atonement. In one of her essays, she illustrates the point with the example of

Rosamond Lydgate in George Eliot's *Middlemarch*. Rosamond is a selfish, manipulative, prodigal social climber. The question Stump raises is how such a person could be brought to recognize her sin and need for transformation. Superficial changes in light of the values she owns would hardly begin to change her. What she needs, Stump notes, is a thoroughgoing revolution in her standard of values and a corresponding redirection of her will. How could this be accomplished without God directly acting on her will without her assent?

For this to occur without simply overriding her will, Rosamond must begin to recognize the wrong she has done and to see its seriousness. She must come to understand how deeply her sin resides in her will and her need of divine transformation if she is to be genuinely transformed. Moreover, she needs to see that God loves her and is willing to help her. To see this would elicit a desire to draw near to God and would even begin to produce some feelings of love for him.

Such a change of outlook does not typically occur instantly but is more likely to be achieved by numerous "providentially ordered circumstances." But when these have done their work, Stump suggests, and the choices of Rosamond's life "have left her ready, the passion and death of Christ will be the wedge which cracks her heart." In this way, "the Atonement figures significantly in justification because of its role in eliciting the assent to moral rebirth requisite for justification."[28]

It is important to stress that grace enables this assent. Indeed, the power of the atonement in helping to elicit assent is surely an aspect of God's initiative and grace. Moreover, the importance of moral rebirth can hardly be overestimated. This underlines the fact that fallen sinners cannot reform themselves or achieve sanctity by their own efforts. Not to recognize this is to slide into Pelagianism.

The specter of Pelagianism, has, of course, always hung over accounts of the atonement that emphasize its moral influence on us. Abelard is the fountainhead of moral influence theories, and his views were condemned by the church of his day. Abelard, however, has recently been defended among philosophers by Philip Quinn. Quinn shows that Abelard clearly endorsed—contrary to popular opinion—the notion of penal substitution in his explanation of the atonement and argues that he should be classified as a "hierarchical pluralist."[29] That is to say, Abelard, like Aquinas, offered an account of the atonement that "has a dominant motif to which others are subordinated." The difference is that for Aquinas, penal satisfaction was the primary emphasis, whereas for Abelard what was central was the love that transforms motives and character.

It is Quinn's contention that Abelard's emphasis is the one that accounts for how the atonement can change us in such a way as to fit us "for everlasting life in intimate union with God."[30] In other words, Abelard's theory provides that prospective dimension which a fully satisfactory account of the atonement must include. Part of the appeal of Abelard's theory is its psychological intelligibility. As Quinn notes, we can understand it by analogy with the way merely human love can influence us for the better. But if an Abelardian theory is to be adequate, it must be stressed that the relationship between divine and human love is only one of analogy and not identity. Divine love operates outside the natural order in producing moral and spiritual changes in us: "Above and beyond its examplary value, there is in it a surplus of mysterious causal efficacy that no merely human love possesses."[31] In the end, Quinn concludes that an appropriately modified Abelardian account is "better balanced" than satisfaction theories and gives due emphasis to "the most important purpose the Atonement serves."[32] This is not to deny that satisfaction is also involved in the atonement, and, as we shall see below, Quinn is also prepared to defend a version of the penal substitution theory.

At any rate, such a judgment about the relative importance of what the atonement accomplishes reflects, I think, a particular perspective on the nature of salvation. In particular, it reflects an emphasis on the personal and relational dimension of transformation over the more legal and forensic dimension of forgiveness. In terms of the common Protestant distinctions noted above, it represents an emphasis on the subjective aspect of sanctification over the objective factor of justification. From this perspective, the primary purpose of salvation is to change us in such a way that we can be united to God in a loving relationship. God's love and desire for a relationship with us is constant on this account and the barrier between us and God comes from our attitude toward him, not his attitude toward us. It is this which must be changed before reconciliation is possible.

On the other hand, those who emphasize the element of forgiveness in salvation tend to stress the objective component of the atonement. That is, they accent the notion that Christ accomplished something objective that makes forgiveness possible. Some of these hold that the atonement pays the penalty for sin and thereby appeases God's wrath so that he can justly forgive the sins of those who have faith in Christ. These accounts of atonement and salvation by faith are easily twisted to suggest that real change and transformation is unnecessary since the penalty of sin has been paid by Christ. These accounts of justification by faith are vulnerable to the sort of moral critiques leveled by Kant and others.

Let us turn now to examine some recent accounts of atonement in this broad tradition. I want to show that objective accounts of the atonement are not inherently morally irresponsible and that careful statements of such theories can avoid moral objections. Let us consider first a version of the sacrifice theory articulated by Colin Gunton, drawing upon insights from the nineteenth-century Calvinist theologian Edward Irving. This is an appropriate place to begin because this view has certain affinities with the view I discussed earlier. Irving emphasized that Christ's incarnation involved taking on the same sort of flesh we all share. His offering to his Father of a life of perfect worship and obedience was through the power of the Holy Spirit. Thus, his life was not only a representative offering to the Father on behalf of all humanity, but it also has implications for how we can likewise offer our lives to God through the same power he did. The Trinitarian dimensions of this are spelled out by Gunton as follows: "The Son's giving of himself in and for the world is the outworking, realized through the Holy Spirit, of the Father's giving up of the

Son in pursuit of his eternal will for communion with the creature. In that dimension, the Atonement must be understood as the eternal love of God, 'contracted to a span' in the historical incarnation of the Son."[33]

The practical implication of such extraordinary love is that those who know it are called to offer their lives in the same sort of sacrifice to the Father. The Holy Spirit is the link between Jesus' sacrifice and ours. "On such an understanding the Spirit is God enabling believers to realize, through the once-for-all Atonement of Christ, the form of life that the Atonement made possible."[34]

Another well-known version of the sacrifice model is that of Swinburne, who defends it not only as the most satisfactory model available but also because he believes it is most widely based in the New Testament. The notion of sacrifice, of course, has its roots in the Old Testament, where a sacrifice was an offering of something valuable to God that God in turn shared with those who offered it. Following this model, Christ offered a sacrifice to God of the most valuable thing he had, namely, his perfect life, with the purpose of sharing the benefits of his sacrifice with others. But as Swinburne notes, since Christ is God, he cannot offer a sacrifice to himself. Thus, the model must be modified to some extent. The key revision is that God makes the sacrifice available but we must offer it. "Christ's laid–down life is there made available for sacrifice, like a ram caught in the thicket. Any man who is humble and serious enough about his sin to recognize what is the proper reparation and penance for it may use the costly gift which another has made available for him to offer as his sacrifice."[35] Christ's perfect life is appropriate reparation because it represents the sort of life we should have led.

On this model, Christ's death has no efficacy until we choose to offer it in atonement for our sins. This is a crucial point for Swinburne, for he thinks we must be involved in the process of removing our sins or God would not be taking us or our sins seriously. Specifically, to claim Christ's atonement requires repentance and apology. Thus, to plead Christ's sacrifice to atone for our sins cannot be a morally frivolous act. As Swinburne put it, we must be humble and serious about our sin. This point is underlined by the recognition that in pleading the atonement we are acknowledging that Christ represents the sort of life we should have led. To so acknowledge, moreover, is to repudiate our sinful past and to desire and resolve to live differently in the future. Without this, we are not truly serious about our sin and have not sincerely repented.

In the same vein, Quinn defends a version of the penal substitution view of the atonement but with the same sort of qualifiers as Swinburne insists upon. He rejects the notion that moral guilt can be transferred from a wrongdoer to an innocent person. But while he does not think the idea of guilt transfer is defensible or intelligible, he argues that we can make some sense of how an innocent person can pay the moral debt of another. In brief, he thinks "there is a case to be made for the variant of the theory according to which, though guilt for the sins of others is not transferred to Christ, it is removed from those among them who repent and apologize for their sins once Christ has paid the debt of punishment they owe, if they acknowledge Christ's action on their behalf."[36] Again, the point to be stressed for our purposes is that the atonement does not exempt the one pleading it from moral reform and renewal. The very act of pleading the atonement involves a change of heart that, if sincere, will eventuate, with God's gracious assistance, in moral and spiritual transformation.

Let us turn finally to consider the recent defense of a "qualified version" of penal substitution by John Hare. The larger framework Hare uses to explicate his understanding of atonement is the New Testament notion that believers are incorporated into Christ and his death. He approaches the penal side of the term by addressing Swinburne's concern that punishment does not seem to be the correct category since Christ willingly accepted his sacrificial death. Hare argues, however, that it is not essential to punishment that it be applied without consent. What is true, he thinks, is that punishment must be exacted, not that it be forced upon the one receiving it. In view of this, Hare believes Christ's death could be rightly understood in terms of punishment.

Another objection to penal theories comes from resistance to the retributive theory of punishment. Hare responds to this challenge by arguing that penal theories can be construed in terms of the "expressive" theory of punishment. Unlike classical retribution theory, it does not hold that harm inflicted by, or on behalf of, the victim is self-evidently justified by the fact that it is a response to the initial harm. Instead, it views retributive punishment as a way to the good end of vindicating the value of the victim.

> The basic idea here is that the offender's wrongdoing demeans the victim by giving expression to the view that the offender's value is high enough to make the treatment of the victim legitimate or permissible. For a vivid example, take the case of the bully in the school playground. The demand for retributive punishment is then the demand that this false elevation of the offender's value be corrected visibly. . . . [I]t is the insistence on the recognition of a moral value, the correct relative value of wrongdoer and victim.[37]

So much for how Hare proposes to understand the penal side of the equation. What about the other side of the term, namely, substitution? Hare finds help for understanding this notion in 2 Corinthians 5:14: "For the love of Christ constraineth us; because we thus judge, that if one died for all, then were all dead" (KJV). The puzzling suggestion of this text is further illumined by its larger context, where Paul describes Christians as ambassadors for Christ. The ambassador presents us with a situation where a representative is a substitute. That is, the ambassador is the one who actually travels abroad in place of her fellow citizens and is thereby a substitute. But when she makes a commitment, they make it as well. In that sense, she is a representative. In view of the idea that believers are incorporated into Christ, Hare proposes a view of substitution such that "it is true both that Christ had to suffer what we do not suffer, and that we share in his death and resurrection."[38]

Hare is willing to defend what most recent interpreters of the atonement have backed away from, namely, the idea that our guilt is transferred to Christ. He reminds us, however, that the relation between Christ and believers is a complex one that surpasses relationships between mere human beings, and that more is involved in this relationship than transmission of liability. Hare explicates the notion of believers' incorporation into Christ by exploring several contexts in which there is a "partial merging of identity" between persons. In particular, he examines some biblical analogies that depict the unity between Christ and believers. In one of these, he asks us to imagine a family who adopts a child and thereby assumes responsibility for his wrongdoing. "If the child steals, the parents pay. It may be that the only way the child can be cured is through the sufferings it causes the adoptive family; the sufferings may be great enough practically to destroy the family. We can imagine, though, that there is a kind of life which the family leads which eventually becomes the kind of life the child leads."[39] As Hare notes, there is here a sort of mutual transmission in this relationship. The parents bear the shame when the child steals and may apologize for him and help him to apologize himself. Since he is now part of their family, his guilt is in some sense theirs as well. But eventually there will be a transmission of their integrity and love to the child, and he will himself become a person of character.

It is clear I think, that Hare's version of penal substitution does not exempt believers from moral transformation. Indeed, the penal side of the theory involves the notion that the death of Christ is a forceful expression of our true position relative to God. To plead the atonement is to acknowledge the truth it expresses and to open ourselves to be changed by that truth. Moreover, Hare's sense of substitution requires incorporation into the life of Christ. This involves a transforming relationship with Christ and his body, the church. Just as the child in his example comes to share the character of his family, so believers come to share the character of Christ as it is transmitted to them through the church.

IV

We have now examined several recent accounts of the atonement, and I have shown in each case that faith in the atonement entails real change on the part of the believer. Again, my goal is not to defend one of these theories at the expense of the others but rather to show that what is common to them all is some explanation of how faith in the atonement is morally and spiritually transforming. But let us turn now to the claim that salvation requires belief that Jesus is God the Son incarnate. Why is this belief necessary for salvation?

I wish to answer this question from the perspective of the assumption that the central claims of Christianity are true and that, thus, Jesus is indeed the Son of God incarnate. This claim has, of course, been defended at great length by Christian apologists from the earliest days of Christianity until now, and to reiterate the arguments in even summary form would require another book. That is not my purpose here. My task here is the relatively modest one of showing why it follows from orthodox beliefs about Jesus that salvation requires belief in his deity.

The reason follows rather straightforwardly from the view of salvation I have been defending, namely, that salvation is about a perfect relationship with God.

If God is a Trinity and Jesus is God the Son incarnate, as Christians teach, then a perfect relationship with God entails knowing Jesus is God the Son. Not to believe Jesus is God the Son would involve a fundamentally mistaken understanding of God, which would be incompatible with a perfected relationship.

According to traditional Christian belief, the truth about Jesus' identity has been given through revelation. Moreover, the revelation is sufficiently clear that those who have access to it are responsible to believe it. The basic logic of this is provocatively stated by Pascal: "The prophecies, even the miracles and proofs of our religion, are not of such a kind that they can be said to be absolutely convincing. . . . But the evidence is such as to exceed, or at least equal, the evidence to the contrary, so that it cannot be reason that decides us against following it, and can therefore only be concupiscence and wickedness of heart."[40]

Notice that Pascal is somewhat vague about how convincing the evidence is. The reason for this is that we cannot judge what degree of clarity is optimal to elicit a positive response of faith from beings who are free as well as rational. But the point is that a revelation from a perfectly good and wise God must be sufficiently evident that unbelief must finally be judged a matter of culpable unwillingness to believe. That is what Pascal means in ascribing unbelief in properly informed persons to "wickedness of heart." Let me emphasize again that my purpose here is not to marshall the relevant evidence that Christianity is true. My point is the conceptual one about what is involved in the claim that God has revealed himself in the manner Christianity claims and for the purposes it claims. Such a revelation would be of extreme importance for all people, and God would surely reveal it in such a way that it would be sufficiently clear, at least in its main lines, that any properly informed person of good will could see its truth.

On this picture, belief in Jesus is nothing like Richard Robinson describes it in the quote at the beginning of this chapter. That is, it is not a matter of trying to believe what does not seem true or probable. To the contrary, belief in Jesus comes readily to one who is properly informed and rightly disposed to believe the truth. Indeed, it is unbelief that reflects an unwillingness to accept what is true. Of course, belief is not an exclusively cognitive operation for Pascal since it also involves a heart that is rightly disposed. But this only underlines the point that on the Christian account of things, belief in Christ is an honest response to divinely disclosed reality.

In another passage, a couplet, Pascal succinctly states what God owes us by way of revelation and what we owe him by way of response.

> Men owe it to God to accept the religion he sends them.
> God owes it to men not to lead them into error.[41]

It is implicit in the very claim to revelation that we must believe what God has revealed in order to be rightly related to him.

It is also important to note that belief in the deity of Jesus is essential to the whole notion of atonement we discussed. The belief that Jesus was God the

Son incarnate who willingly laid down his life provides atonement theology its power. This points up how tightly connected are the basic Christian doctrines of Trinity, incarnation, and atonement. We cannot begin to have an adequate grasp of either the shape or the depth of divine love until it is revealed to us in these terms.

V

It is time now to summarize and draw together the discussion to this point. I will do so by stating what I believe is the correct account of saving faith in view of the preceding material.

The central idea I want to affirm is the notion suggested by Marilyn Adams that a genuine relationship with God must be based on truth. That is, it must be a relationship in which we fully acknowledge and own the truth first about God and then about ourselves. Saving faith is thus the very opposite of sin and by its very nature must eventually eliminate sin from our lives.

Sin arises from attitudes of mistrust toward God or from ingratitude for his love and goodness. To know the truth about God is to recognize both his perfect wisdom and unbounded love for us. I believe it is central to the atonement to demonstrate God's love in this fashion as a means of breaking through our spiritual blindness and mistrust. It is not the case that God has turned his back on us, but that we have turned away from him. The heart of salvation is to change us so we gladly love and obey God. This is how we are united to him in a relationship of mutual love. He has always loved us, but we have not always loved him in return. The heart of atonement is eliciting our trust and willingness to be changed in the confidence that God's will is really for our true good and flourishing.

I am, however, inclined to think that no single model of the atonement captures all of what it accomplished and that penal substitution, properly qualified, is a part of it, although a secondary part. The essence of salvation is the real transformation that allows us to love God and enjoy fellowship with him. The element of forgiveness, although crucial, is secondary to this. The point of penal substitution is not that God needed to be placated, for Christ himself is God and he is the one who gave his life as a sacrifice.[42] However, in keeping with his truthful relation with us, God must take our sin seriously. Hare's account of the penal nature of Christ's death dovetails nicely with this emphasis on truth. It demonstrates the true value of him whom we have disobeyed and disregarded and displays our value relative to him. It vividly expresses how wrong we have been in treating God with mistrust, ingratitude, and contempt, while vindicating his perfect goodness.

Sacrifice theories also exhibit truth, for they involve Christ living the sort of life we ought to have lived. We cannot truthfully plead the atonement as either sacrifice or penal substitution without acknowledging our sin and heartily repenting of it. We cannot honestly plead the atonement and simultaneously wish to remain the same sort of persons who required such a sacrifice in the first place. To think we can is to have a false picture of God. It is to imagine that he does not really take our sin seriously or that we can use his grace and mercy for our own distorted purposes. To plead the atonement, we must acknowledge God as God. We must own his purposes for our lives and recognize them as good. That is, God's purposes for us are indeed for our well-being and ultimate happiness and satisfaction. But we cannot merely ask God's forgiveness and proceed with our purposes apart from God. To attempt to do this is to operate with a false valuation of both ourselves and of God. The atonement expresses the truth that radically undercuts this profoundly false picture.

Honest acknowledgment of the atonement also involves grateful worship of Jesus as God. The Christian requirement to believe that Jesus is God incarnate is not an arbitrary demand. It is, at the most basic level, an instance of the more general moral requirement to admit the true status of our superiors and offer gratitude for benefits and favors they have granted to us. To do otherwise if Jesus is who Christians say he is would be a profound act of dishonesty and ingratitude. But genuine worship is not demeaning or contrived. It is sincere ascription of value and praise to one who deserves it.

Of course, we cannot grasp the full force and implications of these truths immediately. The process of sanctification involves our coming more and more to believe these truths at all levels of our personality. Such belief embraces our emotions and our will as much as our intellect. Entire sanctification is achieved when the truth about God and ourselves has permeated and engaged our entire being.

All of this naturally restores our relationship to God, and to be so restored is both the aim of salvation and the essence of heaven. This is eternal life itself, "the happy and holy communion which the faithful have with God the Father, Son and Holy Ghost."[43] The daring idea is that redeemed persons who have been transformed by the love of God have entered into a relationship with him in such a way that they are part of the eternal love and fellowship of the Trinity. When the climax of this relationship is reached in heaven, faith is no longer unnecessary; but what I have been trying to show is that faith which saves must equip us with the love which fits us for this end.

VI

If salvation is essentially a matter of transformation, as I have argued, this raises an issue of considerable practical urgency. This issue is posed in an article by Philip Nobile written before the first anniversary of the death of Princess Diana, in which the author raises what he terms "an indiscreet theological question: Where is she now?"[44] According to Christian theology, he notes, the options are heaven, purgatory, or hell. Given Diana's well-publicized lifestyle, Nobile suggests that the case for heaven is weak. A better case can be made for hell, given the likelihood that Diana was in a state of mortal sin at the moment of her death. In view of this, he finds it curious that the pope gave positive indications about Diana's salvation, as suggested by the following, which was sent

on his behalf to Queen Elizabeth: "The Holy Father has offered prayers sum-
moning her to our Heavenly Father's eternal love." This remark, Nobile observes, implies purgatory.

Nobile thinks his analysis points to a "chilling core" in Christianity, and his
article is not intended as a defense of orthodoxy. In fact, however, it raises a
substantive issue that believers who take the afterlife seriously cannot evade.
Most believers have probably attended funerals in which recently deceased
persons who would hardly be suspected of sainthood were declared to be surely
enjoying all the glories of heaven. At best, such occasions are understandable
pastoral efforts to comfort grieving loved ones. At worst, they may be sentimental exercises that trivialize the most central beliefs of the Christian faith.

Here is the question that must be faced. If salvation is primarily about transformation and in the very nature of things we cannot be united with God unless
we are holy, what should we think about those who plead the atonement but
die before they have been thoroughly transformed? That is, they have accepted
the truth about God and themselves but this truth has not fully worked through
their character. Their sanctification has begun but it is far from complete. The
problem is that such people do not really seem to be ready for a heaven of
perfect love and fellowship with God, with others who love him wholeheart-
edly, but neither should they be consigned to hell.

This basic difficulty led to the formulation of the doctrine of purgatory. While
the doctrine was not fully developed until the Middle Ages, the seeds from
which it grew go back at least to the church fathers. Cyprian, for instance,
struggled with the question of what to think about Christians who had weak-
ened under persecution. Augustine, the fountainhead of all Western theology,
reflected in several passages on the sort of issues that would eventually be resolved in Roman Catholic theology by the doctrine of purgatory. Yet another
important factor in the formation of the doctrine is the conviction of popular
piety that the living might in some fashion influence the dead, particularly by
prayer.[45]

While the doctrine is most fully developed in Roman Catholic theology, a
version of it is also affirmed by some Eastern Orthodox theologians. The main
difference is that Roman Catholics have traditionally viewed purgatory as a
place of temporal punishment for sins that have not been repented of before
death, whereas Eastern theologians view it as a process of growth and maturation for persons who have not completed the sanctification process.

Despite such impressive support for some version of the doctrine of purgatory, Protestants, by and large, have traditionally rejected the whole notion
out of hand. The roots of this rejection go back, of course, to the Reformation. Purgatory was deeply connected with the most basic and bitter disputes
that split the Western church. Moreover, the prevailing doctrine of purgatory
was related to much of the worst corruption of the time, particularly the sale
of indulgences. The passion surrounding this issue is reflected in Calvin's insistence that "we must cry out with the shouting not only of our voices but
our throats and lungs that purgatory is a deadly fiction of Satan, which nullifies
the cross of Christ, inflicts unbearable contempt upon God's mercy, and over-

turns and destroys our faith."[46] The attitude had not changed much in Reformed theology by the nineteenth century when Charles Hodge, the great Princeton theologian, wrote his landmark systematic theology. Hodge noted that Roman Catholics tended to present the doctrine in rather mild terms in works aimed at Protestant readers, while depicting it in very severe terms otherwise. In view of this, he saw purgatory as "a tremendous engine of priestly power. The feet of the tiger withdrawn are as soft as velvet; when those claws are extended, they are fearful instruments of laceration and death."[47]

In the past few decades, by contrast, purgatory has lost much of its controversial edge. This is probably due largely to the fact that there has been a decline of interest in the doctrine among Roman Catholics, even among those who would continue officially to affirm it. And while Protestants still generally repudiate the notion, the matter incites much less fervor than it did in previous generations.

I want to argue, however, that the issues traditionally dealt with by the doctrine of purgatory must be addressed in any serious treatment of heaven. How have Protestants who reject that doctrine resolved the problem of sin and moral imperfection that remains in the lives of believers at the time of death? They agree, after all, that nothing impure or unholy can enter heaven, and they also typically hold that most, if not all, believers are far from perfection when they die. The answer generally given is expressed eloquently by Jonathan Edwards.

> At death the believer not only gains a perfect and eternal deliverance from sin and temptation, but is adorned with a perfect and glorious holiness. The work of sanctification is then completed, and the beautiful image of God has then its finishing strokes by the pencil of God, and begins to shine forth with a heavenly beauty like a seraphim.[48]

The basic idea is that the work Roman Catholics ascribe to purgatory is accomplished immediately, and apparently painlessly, by a unilateral act of God at death.

An important variation on this theme appears in the theology of John Wesley. Unlike most Protestant theologians, Wesley believed that entire sanctification is possible in this life. In his model of the order of salvation, entire sanctification can be received in a moment of faith analogous to the way justification is accepted by faith. Wesley also stressed the processive dimensions of sanctification and thought that entire sanctification could not normally be received without years of gradual growth and progress in grace and holiness. But what is interesting for our purposes is that Wesley believed that the normal time of entire sanctification is "the instant of death, the moment before the soul leaves the body."[49]

It is interesting to note, in this connection, that much contemporary Roman Catholic thought seems to be converging with Protestantism at this point. According to Zachary Hayes, a Roman Catholic proponent of the doctrine, "contemporary theologians tend to situate a process of purification within the experience of death itself. Death is, in much of contemporary Roman Catholic thought, the moment of our final decision for or against God."[50] Certainly there are differences between these three positions, but they are arguably minor compared to the agreement that our sanctification is completed at or during the moment of death.

I want to argue, however, that there are good reasons to hold something like the traditional doctrine of purgatory, for Protestants as well as Roman Catholics. The fundamental issues are the following, assuming that salvation is essentially a matter of transformation, as I have argued in this chapter. First, is our free response necessary for our transformation? Second, are we essentially temporal beings whose thorough moral and spiritual transformation cannot occur without a significant temporal process?

Let us begin with the second question. This has implications for the traditional Protestant view that sanctification is instantly completed at the moment of death. The difficulty with this notion, as David Brown has pointed out, is that "there is no way of rendering such an abrupt transition in essentially temporal beings conceivable."[51] One way to avoid this problem is to appeal to the highly controversial doctrine of God's timelessness and to maintain that after death we share in this condition, so temporal considerations are irrelevant. The matter of God's relationship to time is one of the most difficult and vexing problems in the philosophy of religion, and it would take us far afield to discuss it. I will simply register the fact that I have doubts about the coherence of the doctrine of timelessness, so I do not think this move solves the problem. A more plausible move is to point to the phenomenon of dramatic conversions, which are often rather abrupt. But as Brown points out, there is good reason to think that such dramatic turnarounds have important antecedent causes that lead up to and prepare the way for them. Moreover, outward change of behavior may occur in a rather vivid fashion, but internal change of character is another matter. Real virtue is achieved over a period of time by numerous choices and decisions, often in the face of adversity. Brown concludes that if man is essentially temporal, "his capacity for moral perfection is likewise. No clear sense attaches to the claim that a human being could become instantaneously virtuous, morally perfect, and so, if God is to respect our nature as essentially temporal beings, he must have allowed for an intermediate state of purgatory to exist."[52]

This is the sort of reason Wesley had for insisting that entire sanctification must normally be preceded by a significant period of growth and maturation. Without this process, one is not prepared to receive the fullness of grace represented by entire sanctification. If this basic line of thought is correct, there is good reason to think that something like purgatory is necessary for those who have not experienced significant growth and moral progress.

This brings us to the first question, which I also believe is first in importance for this issue, namely, whether our free response is required for our transformation. While the necessity of a response on our part has seldom been explicitly denied in the Christian tradition, the nature of our free response has been extensively debated. On the one side of the great divide are those who believe that God determines all things, including our choices. The philosophically sophisticated who take this view and also believe we are free in some sense typically recognize that they must hold to a soft determinist or compatibilist account of freedom. The essence of this view is that an act can be free so long as it is not coerced. That is, if one does as he wills to do, then he is free even if he has been determined to will as he does. On the other side are those who believe that freedom and determinism are not compatible. For an action to be truly free, they maintain, it must be up to the person whether or not he performs it. It must be in his power to perform the act and also to refrain from it.

This is a crucial issue, and the position we take on it has profound implications for our whole theology, particularly our view of the nature of salvation and how it is accomplished. I have written about these issues at some length elsewhere and I will not review those arguments here, but there is one consideration I believe is decisive for those who believe in a perfectly good God.[53] If God determines all things in the way theological compatibilists believe, there is no plausible way to account for why our world is so full of evil, particularly moral evil. If freedom and determinism are compatible, then God could determine all persons freely to choose the good at all times. He could determine all persons freely and gladly to do his will in all respects. If God could do this but has chosen instead to determine many persons freely to choose evil and even be damned, then he would not be good in any meaningful sense of the word, let alone perfectly good.

In view of this, I think we must conclude that God has given us incompatibilist or libertarian freedom and that he takes our freedom very seriously. This is the most satisfactory explanation for the bewildering array of moral good and evil in our world. It is because God takes our freedom seriously that even those who have made the decision to follow his will often make only sporadic progress in carrying out their resolutions.

The reality of such freedom is the major consideration in favor of some version of the doctrine of purgatory. Freedom is central to another of Brown's arguments for purgatory, namely, what he calls the argument from "self-acceptance." The key claim of the argument is that it is a moral obligation to give due value to other persons and that this requires persuading others only in ways they can fully own and endorse. This does not mean that the only sort of considerations that may be introduced are those that others are already aware of and embrace. But it does mean that legitimate persuasion is only accomplished when the persons involved understand and own the insight that is offered. On this model, God enables our transformation each step of the way, but our cooperation is necessary for our sanctification to go forward.

If God deals with us this way in this life, it is reasonable to think he will continue to do so in the next life until our perfection is achieved. Indeed, the point should be put more strongly than this. If God is willing to dispense with our free cooperation in the next life, it is hard to see why he would not do so now, particularly in view of the high price of freedom in terms of evil and suffering. And the uneven, inconsistent way in which most people grow in sanctity is powerful evidence that God does not dispense with freedom in this life.

Eleonore Stump has explicated the sanctification process by employing Harry Frankfurt's notion of a self as hierarchically ordered desires. Of particular interest is the distinction between first-order and second-order desires. First-order desires are basic desires such as, for example, Abelard's desire to seduce Heloise. Second-order desires are desires about first-order desires. So, recognizing the spiritual and moral liabilities in seducing Heloise, not to mention the possibility of inciting her uncle's wrath, Abelard may wish he did not have such desires for Heloise. That is, he may have a second-order desire that his first-order desires were different.

Stump suggests that sanctification occurs with our freedom intact if God changes us at the level of our first-order desires in response to our second-order desires that he do so. Of course, God's grace also enables our second-order desires, as I noted earlier in the discussion of Stump's account of how the atonement figures in this. But Stump's picture raises another question about the nature of the divine-human cooperation in sanctification. Why wouldn't one's sanctification be complete the instant he formed the second-order desire to be sanctified? The answer, Stump replies, is that

> the content of this volition is vague. It consists in a general submission to God and an effective desire to let God remake one's character. But a willingness of this sort is psychologically compatible with stubbornly holding on to any number of sins. . . . Making a sinner righteous, then, will be a process in which a believer's specific volitions are brought into harmony with the governing second-order volition assenting to God's bringing her to righteousness, with the consequent gradual alteration in first-order volitions, as well as in intellect and emotions.[54]

Stump goes to comment that this is a "process extending through this life and culminating in the next."[55] Although this is not an explicit statement of purgatory, it seems to be the natural extension of her line of thought.

The reason that the desire for sanctity may be psychologically compatible with holding on to any number of sins is that one may not clearly recognize them as sins or perceive their destructiveness to the point of truly wishing to be delivered from them. The process of sanctification involves coming to see the truth about not only our overt sinful actions but also about the more subtle sinful attitudes we may cherish. A broad desire to be sanctified simply may not recognize all that is involved, and that is why it takes time and growth for grace to penetrate the deeper recesses of our sinful characters.

Of course, the process must culminate sometime, and there is no good reason why it may not culminate in an act of faith in this life as Wesley believed. But the point now is that considerable growth is required before we know what such an act of faith really involves. If this growth has not occurred in this life, purgatory seems necessary if God is to complete the job with our freedom intact.

Freedom also figures prominently in Swinburne's account of purgatory. Swinburne's position depends crucially on his conviction that if life is truly a gift from God, then God cannot entirely restrict how we may use our lives. There must be a range of freedom for us to choose as we please. Included in this range of freedom is not only the choice of whether we shall seek salvation or not but also whether we shall forward our salvation most directly or whether we shall do so more indirectly "If this life is all the life we have in which to form a saintly character, the most direct route will be the only one with any prospect of success. For to form that character is likely to require all our earthly life and our utmost effort."[56]

Given this scenario, God could grant salvation only to those who achieve sanctity in this life, or else drop the requirement of sanctity. The latter option is unacceptable not only because all Christian traditions have held, at least in theory, that sanctity is necessary to enter heaven but also because compromising this teaching would trivialize Christianity. The former option, however, would deny us the freedom to pursue salvation in anything other than the most direct manner. Therefore, this option would be incompatible with God's perfect goodness in giving us a range of significant freedom as part of the very essence of the gift of life.

It follows, then, that if sanctity is required for heaven and God has granted us the freedom to pursue salvation at a different pace than most directly, that there must be further opportunity to pursue sanctity beyond this life. In other words, a doctrine of purgatory is entailed by Swinburne's view about what it means for our lives to be a gift from God, along with the traditional doctrine of sanctity.

Zachary Hayes has also put his finger on the crucial issue of our free response: "The Protestant problem with purgatory, it seems to me, does not begin in the afterlife. It begins already in this life, in the doctrine of justification and grace."[57] Hayes is referring to the Protestant emphasis on grace as a matter of forgiveness on a forensic model. By contrast with the forensic model, Hayes stresses that a transformation model requires our open responsiveness to God's initiative throughout the whole process of salvation. Hayes explicates the controversial question of merit in just these terms.

> The issue of "merit" for good works, then, does not mean that we receive something extrinsic to the work itself. We receive nothing other than the very self-gift of God. And in the reception of that gift, we are profoundly changed. What we "get," then, is the intrinsic effect of God's presence on the human person.[58]

It is precisely the intrinsic nature of the gift that entails transformation. To dispense with transformation is to dispense with the gift itself. But accepting the fullness of this gift cannot be done in an instant, and God will not give us more of himself than we are ready and willing to receive. That is why purgatory is required for those who have only begun to receive what God wants to give of himself.

These accounts of purgatory that emphasize freedom underline the notion that no one can be exempted from the requirement of achieving perfect sanctity in cooperation with God's grace and initiative. Using Swinburne's terms, no one can choose to pursue salvation only indirectly in this life and expect that God will unilaterally effect what they chose not to further in this life. The temporal dimension that Brown emphasizes is also integral to the notion that transformation is a cooperative venture. It takes time to gain understanding of the various layers of our sinfulness and self-deception and to own the truth about ourselves. This is not to say that time after death must be on the same clock as our world.[59] But discerning truth and allowing it to sink into our character is an essentially mental experience that requires time for finite minds. The doctrine of purgatory makes clear that there is no short-cut to sanctity.

The doctrine of purgatory also reminds us that the most pervasive and deadly sins are sins of the spirit. Spiritual sins are not cured merely by dropping our old bodies and receiving new ones. Consider in this light the words of Edwards: "The saved soul leaves all its sin with the body; when it puts off the body of the man, it puts off the body of sin with it. When the body is buried, all sin is buried forever, and though the soul shall be joined to the body again, yet sin shall never return more."[60] Implicit in this argument is a sort of gnosticism that locates sin in our physical bodies. It is as if sanctification were largely effected by releasing the soul from the body. Again, this makes sanctification a passive matter that requires no cooperation on our part.

It is at this point that Protestant objections to purgatory are most pointed, even in our ecumenical age. To take seriously our role in sanctification is to elicit protests of works righteousness. Contemporary evangelical theologian Millard Erickson puts this argument as follows: "In both this life and the life to come, the basis of the believer's relationship with God is grace, not works. There need be no fear, then, that our imperfections will require some type of postdeath purging before we can enter the full presence of God."[61] In the same vein, William Crockett responds to Hayes's defense of purgatory by insisting "that in solidarity with Christ, believers *already* have forgiveness of sins. . . . To suggest, as Hayes does, that most believers are not ready for heaven, smacks of the kind of works theology Paul so strongly opposed."[62]

Similarly, John MacArthur sees purgatory as a denial of justification by faith: "Deny that we are justified by faith alone, and you must devise an explanation of how we can make the transition from our imperfect state in this life to the perfect state of heaven."[63] In his view, glorification is the instantaneous comple-tion of the process of sanctification that is begun in this life. In view of this, MacArthur chides C. S. Lewis for his endorsement of the doctrine of purga-tory, particularly in the following well-known passage.

Our souls *demand* Purgatory, don't they? Would it not break the heart if God said to us, "It is true, my son, that your breath smells and your rags drip with mud and slime, but we are charitable here and no one will upbraid you with these things, nor draw away from you. Enter into the joy"? Should we not reply, "With submission, sir, and if there is no objection, I'd rather be cleansed first." "It may hurt, you know."—"Even so, sir."[64]

MacArthur replies that "nothing in Scripture even hints at the notion of purgatory, and nothing indicates that our glorification will in any way be painful."[65]

The claim that purgatory is not taught in Scripture has, of course, been a stock objection to the doctrine since the Reformation. Certainly it lacks explicit biblical support, but the deeper question is whether it is a reasonable inference from what is clearly taught there.[66] Scripture is rather sketchy in matters eschatological, so it is perhaps inevitable that theologians and philosophers must engage in more speculation than on other topics if they are to say anything substantive about these important matters. This, no doubt, partly accounts for the fact that, as Thomas Oden has noted, eschatology "remains less consensually matured than other articles of the creed."[67] In view of this situation, there is surely room for a measure of speculation that attempts to take account of both the clear teaching of Scripture as well as the facts of empirical experience. If this is granted, purgatory can hardly be dismissed with a wave of the hand on the ground that Scripture does not explicitly articulate it.

What about the objection that purgatory denies the doctrine of justification by faith? It depends on what one means by justification and by faith. Recall McGrath's point that the traditional view is that justification involves actually making us righteous and that this is what finally restores us to a loving relationship with God. It was a Protestant innovation to separate justification from sanctification and to construe the former primarily in legal and forensic categories. The significance of this point here is that justification so understood does not make us actually righteous. Therefore, it is simply irrelevant as an objection to purgatory. Crockett's response to Hayes indicates that he missed altogether Hayes's account of "the intrinsic effect of God's presence on the human person." The "work" required to experience this is simply openness to God's transforming presence. Nothing is earned by this openness in the sense that we have deserved salvation as a reward. Rather, salvation is itself the relationship.

Erickson's objection to purgatory is wide of the mark for the same reason. To insist that we must be fully transformed by freely cooperating with God before we can fully enter his presence is not a denial of the fact that grace is the basis of our relationship with him, for his grace is what takes the initiative and enables our transformation. Erickson's objection to purgatory implies that grace is primarily, if not exclusively, a matter of forgiveness.

To appeal to the fact that God has forgiven us does nothing to address the fact that many Christians are imperfect lovers of God and others at the time of their death. This is not to say that the experience of being forgiven does not change us. Indeed, gratitude for God's free offer of forgiveness is a powerful incentive for the believer to love God in return. But forgiveness alone, especially on a legal model, does not change us in a subjective sense. That is the point of Lewis's quote. Forgiveness alone does not eliminate unpleasant odors, and lack of condemnation does not clean up soiled clothes. Other remedies are necessary, and, as Lewis suggests, they may involve pain.

The invocation of pain has also been a major source of resistance to the doctrine of purgatory, as MacArthur's response indicates. At its best, this is an understandable reaction to the rather lurid depictions of purgatory that have appeared in Roman Catholic writers in the past. At worst, however, it smacks of the sort of cheap grace which implies that mere mental assent to some basic Christian doctrines is all that is necessary for salvation. On this picture, salvation is a perfectly painless thing that requires nothing of the believer but simple belief.[68]

What Lewis wanted to insist, by contrast, is that the moral transformation necessary for salvation is essentially painful. The pain of moral growth and progress is not an arbitrary punishment that God attaches to it, but rather is intrinsic to it. Gregory of Nyssa maintained that the pain involved when God draws people to himself is not due to hatred or blame for their evil lives. Rather, "He, who is the source of all blessedness, draws them to Himself for a higher purpose. The feeling of pain comes of necessity to those who are being drawn up."[69]

Lewis makes this point in several vivid images in *The Great Divorce*. For instance, the fact that the grass in heaven hurts the feet of the ghosts from the grey town (purgatory for those who choose to leave it, hell for those who stay) shows that becoming conformed to the life of heaven is uncomfortable for sinful persons. "Reality is harsh to the feet of shadows."[70] The promise is given, however, that those who are willing to persevere will eventually become more substantial and will be comfortable in heaven; indeed, they will come to flourish there.

Purgatory means coming fully to terms with reality. Richard Purtill has suggested that the period between our death and resurrection will be a time of "reading" our lives like a book. The entire book would be present to us and we could reread past sections, skip ahead, and so on. All of this reading would be done in what he calls "Godlight."[71] That is, it would be a matter of coming to see our lives as God sees them. This would involve, for instance, seeing the full force of how our sins affected others. "The only adequate purgatory might be to suffer what you made others suffer—not just an equivalent pain, but that pain, seeing yourself as the tormenter you were to them. Only then could you adequately reject and repent the evil."[72] The other side of the coin is that we "would see with love even those who have hurt us, because God saw them with love."[73]

Indeed, the accent here should fall on grace, for to see things in "Godlight" is to see them illumined by God's perfect love for all persons and his will to redeem us from our sins and unite us to himself and to each other. Continuing the reading analogy, Purtill points out that the first time we read a book we may hardly appreciate it but that a subsequent reading may fully disclose its beauty and richness.

> As we may write a commentary on a book that has meant much to us, so part of our afterlife could be an appreciation and correction of our present lives. Even if our present lives have been almost a failure—even if we are barely saved after a life of folly and waste—we could still make these wasted lives the foundation of something glorious—a "commentary" much better than the "book."[74]

Purgatory so conceived is not only a matter of taking our choices and our freedom seriously, it is more importantly a matter of taking seriously God's overwhelmingly gracious love to us and his power to redeem our lives, even "wasted" ones.

Construed along these lines, purgatory can be rightly be characterized, as Peter Kreeft has done, in terms of joy.[75] Indeed, Kreeft suggests that we should think of purgatory as a part of heaven rather than a separate place. The suggestion that purgatory should be joyful is hardly ironic in view of the fact that the New Testament frequently teaches Christians to rejoice in times of adversity. This is not to trivialize the pain of purgatory but to point out that it should not be dreaded any more than the pain of moral transformation that we experience in this life.

Before concluding this chapter, I want to address one more question that is often asked about heaven, a question that may be raised by my claim that God continues to take our freedom seriously after death. The question is whether we will retain our freedom in heaven and if so, does this mean we could still sin and even lose our salvation?

The correct answer to this question, I believe, is that we will indeed be free in heaven, but that sin will no longer be a live option for us. The reason this is so is precisely because of the sort of transformation I have been describing in this chapter, namely, a transformation in which the truth about God forms our character through and through. This transformation, when it is complete, will be so thorough that we will know with full clarity and profound certainty that God is the source of happiness and sin is the source of misery. Through numerous experiences of progressive trust and obedience, this truth will have so worked through our character that sin will have lost all appeal for us. The illusory notion that we can promote our well being by disobeying God will be so entirely shattered that sin will be a psychological impossibility for us. At this point, our character will be unalterably confirmed in goodness and holiness and we will gladly and spontaneously worship and obey God.

In heaven then, we will be free in something like the compatibilist sense with respect to our choice of God and the good. That is, we will invariably act in accordance with our transformed character, but we will do so willingly. This does not mean, however, that all of our choices will be determined, as compatibilists hold. While our character will rule out any choice of evil or disobedience to God, we will still retain libertarian freedom within the happy limits of joyous obedience and worship. We will exercise creative freedom as we perfectly fulfill the end for which were made, "to glorify God, and to enjoy him forever."[76]

Moreover, the characters we have in heaven will have been formed by freely cooperating with the grace of God, and the memory and history of that free cooperation will remain forever at the heart of our identity (more on this later). Indeed, the truth that God is the source of happiness and sin the source of misery can be known with true existential clarity only through free cooperation with God's grace. To know this fully in the depths of our being involves much more than mere intellectual insight. It also requires moral and personal development and formation, and such formation cannot be achieved without the personal engagement consisting of freely given trust and obedience. So the fact that our fully formed characters in heaven will no longer retain the possibility of sinning in no way diminishes the importance of libertarian freedom.[77]

I conclude then that the doctrine of purgatory is plausible not only for Roman Catholics and adherents of Eastern Orthodoxy but also for Protestants. For those who take freedom seriously and believe that transformation is the heart of what salvation is all about, it seems to be a fully natural doctrinal development. Indeed, believers of all traditions who have experienced as joy the purging involved in drawing closer to Christ can affirm purgatory as a gracious gift of love.

$$\mathcal{L}\quad 3 \quad \mathcal{L}$$

HEAVEN AND ITS INHABITANTS

I

In 1996 the Southern Baptist Convention adopted a resolution in favor of Jewish evangelism, and their Home Mission Board appointed a missionary to American Jews. Jewish leaders were quick to condemn the resolution. Phil Baum, head of the American Jewish Congress, stated that the Baptists were "misguided" and that the resolution reflected "offensive doctrinal arrogance."[1]

On the face of it, this incident is simply another example of the tensions and mistrust that have characterized relations between Jews and Christians. Beyond this, however, it points up some central and difficult issues that thoughtful Christian believers cannot avoid. Most fundamentally, perhaps, there is the whole question of the relationship between Christianity and other religions. Indeed, other religious believers have their own version of this problem, a problem that has been felt with increasing urgency because of more frequent and common encounters with persons of other faiths. In the past several years, Christian thinkers have devoted considerable attention to this issue because of the large theological and practical implications that ride on it. The incident I have cited brings these into sharp focus. Perhaps the most central of these pertains to the means to salvation. It is germane to the Christian tradition that it offers God's ultimate revelation and way to salvation. Of course, Christianity is not alone in making this claim, but its version of this claim will be my concern in this chapter.

The basic question I wish to address here is who will be in heaven. Of course, this question is broader than the issue of whether adherents of other religions will be saved. Questions also arise about infants and other small children who die before they are able to respond to the gospel in an intelligent way. Further abroad, but still under the umbrella of this large issue, is the question of the ultimate fate of animals. Will the lower creatures also partake of final redemption? Nevertheless, the question of the ultimate fate of believers in other religions remains perhaps the most pressing and difficult of issues under this large umbrella and will accordingly receive the most attention in this chapter.

Because Christians believe they have God's highest word of revelation for salvation, they have been strongly committed to the task of evangelism and world mission. They have traditionally believed that adherents of other faiths need to come to faith in Christ to be saved. To fail to come to faith in Christ is to miss out on salvation, and finally to miss out on heaven, which is man's final end for which he was created. Consequently, to miss out on heaven is the ultimate tragedy a person can experience. This is the basic line of thought behind the Baptist resolution for evangelism of American Jews.[2]

The response of Jewish leaders to the resolution is at least understandable. Strong and even passionate reactions are altogether appropriate when the issue at stake is eternal salvation and one's understanding of the way to salvation is challenged by another religion. Nothing could be more important than one's eternal salvation, and it is unsettling, to say the least, to contemplate the possibility that one might be profoundly mistaken about the way to achieve it. Of course, given the long history of mutual suspicion between the world religions, there are doubtless several factors involved in such passionate reactions, not all of which are religious or theological. But at the heart of the properly religious conflict between different religions lies the dispute over the nature and means of salvation. Conflict appears inevitable as long as one or more religions claim to be the unique or ultimate means to salvation that all persons need to accept in order to be saved.

In what follows, I will sketch out the main positions Christian theologians have formulated on the matter of the salvation of adherents of other religions. I will assess each of these from the standpoint of some basic theological claims that an adequate Christian account of other religions must meet. Among these claims is the concept of salvation I defended in the previous chapter. These claims together provide a framework to answer our primary question of who will be in heaven.

Obviously the questions I shall pursue in this chapter are rather speculative, but this is balanced by the fact that we will approach them under the impetus of the central theological tenets I will shortly specify. Moreover, these issues are not mere idle curiosities but rather matters of urgent existential concern since they inevitably arise from reflection on crucial Christian claims about the availability and conditions of salvation. To put the point another way, the basic theological claims I shall spell out not only generate the issues we will consider but also suggest answers to them. So while an appropriate degree of modesty should be maintained concerning any proposed answers, they can be defended as plausible if they are implications of basic convictions one takes to be true.

II

Before I spell these claims out, I want to consider the views of J. A. DiNoia, who has proposed an ingenious way to maintain the unique claims of Christianity while eliminating the element of offense to other religious traditions. The essence of his argument boils down to the claim that the Christian notion of salvation is fundamentally different from that of other religions. Specifically, the aim of salvation is eternal communion with the Trinity, a communion in which our individual identity is maintained and fulfilled. This is markedly different from, say, the Buddhist goal of nirvana, where individual identity is extinguished.

Recognizing this fact has important implications with respect to the claims believers make for their various traditions. As DiNoia notes, a Christian need not feel anxious if informed by his Buddhist friend that he cannot attain nirvana except by following the Excellent Eightfold Path. If this is true, and if he does not pursue the Path, it follows he may never reach nirvana. But, he continues, "since I have as yet no desire to attain and enjoy Nirvana, I am not offended by this reasoning. I have not been persuaded that Nirvana is what I should be seeking."[3] In the same vein, DiNoia quotes the revealing remark a rabbi once made to him: "Jesus Christ is the answer to a question I have never asked."[4]

The upshot of this is that Jesus can be recognized as the unique mediator of salvation as Christianity conceives it. However, not all persons apparently desire such salvation, so it is not offensive to insist that Jesus is the necessary means to it. This can be as readily granted as the fact that one should travel south from the United States to get to Brazil or Chile. This will not concern those persons whose goal is to travel to Great Britain.

DiNoia's main argument is surely sound. Christianity offers a distinctive account of salvation and not everybody who is religious shares the Christian hope of eternal communion with the Trinity. He is mistaken, however, to advance this point as a way for different religions to avoid giving the offense that seems inevitable from the fact that they claim their religion is the unique way to salvation, nirvana, or whatever they claim is the eternal good. The difficulty is suggested by one of the sentences just quoted, namely: "I have not been persuaded that Nirvana is what I should be seeking." The issue is precisely that, from a Christian standpoint, there are some things that all persons *should be* seeking.

To bring this point into focus, let us reflect on the Christian claim that Jesus is the only way to communion with the Trinity. Since Christians claim there is only one God and that God is the Trinity, it follows from Christian premises that those who do not want eternal communion with the Trinity do not want an eternal relationship with the only God there is. This has serious implications when we consider that such a relationship is, from the Christian standpoint, the highest good for which all persons were created, indeed the only good that can finally answer the human longing for happiness and satisfaction.

Consider the implications of this for the Buddhist who desires extinction or the rabbi who says Jesus is the answer to a question he has never asked. Can the Christian avoid the conclusion that Buddhists *should* desire eternal communion with God and that the rabbi *should* be asking the questions for which Jesus is the answer? And if they do not, then either they misunderstand Christianity or they do not will what God wills for them. And if they do not will what God wills for them, does this not involve the sort of judgment that must inevitably be offensive?[5]

I will come back to the issue of offense, but for now, I simply want to emphasize that there is no simple way to avoid offense by stressing the distinct conceptions of salvation in different religions. Moreover, there are more important concerns than avoiding offense, if indeed this is even possible. I shall argue that it may not be possible to avoid offense in the end.

III

Let us turn now to consider the crucial considerations that a satisfactory Christian account of the fate of adherents of other religions must meet. Some of these are theological in nature and others are more straightforwardly empirical.

The main thrust of these statements is to meet the major moral objection against the Christian doctrine of heaven, namely, the charge that it is unfair. More specifically, it is unfair that something as monumental as eternal salvation should be exclusively available, or even more readily available only to certain persons, in particular, those persons who have the good fortune to be faithfully taught the Christian message in this life. I shall contend that if the following statements are all true, this objection is turned aside.

1. God is perfectly good, perfectly wise, and perfectly powerful.
2. A perfectly good God would love all his human creatures impartially and desire each of them to have a full and fair opportunity to freely receive the gift of eternal salvation.
3. Eternal salvation involves a perfected relationship with God, and such a relationship requires acknowledgment of Jesus as the Son of God who atoned for our sins.
4. A perfectly wise and powerful God could provide each of his creatures a full and fair opportunity to acknowledge Jesus and achieve a perfected relationship with himself.
5. Not all persons have access to the truth about Jesus in this life.
6. Despite a full and fair opportunity for all, some will refuse to acknowledge Jesus and decline forever God's offer of eternal salvation.

The first of these is obviously essential to theism and would be accepted by all orthodox Christians. Number three is also a given of the broad tradition of Christian orthodoxy as I argued in chapter 2, and I shall not defend it further here. Number five is a rather obvious empirical claim, which few of any religion would dispute. Number six is more controversial and would be challenged by those otherwise orthodox Christian theologians who affirm universal salvation or at least the possibility of universal salvation.[6] There are important philosophical considerations against universalism, but the main reason it has been rejected is because it seems to be incompatible with clear New Testament teaching, including the words of Jesus himself. Universalism is a growing trend even among conservative theologians, and universalists would readily challenge my claim about the New Testament with alternative interpretations of the relevant texts. It remains beyond serious dispute, however, that universalism has been rejected by the broad consensus of orthodoxy. For the purpose of this discussion, I shall assume that that consensus is correct.[7]

Number four is also controversial to some degree, and I shall say more about it in the discussion that follows. But the most controversial of the statements is number two. Since it is crucial to the position I shall defend, I want to spell it out in more detail and offer a preliminary defense of it. In saying God loves all impartially, I mean to reject the view that love is essentially a matter of preferring some to the neglect of others. Carl F. H. Henry has expressed this position in claiming that "all love is preferential or it would not be love."[8] While this is arguably true in the case of finite lovers, such preference seems to be incompatible with a perfect lover of infinite resources as Christians believe God is.

The most characteristic kind of divine love is agape, a love that is selflessly directed to the well-being of the beloved. God is capable of such love because he is perfectly self-sufficient and needs nothing from his creatures. His resources of love are unlimited and therefore need not be parceled out in a discriminate fashion. In view of this, we need not worry that we may "be more generous than God has revealed himself to be."[9] God has shown himself to be perfectly generous, and there is little danger that we may be more generous than God. We may be more indulgent or more permissive, but generosity is another matter altogether.

If God loves in this fashion, it seems clear that he would be willing to offer his grace equally to all persons. That is, he would desire to distribute his grace fairly so that all persons receive a full opportunity to respond to it. That is, God would not give some persons many opportunities to repent and receive his grace while giving others only minimal opportunities, or even none at all. Indeed, it seems a God of perfect love would do everything he could, short of overriding freedom, to elicit a positive response from all persons. The presentation of grace would vary from person to person, for different individuals may respond differently to different things. Let us call such grace *optimal grace*. Moreover, a God of perfect love would not easily take no for an answer. Indeed, the very idea of optimal grace entails that each person must make a fully decisive response to it. Half-hearted, superficial, or unformed responses would not be decisive. What would count in the end would be one's fully deliberate

and committed response. Only such a positive choice would achieve a perfected relationship with God, and only such a negative choice would finally
be accepted by God as a rejection of his grace and love.[10]

IV

Now I am prepared to spell out the main positions on the salvation of adherents of other religions and others who have not heard the gospel in this life.
There are various names for these positions and different ways to nuance each
of them. The three broad positions I shall discuss I shall label *particularism*, *pluralism*, and *inclusivism*. I will spell these out in turn and critique them in light of
the six considerations.

Let us begin with particularism, also called *restrictivism* and *exclusivism*. The
heart of the particularist position is that persons can only be saved by explicit
faith in Jesus, faith that must be exercised in this life in response to the preaching of the gospel. Consequently, those who die without explicit faith are lost
forever. The main thrust of this view and its implications for missionary activity is expressed in the following statement from the 1960 Congress on World
Mission in Chicago: "In the years since the war [i.e., since 1945], more than
one billion souls have passed into eternity and more than half of these went to
the torment of hell fire without even hearing of Jesus Christ, who He was or
why He died on the cross of Calvary."[11]

Despite its potential for inspiring missionary endeavor, this view has obvious drawbacks. The most glaring of these is the profound unfairness that seems
to pervade this position, for it appears to make salvation depend on such contingencies as the time or place of one's birth or the circumstances of one's
upbringing, none of which one has any control over. If one is born into a
country where the gospel is readily available and, moreover, into a family that
meets one's emotional, educational, and spiritual needs, then one has a much
greater chance of coming to faith in Christ than if one is born in a country
where the gospel has never been preached. Such a privileged person has a much
better chance than one who is educationally neglected, emotionally abused,
and spiritually uninformed. But the implications of this are surely morally troubling. More specifically, it seems morally intolerable that chance should have
a role at all in something of such extreme importance as one's eternal salvation. Clearly enough, chance and contingency play a major role in determin-
ing one's lot in this life, but it is another thing altogether to think matters of
supreme importance could be decided by such factors.

Particularists have felt the force of this difficulty and have attempted to mitigate it in several ways. One common strategy is to argue that those who have
never heard the gospel are not condemned for rejecting Christ but rather for the
response they make to the light they actually have. The crucial question for those
who make this move concerns the nature of this light. They must maintain the
delicate balancing act of insisting on the clarity and significance of this light while
also denying that such light is sufficient to enable a saving response on the part of

those who receive it. The difficulty of this is illustrated by Carl F. H. Henry, who criticizes his fellow particularists for failing in one of these two directions. Some of them dim the light to such an extent that it is hard to see how anyone could be guilty before God if they had nothing else to go on. Others, he thinks, exaggerate its luminosity to the point of suggesting that it provides a universally shared body of knowledge about God.

The reason general revelation is not adequate to provide saving knowledge of God, according to particularists, is because of the fallen condition of humanity. Sinful rebellion distorts the light of natural revelation, but the light is enough to render the rebellion and the distortion culpable. The revelation of Scripture is needed for even a proper understanding of general revelation. The correct balance as Henry sees it is that "General revelation attests God's eternal power and moral majesty and renders rebellious humankind guilty. But it declares nothing of God's redemptive grace and the atoning work of Jesus of Nazareth that provides salvation for sinners."[12] In the same vein, R. Douglas Geivett and W. Gary Phillips hold that "general revelation is epistemically valuable, even if it is not soteriologically efficacious."[13]

This is a difficult balance to achieve for the simple reason that it is hard to see how light can be sufficient to condemn but not to save. To grasp this, let us ask what light must be like in order to render culpable those who receive it. It would seem that such light must provide at least reasonably clear direction on what we should believe and how we should behave. If it does not, then how could anyone be guilty for not responding to it? But if it is clear in this fashion, then it seems the recipient could respond positively to it, at least insofar as it is simply a question of adequate light.

Of course, according to traditional Christian theology, it is not simply a matter of light. In addition to light, sinners need the assistance of grace in order to respond favorably to the truth God reveals to them. This is the case even for those who have the privilege of hearing the gospel fully and clearly preached. Sinners still need the help of the Holy Spirit to believe and obey the truth.

If the light of general revelation is at least reasonably clear in showing sinners what they ought to believe and how they ought to behave, then presumably the only thing lacking to enable a positive response is God's grace, the same sort of grace sinners who hear the gospel receive. And if God loves those persons who receive only the light of general revelation and desires to save them, then would he not be willing to give them the grace to enable a positive response? There seems to be no reason to think he could not or would not.

I conclude that particularists cannot walk the tightrope they wish to walk on the subject of the light of general revelation. If such light is sufficient to condemn, then it is sufficient, along with accompanying grace, to enable a positive response. If it is not adequate to enable a positive response, then it is not clear enough to render culpable those who receive it.

Particularists themselves sometimes concede in a very telling way that they cannot keep their balance on the tightrope they have stretched across this issue. Specifically, they allow that it may be possible for some to be saved who have not heard the gospel in this life. Geivett and Phillips, for instance, gesture in this direction when they write that "except perhaps in very special circumstances, people are not saved apart from explicit faith in Jesus Christ, which presupposes that they have heard about his salvific work in their behalf."[14] What is interesting here is the muted acknowledgment of exceptions in special circumstances. Likewise, the traditional missiologist J. Herbert Kane, while expressing serious doubts that anyone could be saved with only general revelation, admits that "we must not completely rule out the possibility, however remote, that here and there throughout history there may have been the odd person who has got to heaven without the full light of the gospel. In that case *God* is the sole judge. He is the sovereign in the exercise of His grace."[15]

These exceptional cases are interesting, but they raise more questions than they answer. More specifically, the pressing question is why there should be any exceptions at all on particularist grounds. What separates the odd or exceptional person from others who are simply lost without the benefit of hearing the gospel? Is there something exceptional about these persons themselves? Are they more religiously or morally discerning than their peers? Are they more intelligent and therefore capable of seeing the light of general revelation? Are they more conscientious in their efforts to live out the moral truths they grasp? None of these suggestions would be acceptable to an orthodox Christian, for they all imply salvation by some sort of human merit or excellence.

The possibility that some might be saved apart from explicit faith in Christ is more typically construed along the following lines. Some persons may have a sense of their guilt through the law written on their hearts. They may cast themselves on the mercy of God even though they know very little about God or his love for us. Such persons would be saved by the merits of Christ even though they had not heard of him in this life.

This view is certainly plausible, but it still raises the same sort of questions as mentioned earlier. Why are only a very select few sensitive to their guilt and need for mercy? Why does only an occasional odd person here and there come to this recognition? Kane suggests an answer in the sovereignty of God. It is he who dispenses the appropriate amount of light from general revelation and sovereignly chooses whom he will save through it.

This account certainly gives some explanation of why some are saved with only the benefit of general revelation. But again, it raises more questions than it answers. Most obviously it raises the question of whether God could sovereignly choose to save others, besides the occasional odd person here and there, through general revelation. Indeed, if it is simply a matter of sovereign choice, could not God choose to save all persons, some with the benefit of special revelation and others with only general revelation? And why would he choose not to if he could do so? The appeal to sovereignty solves nothing. It only exacerbates the question of why only by rare exceptions could anyone be saved without explicit faith in Christ in this life.

In short, the granting of the possibility that some might be saved without benefit of special revelation appears to be an ad hoc maneuver to blunt the sharp sense of unfairness in the particularist position without diminishing to any significant degree the urgent motivation for missions in that view. The suggestion that some sincere seekers of truth might be saved by casting themselves on God's mercy is meant to mitigate the severity of the particularist position. But the claim that such persons are extremely rare, if indeed they even exist at all, keeps the edge of missionary motivation sharp and pointed.

Maintaining this position is, like the particularist stance on general revelation, a delicate balancing act. It is, however, a decidedly unstable position because it lacks any clear or consistent theological account for why occasional unevangelized persons may be saved. It also appears to be largely sustained by the pragmatic concern to keep missionary activity as urgent as possible. Both its arbitrary nature and its pragmatic motivation point to its lack of consistent and coherent theological grounding.

This brings us to a more recent and philosophically sophisticated attempt to defend particularism. This strategy involves an appeal to God's middle knowledge, a controversial doctrine first defended by Luis de Molina, a sixteenth-century Jesuit theologian. Molina's views were developed in opposition to the theological determinism of some of his Thomist opponents. The basic idea of middle knowledge, roughly speaking, is that God knows from all eternity what all possible persons would do in all possible circumstances, including circumstances and states of affairs that will never be actual. Molina believed that God created and providentially ordered the world in light of what he knew through middle knowledge.[16]

Middle knowledge has significant implications for our question in this regard. It raises the fascinating possibility that God knows of unevangelized persons who would have responded favorably to the gospel if they had been placed in circumstances where they would have heard it. Consider for instance the many generations of persons throughout the world who lived and died before missionaries ever reached their shores. According to the doctrine of middle knowledge, God knows which, if any, of these persons would have believed in Christ if missionaries had come to them and they had heard the gospel faithfully preached and observed persons living it with integrity.

Some particularists have proposed an ingenious answer to this question that is intended to save their position from the charge of unfairness, namely, that *none* of these persons would have believed. William Craig, who has defended this move in some detail, has suggested that "it is possible that God in his providence so arranged the world that those who never in fact hear the gospel are persons who would not respond if they did hear it. God brings the gospel to all those who he knows will respond to it if they hear it. . . . No one who would respond if he heard it will be lost."[17] Following the model of Alvin Plantinga's "Free Will Defense," Craig's primary aim is to show that there is no logical inconsistency in believing both that: (1) God is perfect in goodness, power, and knowledge and (2) that some persons do not receive Christ and are damned. The possibility Craig proposes to show the compatibility of these two statements is the key to his argument, for it entails that all persons who would freely respond to the gospel will in fact be saved. Craig argues that perhaps the only persons who are lost are those who would not receive Christ in any world in which they exist and that God could actually create.

As a bare logical possibility, I think Craig's argument is above reproach. Unfortunately, he does not leave it as a mere possibility but ventures the further suggestion that it is a plausible account of what might actually be the case in our world.[18] When taken on these terms, I find it extremely dubious. Consider some of the places in the world where Christianity is flourishing today, such as Korea and sub-Saharan Africa, places where Christian witness was relatively minimal, if it existed at all, in earlier generations. Is it really plausible at all to think none of the forebears of these contemporary Korean and African Christians would have accepted the gospel if they had heard it? Surely it strains credulity to the breaking point to think none of them would have. Indeed, it seems more likely that many persons would have responded positively, just as they have in our day.

Moreover, as William Hasker has pointed out, Craig's theory has dubious implications for mission work. Hasker asks us to consider Parson Peter, the minister of a thriving American congregation. While enjoying his ministry, he wonders whether his efforts might be better spent taking the gospel to those who would otherwise never have a chance to hear it instead of remaining among those who have had many opportunities. He wants his life to make a difference, and he wonders whether he would be able to do so by going abroad. While pondering this question, he happens to read Craig's article and arrives at an affirmative answer. In particular, he draws inspiration from Craig's claim that "it is our duty to proclaim the gospel to the whole world, trusting that God has so providentially ordered things that through us the good news will be brought to persons who God knew would respond if they heard it."[19] Parson Peter concludes that there likely are persons who will be saved if he goes to the mission field, who otherwise would be lost.

But then Parson Peter considers the question from another angle. He wonders whether, if he stays where he is, there are people who would then be lost but who would have been saved if he had gone to the mission field. Surprisingly, using the same reasoning as before, he arrives at the conclusion that there probably are no such people. Those who are lost would not have believed even if the gospel had been preached to them. In short, Craig's position leads to a paradoxical result on a central issue for particularists, namely, the rationale for missionary activity. Surely this is a good reason for particularists to avoid appealing to middle knowledge to defend their view against the charge of unfairness.

This brings us to the final move I want to discuss that particularists might employ to defend their position against moral objections. Particularists might challenge statement number four. That is, they might deny the claim that God could provide all persons with a full and fair opportunity to accept Christ. Geivett and Phillips, for instance, have suggested, "For all we know, there may be something about the nature of unregenerate human persons which, in conjunction with the requirements of divine justice, limit the ways that God might make his salvation available."[20] They go on to point out that we are entirely dependent on God's revelation if we are to know the truth on such matters, and in their opinion God has revealed that the condition for salvation is proclamtion of the gospel and belief on the part of those who hear it. "Certainly, if God has revealed his method for saving individuals, his veracity limits his flexibility."

These are interesting and relevant suggestions, but the question is whether they provide a good reason to think God could not provide a full opportunity for all persons to respond to Christ. I think not. Surely it is hard to see what there is about the nature of unregenerate persons that could place limits on making salvation available. According to orthodox Christian teaching, such persons are helpless without grace and it is up to God's gracious initiative to reveal the truth to them and enable them to respond to it. Surely God is up to the task, and unregenerate hearts do not pose an insurmountable obstacle to his at least making salvation available to all persons. Nor does it help to appeal to divine justice in this regard. Indeed, if justice is a consideration, it is a good reason to believe that God would make sure all persons have a fair chance to respond to the gospel. In other words, God's perfect justice is a constraint on any suggestion that the resources of salvation might be distributed unevenly.

This brings us to the dictum that God's "veracity limits his flexibility." It is noteworthy that Geivett and Phillips agree that "if there were not strong biblical evidence to the contrary, God's salvation arrangements might be more inclusive."[21] The suggestion here is that God could have arranged things so that more people could be saved but that he has chosen not to. Moreover, he has revealed his more exclusive arrangements and he cannot go against what he has revealed. The limits of mercy are drawn by veracity.

I would argue in response that God's mercy and perfect love are the ground of his veracity and that there is no conflict at all between these. God would not reveal anything that would limit the exercise of his perfect love and goodness. God does not make arbitrary promises or commitments that would restrict his ability to exercise his perfect love in the best interest of his creatures.

Of course, Geivett and Phillips believe that "strong biblical evidence" requires their position even though it might be doubtful on other grounds. It would take us too far afield to engage in an exegetical debate, but it is at least worth noting that many scholars find the biblical material much more open than Geivett and Phillips suggest it is. Indeed, there is a significant Christian tradition that has held a much more hopeful view of the fate of the unevangelized than particularists hold, and it is misleading for particularists to imply that their view has the unambiguous support of Scripture and the Christian tradition. Many would agree that Scripture simply does not say much directly about how God will deal with those who do not hear the gospel in this life.

Scripture and the Christian tradition are certainly clear that salvation is through faith in Christ and that those who persist in unbelief will be lost. This obviously applies to those who have heard the gospel and have truly understood it. But as John Wesley remarked, this does not concern those to whom the gospel has not been preached. It was his view that "we are not required to determine any thing touching their final state. How it will please God, the judge of all, to deal with *them*, we may leave to God himself."[22] Wesley took the authority of Scripture with full seriousness, and his agnosticism on this question cannot be charged to a desire to evade its clear teaching. Given the time in which he wrote, it is also worth stressing that his views on the matter cannot be attributed to the pressures of late modern or postmodern sensibilities.

Another way particularists might argue that God cannot give everyone a full chance to respond to the gospel is as follows. They might argue that God has chosen to make the gospel known exclusively through the human instrumentation of the church in this world. It is the task and privilege of the church to evangelize the world, and if it fails in its task, the price to be paid is that many persons will be lost who otherwise would have been saved. This is admittedly a heavy responsibility to place on human shoulders, but it shows God takes us and our choices seriously. We live in a web of mutual dependence, and this extends even to our dependence on others to make known to us the way to eternal salvation. Since God has chosen to give us such responsibility and to respect our freedom in this regard, there is a very real sense in which he cannot make sure that all persons have a full chance to accept Christ.

This argument is a variation on the particularist's rationale for missionary motivation, and there is surely something to this version of it. We are interdependent, and our choices do affect others in many ways, some of which we are not even aware. This is what constitutes the fabric of human community and accountability, and most view this community as a good thing. In view of this, we may be inclined to agree with Richard Swinburne's judgment that "It is good that the fate of men should depend in small part on the activity of other men, that men should carry the enormous responsibility of the care of the souls of others."[23]

It is not altogether clear what degree of dependence Swinburne means to endorse by his phrase "in small part." At any rate, I would agree with him, unless he means to suggest that whether or not one has a full chance to receive eternal salvation depends on the activity of others. Surely our activity can influence others to believe or disbelieve, and we can affect when people come to faith, how deeply it matters to them, and the like. But just as surely it cannot be the case that whether or not someone else has a full and fair chance to receive salvation depends on our choices. If it did, then some, perhaps many, would experience the misery of eternal damnation because of the failure of others. It will not do to reply that none are lost except for their own sins if it is the case that such persons would have been saved if others had not failed in their behalf. The conclusion is inescapable that such failure contributed largely, if not decisively, to their damnation. It is hard to see, moreover, how the saved who failed in their responsibility to reach the unevangelized could enjoy their eternal salvation knowing many persons were eternally lost as a result of their failure.

Surely a perfectly wise, powerful, and loving God would not allow the opportunity for salvation to be limited to the inconsistent and sometimes haphazard, albeit loving, effort of his human servants to spread the gospel. As Alister McGrath has argued, God's sovereignty will not allow human failure to defeat his good purposes. While not denying the importance of our efforts in God's economy, we should not imagine that God's saving activity is defined by our faithfulness in preaching or evangelism: "A human failure to evangelize cannot be transposed into God's failure to save."[24]

It makes much better theological and moral sense that none can be lost through the failure of others. God loves each person as an individual and will judge each as an individual. For such judgment to be fair, all individuals must be on an equal footing with regard to their opportunity to accept Christ and achieve salvation.

It is important to emphasize that the crucial moral issue here is the opportunity to receive salvation, not whether salvation is actually received. In this regard, we can agree with Geivett and Phillips that "the specific number of the redeemed is not a measure of [Christ's] love."[25] Because of the factor of free will, and especially the possibility of perversity, there is no guarantee that even perfect love will be accepted when it is given.[26] The greatness of the love is not reflected entirely in the response it receives. But God's love is measured by whether he does everything he can, short of overriding freedom, to reach his needy creatures and elicit a positive response from them.

Particularism poses an insurmountable moral problem for the doctrine of heaven because it depicts God as less than perfectly loving. It depicts heaven as a place that is relatively sparsely populated because of the contingencies of time, place, and historical accident. In short, the very notion of heaven as a fellowship of perfect love is compromised by particularism. We need, then, a different account of the unevangelized than this theory offers.

V

Let us turn now to consider pluralism, a position on the other end of the spectrum. I will focus on the best-known and most philosophically sophisticated version of that position, namely, that of John Hick. Hick has been developing his position over several years, having moved from a stance of broad Christian orthodoxy to one of radical pluralism. He has spelled out his position in several essays and books, sometimes in summary form and at considerable length in others. The essence of his view can be stated in three broad claims as follows.

First, the structure of salvation is basically the same in all of the world religions. Despite using different language and telling different stories in their accounts of salvation, in each case it amounts to becoming rightly related to reality. More specifically, it is a change from self-centeredness to reality-centeredness. It is Hick's view that the same thing is going on in worship in the different religions, again despite variations in liturgical practices, cultural factors, symbolism, and so on. Participants are seeking to open themselves to God and to experience transformation in the process.

Second, Hick believes that none of the great religions are salvifically superior to the others. Each of them has produced its saints, and there is no empirical evidence that Christians are morally superior to their counterparts in other faiths. In fact, it was Hick's encounters with saintly persons of other faiths that were instrumental in causing him to rethink his earlier views about the uniqueness of Christianity. We would not expect such equality in morality and sanctity among the religions if Christianity is really God's final revelation and means to salvation. Hick believes his pluralistic hypothesis better explains the observed facts concerning the power of the various religions to transform human lives. Of course, Hick grants that "If we define salvation as being forgiven and accepted by God because of Jesus' death on the cross, then it becomes a tautology that Christianity alone knows and is able to preach the source of salvation."[27] But if salvation is understood as moral and spiritual transformation, then he thinks it is obvious that salvation is being accomplished in all of the great religions.

Third, Hick believes the conflicting claims of the world religions can be accounted for in terms of a Kantian-styled distinction between the divine noumenon, the Real *an sich*, and the various divine phenomena, God as experienced through human categories and receptivities. Indeed, Hick is willing to say that the various divine personae such as Yahweh, Krishna, and Allah "have been formed in the interaction between the Real and different human religio-cultural communities."[28] Hick's use of the word "interaction" here is interesting for it suggests actual contact with or experience of the Real, a suggestion that is hard to understand in Kantian categories. Leaving this difficulty aside, however, it is not surprising, given Hick's Kantian distinction, that the divine reality would be differently conceived, experienced, and worshiped. This does not mean that incompatible things are actually true of the Deity, but it does mean that we cannot know which of the various contradictory claims made about God are really true. "We should therefore not think of the Real *an sich* as singular or plural, substance or process, personal or non-personal, good or bad, purposive or non-purposive."[29] This agnosticism about the actual nature of the Real has deep practical implications for normal religious activity. For instance, it rules out the belief that we are worshiping the Real in itself, and it redefines religious devotion as a matter of adoring one of the various humanly constructed manifestations of the Real.

Hick's defense of religious pluralism is vulnerable to criticism at several points, some of which bear particularly on our concerns. First, it is not all clear that Hick is in a position to make the sort of judgments he makes about the moral and spiritual transformation produced by the various traditions. As Kelly Clark has pointed out, spiritual transformation is not a matter of mere morality, and neither of these are reducible to outward, publicly accessible behavior. Internal motives are crucial for assessing both spiritual and moral progress. Moreover, some religions place full transformation beyond this life. "We lack access both to the post-mortem goals of transformation and to the fundamental principle of a person's action. We simply are not in an epistemic position to make judgments about the equal success of differing religious beliefs at moral and spiritual transformation."[30] This point is particularly telling in light of Hick's Kantian distinction between appearances and reality. His whole position is thus suspect at the fundamental level of its rationale and motivation.

This brings us to a second difficulty, namely, that it requires Christians, as well as adherents of other religions that make exclusive claims, to give up what is distinctive to their faith and accept a generic substitute in its place. Hick denies this, claiming that his position "leaves each tradition as it is, though opening it in dialogue with other traditions to both mutual criticism and enrichment." Hick does concede, however, that to accept the pluralistic view requires the various religions to "deemphasize and eventually winnow out that aspect of its self-understanding that entails a claim to unique superiority among the religions of the world."[31]

With respect to Christianity, this requires nothing less than a radical reinterpretation, if not outright rejection, of incarnation, atonement, resurrection, and Trinity. As Hick recognizes, it is the incarnation in particular that warrants the Christian claim to superiority because that doctrine implies that Christianity was directly founded by God as the means to salvation and that it should supersede all other faiths. Moreover, the doctrines of atonement and Trinity follow logically from incarnation. "To revise the traditional doctrine of the Incarnation is thus, by implication, to revise also the traditional Trinity and Atonement doctrines."[32] Accordingly, Hick has devoted a good deal of energy to promoting a revised doctrine of the incarnation. His move away from orthodoxy was crystalized several years ago when he argued in a much-publicized controversy that the incarnation should be understood as a myth. In the same vein, he argued against accepting the traditional understanding of Jesus' bodily resurrection as a historical event. More recently, he has preferred to refer to the incarnation as a metaphor.[33] Either way, he means to reject the orthodox view that Jesus was God the Son incarnate, with its implications of atonement and Trinity.

What is remarkable is that Hick can protest with an apparently straight face that his pluralistic view leaves Christianity "as it is." The obvious truth is that his view requires a thoroughgoing reconstruction of the central beliefs of Christian orthodoxy that most believers through the ages would hardly recognize as a version of their faith. And this would hardly be an idiosyncratic reaction confined to earlier generations of believers. Contemporary adherents of orthodoxy have been no more friendly to Hick's proposals for reshaping Christianity to fit into his pluralistic procrustean bed.

Third, Hick's claim that the nature of salvation is essentially the same in the various world religions begs some profound questions. Consider particularly the notion that salvation is about being changed from self-centeredness to reality-centeredness. The question that is immediately raised by this definition and cannot be evaded is the nature of reality. Traditional believers would insist that the very doctrines that Hick wants to "winnow" out of Christianity are the very bedrock of reality, which all persons must come to terms with in order to be saved. Becoming reality-centered means coming to acknowledge Jesus as God the Son incarnate who died to atone for our sins. It is to enter into the fellowship of the Trinity. As I argued in chapter 2, the Christian doctrine of heaven is integrally related to the distinctive Christian notion of salvation.

Recall that Hick thinks it is tautological to believe salvation is exclusively through Christianity if salvation is defined as reconciliation to God through Christ. Hick appears to think there is something arbitrary about the way Christians define salvation and that they could easily dispense with their account of it. But they cannot do so without radically redefining the nature of ultimate reality. If Christ is God, as orthodox Christianity believes, then one must acknowledge Christ as God in order to have a right relationship with God. The requirement to believe in Christ is a straightforward implication of belief in the incarnation. Perhaps there is a tautology in the neighborhood, but it is not a matter of an arbitrary definition of salvation. Christians can no more give up their account of salvation than they can dispense with the incarnation. Of course, Hick would readily recommend giving up the doctrine of incarnation. But the point is that to do this is to give up the Christian vision of reality.

George Mavrodes has made essentially the same point by arguing that the Real as Hick conceives it is incompatible with the Trinity.[34] The Real is something Hick believes we must postulate to account for the facts of religious experience. He even goes so far as to say, as noted earlier, that the various religious traditions have emerged out of interaction between the Real and different human communities. It is hard to know what sort of interaction he has in mind, given some of his other claims. But what is clear is that traditional Christians do not believe God is a mere postulate of human reason and experience. Rather, God has revealed himself and his purposes with a striking degree of specificity. Such a strong account of revelation is hardly amenable to Hick's view that we cannot even say whether the Real in itself is personal or impersonal, purposive or nonpurposive, and so on. According to traditional Christianity, ultimate reality has far more definition and purpose than Hick is willing to allow.

This brings us to a fourth difficulty in Hick's position, a problem of great immediate practical significance. If Hick's position is accepted and understood, it has devastating consequences for religious motivation and devotion. Recall the argument of the first chapter that belief in an evil or amoral deity would be profoundly demoralizing. Belief in a good God who supports our efforts, on the other hand, is morally encouraging. This encouragement is enhanced even further by the Christian belief in heaven and the central doctrines that display God's love and resources to transform us.

Hick's position requires us to be agnostic about the very moral and theological resources that have traditionally fired Christian devotion. To put it another way, the central Christian doctrines provide believers not only with an account of the shape and structure of ultimate reality, they also provide powerful inspiration and motivation for spiritual transformation. These doctrines assume that God is profoundly good, that he loves us with an overwhelming love, and that he desires our renewal and perfection. Take as an example the final verse of Isaac Watts's hymn "When I Survey the Wondrous Cross." This verse expresses the devotional response of countless believers who have reflected on the remarkable account of divine love depicted in the earlier verses of the hymn.

> Were the whole realm of nature mine,
> That were an offering far too small;
> Love so amazing, so divine,
> Demands my soul, my life, my all.

It is the particular story of love as revealed in the incarnation and death of Christ that has elicited the love and devotion of believers down the ages.

But on Hick's account of things, we cannot even know that God in himself/itself is even good or loving, let alone that he loves us enough to come among us as a man and die to reconcile us to himself. To be sure, we can know this about the Christian manifestation of the divine, but we must be careful to remember that this particular culturally shaped description of the Real is not to be identified with the Real itself. This sort of agnosticism surely robs normal Christian devotion of its rationale and motivation. The Real itself is shrouded in mystery and, as Kelly Clark has pointed out, we cannot even be sure the Real cares about human transformation or what such transformation would entail. "Whether or not he/it/nothing is actually concerned about human transformation is an enigma. Is Reality concerned for human welfare or transformation at all? Your guess is as good as mine. We aren't allowed a peek behind that veil either."[35]

Human motivation is a complex matter, and I do not want to go so far as to deny outright that someone who held Hick's views could be motivated by the likes of Watts's classic hymn. After all, sometimes people are moved, even to the point of tears, by things they do not believe to be a reality of the sort that should move them in that fashion. For instance, sometimes people are moved in this way by rituals surrounding the flag of their country. Being fired by passion in such a case is not a logical matter, nor is it necessarily tied to any sort of beliefs about ultimate reality.

While this is surely true, I think the earlier point still stands. Christian motivation at its best is not merely an emotional reaction, devoid of thoughtful reflection on what is believed to be the sober truth about God and his love for us. Christian devotion is a way of life that must be sustained even when emotion is at a low ebb. At times like this, orthodox Christian beliefs provide a rationale for devotion and obedience that is sorely lacking when those beliefs are shrouded in agnosticism and obscurity.

Another way to bring Hick's agnosticism into focus is to consider the six propositions stated earlier. Presumably Hick would say we cannot know any of these except for number five, an obvious empirical truth. Even the first of these, which represents the bare bones of theism, cannot be known of the Real itself.

I conclude that Hick's position is altogether unacceptable for anyone who takes seriously anything like a traditional view of heaven. His desire to defend a position that ensures persons of other faiths are taken seriously and treated fairly is commendable, but his means of achieving this goal destroys the substance of Christian faith and the distinctively Christian hope of eternal salvation.

VI

Having rejected particularism and pluralism, I turn now to consider inclusivism. How shall we characterize or define this view? For a start, inclusivism, like particularism, is committed to maintaining intact the core commitments of

Christian orthodoxy. Accordingly, the inclusivist readily admits that there are real contradictions between essential Christian doctrine and the fundamental commitments of other religions. Where this is the case, moreover, the inclusivist believes the Christian claim is true in the realist sense and rejects what is incompatible with it as false. Of course, this does not mean other religions must be rejected as completely false, and the inclusivist can happily affirm as true anything in other religions that is compatible with essential Christian orthodoxy. Like the pluralist, then, the inclusivist is prepared to acknowledge a measure of common ground between Christianity and other religions. Furthermore, inclusivists hold a much more hopeful view of the fate of the unevangelized than do particularists. Indeed, they characteristically view the truth in other religions as preparation for the full truth of the gospel, sometimes suggesting that such partial truth plays a role similar to that played by the Old Testament revelation.

In short, inclusivists insist against pluralists that all salvation is ultimately through Christ, but they also challenge the particularists' insistence that salvation comes only—with rare exceptions—through hearing the gospel and explicitly coming to faith in Christ in this life. They aim for a mediating position that allows them to maintain the integrity of orthodox belief while avoiding the moral difficulties that plague particularism.

These ideas are familiar and have become broadly accepted among orthodox theologians, both Roman Catholic and Protestant. Evangelical theologian and proponent of inclusivism Clark Pinnock writes that it "may even be called the mainline model."[36] In Roman Catholic theology, the Second Vatican Council is an important landmark in articulating an inclusivist position, and the work of Karl Rahner has further developed this line of thinking. On the Protestant side, many examples could be cited, but perhaps the most symbolically significant are the enormously influential apologetic writings of C. S. Lewis. It is worth noting that Pinnock largely credits Lewis for moving him to an inclusivist position because he trusted Lewis as an orthodox thinker.[37]

Is inclusivism a coherent and balanced combination of orthodox belief and moral sensitivity as its advocates think, or is it beset by difficulties of similar magnitude to the views I have rejected? I want to consider one criticism that is germane to inclusivism and, indeed, to any position that purports to offer a third option to what are considered more extreme positions on opposite ends of the spectrum. This is the criticism that such positions are mere compromise measures with none of the integrity of the allegedly more extreme views they intend to replace. As such, they will satisfy no one on either side of the divide. Hick presses this charge when he claims that inclusivism is "an inherently unstable position" similar to the epicycles that were added to Ptolemaic astronomy in order to keep it propped up a little longer in the face of new evidence that seemed to undermine it.[38] So understood, inclusivism is only a sort of rickety halfway house on the way from particularism to pluralism. It is not a secure resting place capable of being sustained in the face of careful scrutiny.

I believe Hick's criticism of inclusivism is wide of the mark on at least two counts. First, there is a significant tradition of inclusivism going all the way back to the church fathers. It is highly misleading to suggest that inclusivism is a new position constructed in an ad hoc way to withstand the pressures of recently discovered evidence or considerations advanced by pluralists in a way similar to the fashion Ptolemaic astronomy was modified under pressure of new data.[39]

But there is a second and more important reason why inclusivism cannot be dismissed in the way Hick attempts to do. That reason, essentially, is that something like inclusivism follows from the fundamental claims of Christian theism as spelled out earlier. In particular, the claim that God could and would provide all persons a full opportunity to achieve a perfected relationship with himself, despite the obvious fact that not all persons hear about Jesus in this life, leads to an inclusivist position. If this is so, then inclusivism is far from an unstable or ad hoc view. To the contrary, it is quite secure and stable since it is deeply rooted in the most basic claims of Christian theism. In other words, all that is needed to embrace an inclusivist view is a commitment to a strong view of God's love and power and a willingness to work out consistently the implications of those beliefs. Of course, not all theists would agree with the account of God's perfect goodness that I have affirmed. It is, however, an intuitively appealing account, rooted in the biblical picture of God as overwhelmingly generous and gracious, and I would defend it as the most satisfactory way to construe God's goodness, as sketched above.

Let us turn now to spell out inclusivism more fully. In particular, I want to emphasize what is involved in believing that God impartially loves his human creatures and would therefore desire each of them to have a full and fair opportunity to receive the gift of eternal salvation. What this implies is that God will do everything he can, short of overriding freedom, to save all persons. This means that, finally, none will be at a disadvantage with respect to the opportunity to receive salvation. Whatever the inequities of this life, in the end, all persons will have equal opportunity for salvation.

I want to stress the notion of equal opportunity for salvation, for this is sometimes resisted even by those who would insist that all persons will receive at least sufficient grace that they could actually be saved. Consider for instance Swinburne's claim that equality cannot be achieved because we are to some degree at the mercy of our particular social influences. God has given us responsibility for our fellow men, and in view of this, not all will have the same chance to achieve the good character necessary for salvation. "The inequality of chance to attain good character for some is an inevitable consequence of giving such serious responsibility to others, of God allowing others to share in his creative activity."[40]

I have already commented critically on Swinburne's claim that the fate of men should depend to some extent on the actions of others. While agreeing with this broadly construed, I argued that all of us are finally loved as individuals by God and are individually accountable to him. Accordingly, whether or not we are saved cannot depend on the faithfulness or failure of others. Now

I want to argue that the logical extension of this line of thought is that equality of opportunity cannot depend on the contingencies of human faithfulness in this life.

Let us begin with the assumption that all persons have at least some chance to be saved. Many inclusivists would grant this, and it is clear that Swinburne would agree.[41] Here is the question: If God can ensure that all persons have at least some chance, then is there any good reason why he could not ensure that all persons would have a full and fair chance? So far as we can determine, and insofar as opportunity for salvation depends on human faithfulness, it would appear that many persons have no chance at all. Certainly many never hear the gospel in this life. So it is obvious that if all persons are to have a real chance to be saved, that chance must be understood in terms of something other than explicitly hearing the gospel in this life.

There are at least four possibilities here. First, there is the notion of evangelism occurring at the moment of death. According to this view, all persons encounter Christ in the moment of death and make a fully free and decisive choice to accept or reject him. Second, there is the suggestion that God will judge people on the basis of his middle knowledge. On this view, God knows through middle knowledge of some persons who would have accepted the gospel if they had heard it, and in his mercy he saves them on this basis. Third, there is the theory of postmortem or eschatological evangelism. Some defend this as a straightforward inference from the belief that explicit faith in Christ is necessary for salvation, that God is perfectly fair, and that none are damned except for deliberately rejecting Christ. This view is further bolstered by those rather difficult New Testament texts that speak of Christ's descent into hell and his preaching of the gospel to those who have died.[42] Fourth, there is the notion that God will judge all persons according to the light they have. That is, all have a degree of light and God only requires a response in proportion to the degree of understanding one enjoys. What is crucial for salvation is the moral response of the heart rather than the degree of one's cognitive clarity. Some in this tradition distinguish between Christians and believers and hold that all believers are finally saved while only Christians have the benefit of full assurance and understanding in this life. All who are saved are saved through Christ, even if they do not understand or believe this in their present life.

The point I want to emphasize is that there is no decisive reason, on any of these four accounts, why all persons could not have equal opportunity for salvation, although the first of these poses the greatest difficulty. I will consider each of them in turn.

The first is most difficult because it is hard to see how an equal chance could be offered in an instant, namely, the instant of death. Consider two persons. The first has been raised by a loving family in a strong Christian community where the faith is sincerely taught and lived. He has been consistently nurtured in the faith by teachers and mentors who were clear, informed, honest, and emotionally sensitive. The second has been raised in a culture that is strongly opposed to Christianity and has heard only a garbled and distorted version of it, which repulsed him. The question is, How could the second person receive in an instant the same sort of opportunity to respond positively to Christ as the first person has had? How could all his resistance, built up over many years, be overcome in an instant? One answer that proponents of this view have suggested is that at the moment the soul leaves the body it can for the first time make a truly free choice. As John Sanders explains this position, "This fully free act is similar to the decision the angels made—in full knowledge of the truth, unhindered by any constraints. The soul is fully awake and aware of the situation."[43]

If I understand this position, it amounts to abstracting a person from all his previous choices and the character he has formed. It is as if the soul, apart from the body, possesses immediate and full clarity and can for the first time make really significant moral and spiritual choices. All that a person was before, including his physical nature, is dismissed as a hindrance to positive moral choice.

Such a suggestion obviously poses serious problems. In the first place, it verges on an extreme Platonic dualism if not gnosticism in its attitude toward the body. Orthodox Christianity has characteristically taken very seriously the significance of deeds "done in the body" and has insisted that we will be judged for these. This view seems to trivialize all choices made prior to the moment the soul is released from the body. This also raises questions about personal identity. How is continuity of identity maintained on this view if one's previous choices and character are simply eliminated as hindrances? This recalls the point of David Brown, discussed in the previous chapter, namely, that real conversion and character change is an essentially temporal matter, which requires a series of choices and acts of understanding. Truth must be grasped, accepted, and acted upon to produce real conversion and transformation.

The essentially temporal nature of such change also poses difficulties for another move that might be made to defend the notion of conversion at the instant of death, namely, an appeal to timeless eternity. That is, it might be suggested that the necessary growth in understanding, change of mind, and so on needed to convert even a person who had built up layers of opposition to Christianity could be achieved in an instant of timeless eternity. But as I indicated in the previous chapter, I have doubts about the coherence of the timelessness position, so I reject this appeal as a way to resolve this difficulty. I conclude then that there are ways to maintain the equality of grace and opportunity for those who support the notion of evangelism at the moment of death. The difficulties in doing so are severe, however.

Let us turn now to consider how equal opportunity for salvation could be achieved using the resources of middle knowledge. The answer, in brief, is that God could know through middle knowledge whether or not there are circumstances in which one could be moved to freely accept grace and be saved. Consider the two persons described above. What if God knows through middle knowledge that the person who was raised in a culture hostile to Christianity would have become a devout believer if he had all the advantages of the first person? Does it not seem unfair that such a person should be lost? Could not a perfectly wise God find a way to elicit the positive response of grace that he knows would have been elicited in different circumstances?

While we might be inclined to think God would do this if he could, we may wonder if it would actually be possible. How does the fact that a person would have become a devout believer in different circumstances show that he can be brought to believe in the actual world? Perhaps he would have believed given optimal opportunities, but in the actual world he has become so hardened and bitter he will never be willing to believe. The question is how can faith be elicited in the actual world.

One suggestion might follow along the lines of the view I discussed earlier. That is, God might simply eliminate the second person's present character and negative memories and restore him, as it were, to a condition of innocence and then put him in the circumstances that will elicit faith. The problem, of course, is that such a suggestion raises the same sort of problems for personal continuity and identity we noted above. So the question remains of whether there is any way to elicit a positive response while respecting the freedom and integrity of the person we described.

It seems plausible to think God could do this. It would no doubt take a great deal of patience and insight to move through the layers of resistance and misunderstanding that presently keep the person from faith. But if there are circumstances in which the person would have made a genuinely free response of faith, then it seems plausible to think the factors that have led him to unbelief could eventually be sifted out of his thinking and character. Once this was accomplished, he would make the response of faith he would have made if his original circumstances had been different. A reasonable case can be made then for equal opportunity on the middle knowledge account of inclusivism.

Let us turn now to postmortem evangelism. On this account, it is relatively easy to make a case for equal opportunity, for if such evangelism should occur, presumably it would be God's intention to convert as many persons as possible through it. That is, such evangelism would be as effective and persuasive as it could be. Optimal persuasion may require hearing the gospel more than one time and from more than one angle, just as it typically does in this life. It would surely take time, patience, and sensitivity to penetrate the defensive barriers that many persons have built up to Christian faith. But the point is that, given such resources, it seems likely that the Gospel could be presented in an optimal way to all persons so that in the long run, all have an equal opportunity to accept it.

Finally, let us consider the notion that God judges all persons according to the light they have. Again, this account readily lends itself to the notion of equal opportunity. Indeed, the concern for fairness seems to be the driving motivation for this view. If God judges people according to the light they have, then ultimately no one should be at a disadvantage with respect to salvation, not even those who receive only minimal light, for presumably God only requires a minimal response from those who receive only minimal light. The very notion that the response required is proportionate to the light received has built into it a commitment to fairness and even treatment.

I conclude then that there is no reason why God could not give all persons an equal opportunity for salvation. Although the first of the theories surveyed poses serious difficulties, the other three at least allow equal opportunity, and the second and fourth appear to assume such fairness as their rationale.

If God could provide equal opportunity, I want to argue he would do so. Why would he do any less? Surely God is not concerned merely to provide all persons at least some genuine opportunity for salvation in order to meet some minimal standard of fairness in a legalistic way. The biblical picture of God is that he is a being of overwhelming grace and compassion who earnestly loves and desires to save all persons. This is why the notion of equal opportunity makes the best theological sense. It is not a matter of modern democratic principles or human rights. It is a matter of God's perfect love, his sincere desire to have a loving relationship with all his free creatures, and his infinite resources to provide opportunity for his creatures to accept his grace. Because he truly loves all and desires all to be saved, he will bestow optimal grace on all persons.

Having so concluded, the question naturally arises of which of the previous theories makes best sense. Some may see this as a pointless question that we cannot hope to answer. Paul Griffiths, for instance, has remarked that some such theory may be necessary for Christians to maintain their orthodox convictions about the necessity of faith in Christ for salvation but that to pursue the "details has an air of solemn and faintly absurd blasphemy."[44] While this is a salutary caution, it is still worth asking whether one of these theories coheres best with one's other theological convictions, especially one's account of the nature of salvation. If so, one has reason to prefer that theory. So the question we can legitimately ask is which, if any, of these theories makes best sense in relation to the transformational account of salvation I discussed earlier.

I would propose that the postmortem theory coheres best with a transformational soteriology. Moreover, I would suggest that both the theories that God judges the unevangelized according to his middle knowledge and that he judges them according to the light they had require some sort of postmortem evangelism to make full sense. Take the middle knowledge view. As I sketched this out earlier, it involved God finding a way to cut through the layer of resistance that unbelievers have built up in order to restore them to a condition wherein they are susceptible to belief. The free responses of the person involved all along the way are necessary for real conversion and transformation. Salvation is not a matter of God simply accepting persons on the basis of the fact that they would have believed in different circumstances. Actual belief and transformation, freely given, are necessary for a real relationship with God.

The same essential argument applies to the view that God judges people on the basis of the light they had. Surely this does not mean God leaves such persons for all eternity with only the minimal light they had during this life. Rather, God will give such persons the full light of the gospel and the grace to achieve the complete transformation that salvation aims to achieve. What this means is that such persons will need to be informed about the incarnation, atonement, and so on. In other words, they will need to be evangelized. Those who responded to minimal or obscure truth would respond positively to the fullness of truth, for the truth is a whole, and those who embrace partial truth would naturally embrace it when it is revealed to them more fully and clearly.

Consider in this light Jesus' words in the Gospel of John: "If God were your Father, you would love me."[45] From the standpoint of a fully developed Christian orthodoxy, this is a profoundly (albeit implicit) Trinitarian statement that explicates what it means for Jesus and the Father to be one. If one is positively related to God, then he will respond positively to the Son of God and love him as well, for the Son is the fullest and clearest revelation of the Father. To reject Jesus is to show that one does not know or love God.

Some persons may respond positively to God but have little cognitive or theological grasp of that fact. For them to experience the full transformation and relationship with God that salvation represents requires that they come to understand who God is and what he did to save them. Consider in this regard the view of Olin Curtis. He held that while full Christian experience requires Christian belief, the essence of salvation is a correct moral bearing. Moreover, everyone with a conscience has a full and fair probation in this life. Thus, the essential response God requires can be made even by those who have not heard of Christ or have heard only imperfectly. Curtis appealed to an intermediate state to complete the work of full salvation and Christian experience. He believed the primary purpose of the intermediate state was to "adjust a person's mental life to his moral meaning."[46]

Such adjustment is necessary because fully formed faith is a response of our total being to God as he has revealed himself. Such faith embraces mind, will, and emotion. Complete transformation includes full moral reform, full acceptance of the truth at the cognitive level, and trust and love at the emotional level. Any or all of these may require some degree of adjustment in the intermediate state to achieve full transformation.

VII

Let us bring this discussion into focus by considering the concrete example of one of the best-known saints outside the Christian tradition, namely, Mohandas Gandhi. As one of the most influential spiritual leaders and moral reformers of the twentieth century, Gandhi is surely a good test case for the issue of salvation in religions outside Christianity. He is a difficult case for orthodox Christians because of his saintly life on the one hand, and his rejection of Christianity on the other. One of Gandhi's best friends was the Methodist missionary and evangelist E. Stanley Jones. Despite several attempts by Jones to convert him, Gandhi remained committed to Hinduism. It is highly striking, in view of this, that Jones claimed that Gandhi "taught me more of the spirit of Christ than perhaps any other man in East or West."[47]

Jones cautions his fellow believers not to claim Gandhi as a Christian, for he would likely repudiate that claim. Nevertheless, he saw in Gandhi such a profound affinity with Christianity that more of his operative ideas were shaped by it than by Hinduism. Indeed, Jones goes so far as to say that Gandhi was "a natural Christian rather than an orthodox one."[48] Although he admits the distinction is hard to defend, he thought it fit the facts better than any other description.

Of course, none of us are in a position to make infallible judgments about the heart or final destiny of another person. But for the sake of our discussion, let us assume Jones's assessment of Gandhi is essentially correct. That is, let us assume that Gandhi was significantly shaped by the spirit and teachings of Christ. What are we to make of the fact that he rejected Christianity despite the efforts of several effective Christian evangelists to convert him? Does this show, on orthodox Christian principles, that Gandhi did not have a relationship with God and is therefore excluded from salvation, despite his apparent sanctity?

I would argue that it does not, for we cannot know that Gandhi decisively rejected Christ in a fully informed way. Perhaps his experience made it more difficult to accept Christ than it would have been in more favorable circumstances, and if he had encountered Christ in other settings perhaps he would have accepted him. As Jones points out, Gandhi's early encounters with Christianity were in South Africa and were negatively shaped by the racism he experienced there. On one occasion, Gandhi was not permitted to enter a church where C. F. Andrews, a Christian leader Gandhi admired, was speaking. Jones rightly wonders how Gandhi could see Christ through such obscuring factors.[49] Moreover, the political and social issues to which Gandhi had given himself were complicated by religious alliances, and he may have recoiled from conversion because he suspected it would be exploited by his political opponents.

In short, I am suggesting that several factors converged to prevent Gandhi from seeing with clarity the claims of Christ, so his rejection of Christian faith may not have been decisive. As Alvin Plantinga has pointed out, this sort of analysis naturally follows for an orthodox Christian who recognizes that adherents of other religions sincerely believe things that are incompatible with Christianity. The Christian may grant that such a believer is as internally certain of his beliefs as she is, and in *that* sense equally justified in his beliefs, but nevertheless think there is an important epistemic difference: She "thinks that somehow the other person has made a mistake, or has a blind spot, or hasn't been wholly attentive, or hasn't received some grace she has, or is in some way epistemically less fortunate."[50]

One way to describe the optimal grace that I have argued God would give all persons is in terms of a leveling of the epistemic playing field. This would involve God giving all persons time and opportunity to see through the blind spots they may have from social, political, cultural, or psychological factors. Then the truth would be seen with a clarity that would be optimal to elicit a positive response from free creatures. Of course, optimal grace does not guarantee a positive response. Rather, it makes clear the motives of our hearts. Recall Pascal's comment, cited earlier, that the evidence for Christianity is sufficient to make clear that unbelief can only be due to "concupiscence and wickedness of heart." It is my claim that optimal grace evens the epistemic playing field in such a way that unbelief finally stands exposed as a matter of the will, which is morally culpable.

Here is where the element of offense inevitably enters the picture in the matter of relations between Christianity and other religions. While unbelief may be temporarily assigned to blind spots and other various epistemic disadvantages, in the end it is a very different matter. God saves all he can without overriding freedom, but some will not, or at the very least may not, be saved even on those terms. While orthodox Christians may plausibly hope that unbelief in the likes of Gandhi will give way to faith when epistemic disadvantages are eliminated, they must also conclude that persistent unbelief in the face of optimal grace is proof that one does not love the only God who really exists.

VIII

Let us turn now to consider the fate of infants and others who die at an early age before they have had an opportunity to exercise faith in Christ or develop good character. The connection between this question and the one we have been considering is obvious, since those who die in infancy represent a significant portion of the unevangelized, particularly in ages when the infant mortality rate was much higher than it is today. The issue of infant salvation has received considerable attention since the time of the church fathers, and it has been increasingly recognized that one's position on this matter has implications for one's view of unevangelized adults.

In view of this, it is striking that there is a broad consensus today that all who die in infancy are saved. Of course, this has not always been the case. Throughout the period of patristic and medieval theology, it was generally believed that unbaptized children could not be saved. Some taught that unbaptized babies go to hell, but the view that came to prevail during this period was that unbaptized babies go to limbo, a place that falls short of the joys of heaven but that is also void of the pains of hell. Among Protestants after the Reformation, the debate about infant salvation was framed in terms of the doctrines of election and predestination. Some held that all children of believers who died in infancy were among the elect, while others were agnostic on the matter. Only later was it a matter of general agreement among the Reformed that all who die as infants are among the elect. In a fascinating historical survey of the doctrine of infant salvation, Benjamin Warfield, the great Princeton theologian, argued that only the Reformed doctrine of election provides a consistent basis for the belief that all who die in infancy are saved. Others, he thinks, have to compromise their principles to believe this.[51]

Warfield is surely right in his broad claim that our view of infant salvation should be consistent with our account of the nature and ground of salvation generally. So what follows about infant salvation from the account of salvation I have defended? If salvation is a thoroughgoing moral and spiritual transformation that requires our free cooperation, what does this imply for those who die before such transformation can be achieved? As Warfield saw it, "[T]here is but one logical outlet for any system of doctrine which suspends the determination of who are to be saved upon any action of man's own will . . . and that lies in the extension of 'the day of grace' for such into the other world."[52] Moreover, he points out that there is no guarantee on this view that all who die as infants will be saved on this account. If some freely reject Christ in this life, then it is possible, if not likely, that some would reject him in the next life as well.

Warfield is correct on both counts. Since infants are not capable of moral or spiritual choices, if salvation requires such, then infants must have the opportunity after death to make such choices. Moreover, infants must grow up and mature in order to achieve the character and transformation that is characteristic of a perfected relationship with God. Strictly speaking, then, there will not be any babies or children in heaven or hell. Eternity will bring to full fruit either the choice of sanctification or corruption. Infants and children lack the cognitive and moral maturity to experience either of these. These can only be chosen over a period of time and development.

For such choices to be truly free, they must include a dimension of temptation to evil, just as such choices do in this life. What this points up again is that optimal grace does not mean the elimination of all adversity and moral challenge. These are necessary for morally significant free choices. But the point is that such freedom involves the possibility of choosing wrong just as it does in this life. So if one believes salvation requires our free cooperation with God's gracious initiative, there is no more reason to believe that all who die in infancy are saved than there is to believe all who grow to adulthood in this life will be saved. To put it another way, the time of one's death does not increase or decrease one's chances of being saved. This is another way optimal grace makes even the playing field. A consistent defender of the role of freedom in our relationship to God should not view an early death as either an advantage or a disadvantage when it comes to eternal salvation. Since there is no reason to assume infants who die are assured of salvation, there is no warrant at all to view it as "a great blessing to them if they should be smothered by their midwives or strangled in the cradle."[53] Warfield cites this chilling scenario from one of his fellow Reformed theologians, who argued that we must assume that children of unbelievers are damned if we are not to view such strangulation as a blessing. It is worth stressing, however, that Warfield's own view that all who die in infancy are elect is vulnerable to this sort of argument.

Indeed, his view that all dying infants are elect lacks a clear theological rationale, as David Clark has pointed out. In particular, the question that requires an answer is why God would elect all infants but only some adults. The belief that he would do so seems arbitrary at best, especially if we remember that all adults were infants at one time and if we agree that all infants will be mature adults in eternity. What reason can Warfield give for thinking infants who die receive such preferential treatment in the matter of eternal salvation?

Clark ventures to ask, "Is the salvation of all infants who die held for sentimental reasons?"[54] When sentimentality is stripped from our thinking, it is clear
that Warfield would be more consistent to agree with that strand of his tradition which held that some infants are elect and some are not, and that which
are which depends solely on God's sovereign will. In short, Reformed theology has no more reason to assume all infants are saved than does theology that
insists on free cooperation in the matter of eternal salvation.

The view I have defended has an enormous advantage, however, in that it
provides a persuasive account of God's perfect goodness and desire to save all
persons. He does all he can, short of overriding freedom to save all persons.
None are finally at a disadvantage with respect to the most important thing in
life, regardless of such contingencies as the place of one's birth or the timing of
one's death.

IX

This brings us to a final issue I want to consider in this chapter, namely, the
fate of subhuman creatures. Is there any good reason to think animals will
share in the life of heaven, or is this notion merely the product of pious
sentimentalism?

Let us approach this question from the perspective of the broad theological
conviction that has motivated much of our discussion in this chapter, namely,
the goodness of God. Does the concept of divine goodness I have articulated
have implications for animals as well as for human beings?

One theologian who thought so was John Wesley.[55] He cited several biblical passages that indicate God is concerned for the well-being and happiness
of all his creatures, including animals, and argued that we should take these
with full seriousness. One of the most significant of these is the Pauline passage which teaches that all of fallen creation will share in the final restoration
when human redemption reaches its ultimate goal.[56] Wesley was an advocate
of the *felix culpa* tradition, which argues that the fall is finally a blessing because
greater riches of grace flow to us than would have without the fall. What is
fascinating is how he applies this broad strategy to the animal kingdom as well
as to humanity. For Wesley, this entails animal immortality and participation
in the kingdom of God when it arrives in its fullness.

Theodicy considerations play a prominent role in Wesley's case for animal
redemption. For him, it is a matter of divine justice that animals who have
been mistreated in this life should be compensated in the next. Of course, for
this argument to carry any weight, it must be assumed that animals have moral
significance, sufficient intelligence, and "personal identity" to be appropriately
compensated. Wesley indulged in the speculation that animals may receive an
increase of intelligence in the next life as part of their portion of the greater
blessings that come from the fall and redemption.

More recently, C. S. Lewis has offered a qualified defense of animal immortality. Lewis proposes that domestic pets may enjoy a degree of personal-

ity in relationship with their masters and that this personality has promise of being restored in heaven. He suggests that pets may exist "in" their masters in a way that is faintly analogous to the way believers exist in Christ. Thus, pets may be a part of a web of affection and love that will be a fit object of redemption and preservation. This answers the question of personal identity for Lewis. "In other words, the man will know his dog: the dog will know its master and, in knowing him, will *be* itself."[57]

This is not the place to engage thorny issues such as personal identity and theodicy. It is worth noting, however, that until the period of modernity, it was widely believed that animals possess souls, and this view still has its capable defenders.[58] But insofar as the issue turns on the theological premise of God's perfect goodness, I think a case can be made for animal redemption and immortality. If heaven is the beatific vision exclusively, then there may be no meaningful place for animals in heaven. But if heaven will restore and perfect all that makes this life meaningful, it is another matter altogether.

To put the point another way, if heaven involves truly cosmic redemption, it is natural to believe that the animal kingdom will share in it. Stephen H. Webb has recently defended animal redemption along these lines. He argues that if we take the incarnation seriously as an event with cosmic implications, then it means that the love of God revealed therein cannot be limited in scope to human beings. Rather, wherever there is suffering of any kind, God's love extends through the incarnation to provide healing and renewal. Webb challenges the common assumption that there is a necessary connection between afterlife and moral agency. Since all things find their telos in God, it is not unreasonable to include animals in our hopes and to believe they will be included, to the degree they are capable, in the fellowship of the redeemed.[59]

4

HEAVEN, TRINITY, AND
PERSONAL IDENTITY

I

One of the best resources to consider for understanding the significance of the hope of heaven in the Christian tradition is its hymnody. What the church sings reveals, perhaps as clearly as anything else, what it believes. Heaven has been an important theme not only in the great literary hymns of the church but also in the hymns and songs of popular piety and devotion. The hope of eternal joy and bliss has been expressed vividly in numerous songs popularized in revivals and camp meetings. One such song is "When the Roll Is Called Up Yonder" by James M. Black. The second verse of this song states the hope of heaven as follows.

> On that bright and cloudless morning when the dead in Christ shall rise,
> And the glory of His resurrection share;
> When His chosen ones shall gather to their home beyond the skies,
> And the roll is called up yonder, I'll be there.[1]

The chorus reiterates the confidence that "When the roll is called up yonder, I'll be there."

It is a safe guess that most authors of popular songs give little thought to the philosophical implications of the lyrics they compose. A similar statement could be made about those who sing them. Philosophers will readily recognize, however, that this song raises one of the most difficult of all philosophical questions, namely, that of personal identity. Consider that the scenario depicted concerns an event in the future, perhaps the distant future, many years beyond the time when the author of the song and many of those who have sung it have died. By this time, their bodies will have turned to dust. Undaunted by this prospect, the author envisions that he will somehow be raised in Christ and share the glory of his resurrection. That is, he will receive a new body like the body Christ had when he was resurrected. Thereby, he, James M. Black, the same person who wrote the song, will be there when the roll is called up yonder and will be able to answer for himself when his name is called.

Such anticipation is contingent upon identity. It is not enough that someone who looks like James M. Black and has a similar personality will be there. His hope and expectation is that *he* will be there. But here is where the philosophical difficulties are raised. In particular, the question is how or in what sense the person raised could be the same person. Clearly he does not have the same body. So in what sense is "he" the same person?

As difficult as the issue of personal identity is under normal conditions, it seems to be exacerbated by the claims involved in the Christian doctrine of heaven. Claims about resurrection and life in the mysterious beyond appear only to intensify problems that are already notorious for resisting resolution. I want to argue, however, that the doctrine of heaven is actually a positive resource for dealing with this classically confounding controversy. In what follows, I shall not discuss the issue of personal identity in the abstract. That is, I shall not attempt to provide an account of personal identity independently of my theological convictions that I shall then employ to show that the doctrine of heaven is coherent. Rather, I shall develop an account of personal identity in conversation with the doctrine of heaven. To put it another way, the doctrine of heaven will serve to provide philosophical inspiration as well as a control on what shall count as an adequate account of personal identity.

Compare Thomas V. Morris's treatment of the doctrine of the incarnation of the Son of God in Jesus of Nazareth. In particular, consider his response to the common charge that the doctrine is incoherent because certain essential human properties are incompatible with certain essential divine properties. Morris maintains that it is perfectly legitimate for a Christian philosopher to develop an account of human nature in light of his beliefs about God and, in particular, the incarnation. After all, we do not have a ready-made authoritative account of essential human properties that is nonnegotiable for all philosophical discussions. Morris analyzes the issue as a matter of epistemic priorities. "The orthodox Christian can quite rationally argue that we are less sure that human nature essentially comprises properties incompatible with a divine incarnation than Christians are that Jesus was God Incarnate."[2] Accordingly, Morris goes on to propose an account of essential human nature compatible with the incarnation. This approach does not mean giving the incarnation absolute epistemic priority, for as Morris notes, we must have some idea of humanity and divinity to make even preliminary sense of the incarnation. But the point is that since philosophers are far from a definitive consensus on these matters, there is considerable room for a Christian to give his convictions epistemic priority in formulating a conception of essential human nature.

I shall proceed in a similar fashion by giving basic Christian convictions about heaven a certain epistemic priority in putting forth a conception of personal identity that is compatible with those convictions. Compatibility with the doctrine of heaven is not the only important consideration, however. To be judged adequate, the account of personal identity that results from this investigation must plausibly cohere with our clearest intuitions about what it is that makes each of us the unique persons we are. Moreover, it must mesh with our intuitions about what allows us to identify someone as the same person through time.

II

Let us begin this exploration by reflecting on one of the most suggestive pictures of the essence of heaven, namely, the notion that heaven is being taken up into the very fellowship of the three persons of the Holy Trinity. In a previous chapter, I cited John Wesley, who identified this experience as the climax of salvation. This is also a prominent theme in Eastern theology. According to Vladimir Lossky, "The goal of Orthodox spirituality, the blessedness of the Kingdom of Heaven, is not the vision of the essence, but, above all, a participation in the divine life of the Holy Trinity. . . . It is the Trinity that we seek in seeking after God, when we search for the fullness of being, for the end and meaning of existence."[3]

Two points related to our issue deserve immediate emphasis. First, according to this conception, human beings can achieve fullness of being only by sharing in the life of the Trinity. Another way to put this point is to say that who we are in our God-given nature is such that our true identity is only fully realized in this extraordinary relationship. Second, consider that the doctrine of the Trinity involves some remarkable claims about personal identity. Some of the most famous debates in intellectual history center around the orthodox definition of the Trinity as one God in three persons. Indeed, there is good reason to believe that the concept of a person first emerged in the history of thought from the church's Christological and Trinitarian controversies.[4]

This is a significant observation. It is much more than an example of the fact that some of the most fascinating and vexing philosophical issues are secularized versions of theological counterparts. The interesting point is that since the doctrine of God gave us our concept of person in the first place, it should perhaps not be surprising if the concept of personal identity breaks down when isolated from its original matrix. The implications for personal identity arising from the Christian doctrine of God are particularly striking when we reflect on the nature of the persons who compose the Trinity. I especially have in mind the notion that the divine persons of the Trinity are spiritual beings who have no physical properties in their eternal nature. Thus, they cannot be individuated by means of anything like bodily criteria. I speak particularly of those strands of the Christian tradition that have emphasized a social understanding of the Trinity, namely, those strands that have insisted that priority must be given to recognizing three distinct divine persons and that God's oneness must be understood in this light. Other strands of the tradition, of course, have emphasized oneness and have tended to understand the "threeness" of God in terms of different modes or manifestations of his being.

According to the social model, all three persons of God share a common divine nature. The question persists of how they are to be distinguished or individuated. Characteristically, the three persons of the Trinity have been distinguished in terms of relational properties that constitute their unique personal natures. As Cornelius Plantinga has pointed out, the unity of God is ensured not only by the generic divine nature that each of the persons share equally. It is also the case, somewhat ironically, that the unique personal essences of the three persons unify as well. These personal essences "relate each person to the other two in unbreakable love and loyalty."[5] It is essential to the Father that he is related to the Son in an unbreakable relation akin to the parent-child relationship. Likewise, the Spirit is essentially the loyal agent of the Father and Son, and they have the complimentary property of essentially having the Spirit as their loyal agent. Thus, the personal essence of the Father depends on his relation to the Son and the Spirit just as theirs depends on their relationship to him.

With this background in place, let us turn to explore how these theological resources can assist us in developing an adequate account of personal identity. Before going further, we need to distinguish two aspects of this discussion that are easily confused, namely, the epistemological on one hand, and the ontological or metaphysical on the other. The first of these concerns our warrant for believing that we are indeed persons, whereas the latter asks for the criteria that compose personal identity. While this distinction is important, it should not be exaggerated unduly; indeed, the two questions are often closely related.

Skepticism about the whole notion of personal identity is one of the common threads in the broadly different traditions of continental and analytic philosophy. A major fountainhead on the English-speaking side is, of course, Hume, who, in a famous passage expressed doubts about the existence of a persisting subject underlying the various experiences and thoughts he could identify. On the continental side, Nietzsche comes readily to mind because of his radical doubts about the continuity and persistence of personality. Both of these streams have come together to form the morass of postmodernism with its characteristic themes of fragmentation and flux. A popular postmodern theme is that the self is nothing more than a linguistic construct.

Those who believe in God, especially the Christian God, have powerful resources to resist such cultural currents, not least in the area of personal identity. To see this, let us consider Alvin Plantinga's theistic epistemology, which provides an alternative to both classical foundationalism and the relativism that is often embraced when foundationalism is rejected. The heart of his view is that a belief is warranted if it is produced by faculties that are functioning properly in the environment for which they were designed. Moreover, the faculties must be aimed at truth and there must be an objectively high probability that beliefs so formed are true. In keeping with this account, the more firmly the person involved is inclined to accept a belief, the more warrant it has for him.[6]

What are we warranted in believing about ourselves on this account? As Plantinga points out, what we naturally believe about ourselves is that we have existed for some time, that we have had many thoughts and feelings but that we are not ourselves identical with those thoughts or feelings. That is, we as thinking and feeling subjects are distinct from our thoughts and feelings. But is it not possible that our natural instinctive beliefs about this matter might be badly mistaken? Derek Parfit, following in the Humean tradition, argues that we might not be what we think we are. Perhaps the only things that really exist are the thoughts and feelings themselves. Maybe there are only many series of "person slices" that are linked by the relevant causal relations and apparent memories.

It is useless to appeal to memory to try to rebut Parfit's position. I am presently being appeared to in a computer screen fashion, but an hour ago I was appeared to in a cherry pie fashion. I cannot be both a computer appearance and a cherry pie appearance, so the argument might go, so there must be a continuing subject that underlies both these experiences. But as Plantinga points out, if we do not accept the reality of the subject–experience structure in the case of a normal sense experience, there is no reason to accept it in the case of a memory experience. Neither experience gives us direct awareness of a subject that is distinct from the various experiences. The most that we are directly aware of is a psychologically continual stream of consciousness. Plantinga concedes, then, that our experiences do not conclusively rule out the sort of possibilities Hume and Parfit put forward.

But what exactly follows from this? Much less than is often thought. As Plantinga puts it, Parfit's "fateful inference" is to conclude from this fact that we cannot know or even justifiably believe that there is a distinct subject that exists along with these various experiences.

> Most of my contingent beliefs are such that my experience could be just what it is but the belief false; how is it supposed to follow that these beliefs don't constitute knowledge? How does it follow that (even more alarmingly) I should try to give them up unless I can find some other evidence? We know that there are trees and flowers, even though our experience could be just what it is and there be no trees and flowers.[7]

Plantinga's theistic epistemology is a powerful challenge to the notion that we cannot have knowledge unless we have Cartesian certainty. Cartesian demons have haunted Western philosophy for centuries now, and all claims to knowledge and rational belief have been judged by the criterion of whether they are warranted in spite of the possibility that such demons are doing their utmost to deceive us. What we are warranted in believing is altogether different if we and our world have been created by a good God who wants us to know the truth about a wide range of important things.

Strictly speaking, theistic philosophers have good reason to deny even the possibility of some of the haunted epistemological scenarios modern philosophers have delighted in sketching to undermine confidence in much of what most people naturally believe. Here we can draw a distinction between possibility and conceivability.[8] If God is a necessary being, as most of the theistic tradition has maintained, then all possible worlds are delimited by God's nature. In other words, there are no possible worlds that are not compatible with what a perfectly good and wise God would create. So it may be the case that many of the scenarios that epistemologists sketch involving radical deception are not even possible. Of course, our intuitions concerning what a perfectly good God would do are not infallible, but they can still provide some guidance for our judgments about what sort of worlds are really possible. Many of the worlds we can conceive may not be possible because a perfectly good and wise God would never create them.

Again, the point is that what is warranted belief varies greatly depending on whether we believe in such a God or whether we allow the possibility of evil demons haunting all of our epistemic activity. Of course, even those who believe in a good God will readily admit that we are vulnerable to any number of epistemic foibles such as misleading memories, unreasonable biases, and the like. But the point is that belief in a good God rules out the possibility of systematic epistemic failure.

Let us return to Plantinga's point that those who are willing to doubt the subject-experience structure of normal sense experience cannot exorcise the doubt by appealing to memory. Memory beliefs have the same basic structure, and those who are inclined to doubt the one can just as easily doubt the other. It remains true, nevertheless, that memory has a special significance for personal identity. As Plantinga himself has remarked, "It is of course memory that is the source of my belief that I am a being that persists through time. I couldn't have anything like this sense of myself as a persisting object without memory."[9]

Plantinga's point, I take it, is an epistemological one. That is, he is appealing to memory to warrant the belief that he is a being who persists through time. The metaphysical or ontological makeup of identity may be another matter. Locke, of course, is famous for defending the continuity of memory as constitutive of personal identity, and he did not always keep epistemological and ontological matters distinct. Surely it is a mistake to take continuity of memory as infallible and to suggest that identity consists essentially in such certainty of memory. Antony Flew criticizes Locke in this regard and remarks that "personal identity is in this regard not like pain. The honest testimony of the subject is not with personal identity as it is with pain the last word."[10]

Those who have learned not to hanker after Cartesian certainty in such matters can cheerfully grant Flew's point. But this hardly eliminates the positive significance of memory as a warrant for belief in personal identity. The point, again, is to recognize that memory is not an infallible source of truth about anything, including personal identity. But this does not for a moment discredit our utter and profound reliance on memory for a vast number of our beliefs. Pascal recognized the depth of our need to trust memory in remarking: "Memory is necessary for all the operations of reason."[11] A particularly telling instance of this point is that one cannot even mount an argument against memory's claims without assuming the reliability of memory in the process. That is, one must rely on memory even to keep in mind the premises and logic of an argument. Indeed, memory must be trusted in the very act of spelling out a single premise from beginning to end. Moreover, we must rely on memory to correct memory when we believe it has erred. There is, then, no epistemic foothold for a widespread doubting of memory. We must trust it or fall into radical skepticism.

Richard Swinburne is another contemporary defender of the crucial role of memory as evidence for personal identity. As he notes, the two most commonly cited criteria of identity are brain continuity and continuity of apparent memory. What is interesting is his argument that bodily continuity, especially brain continuity, are only indirect evidence of personal identity. In particular, as he argues, the reason we focus on the brain as crucial is because it is that part of our bodies with which we correlate character and memory. This "suggests that but for a correlation with apparent memory and character we would not use any part of the body as evidence of personal identity."[12] Whereas some argue that bodily continuity is needed to confirm apparent memory, Swinburne maintains that memory is a more fundamental criterion than any bodily one. As he notes, we typically accept memory claims without requiring some other sort of confirmation. Moreover, an apparent memory can be checked by another apparent memory. Of course, Swinburne recognizes the fallibility of memory, but he is surely correct in maintaining that questions of personal identity can be settled as certainly as most other factual questions.

III

Let us turn now to apply these conclusions to some of the particular problems posed for personal identity by the concept of heaven. One obvious and often noted difficulty arises from the doctrine of resurrection. The orthodox Christian account of eternal life is life in a resurrected body. The song cited at the beginning of this chapter refers to this hope. One question that comes readily to mind is how personal identity is maintained between the time of one's death and one's resurrection. Does personal identity cease at death and then resume at the resurrection?

The traditional Christian view of humanity has a ready answer to this issue, namely, that persons are composed of souls as well as bodies and that the soul survives in conscious form during the time between death and resurrection. This dualism has, of course, come under fire from several directions. Most famously, critics have rejected it on the grounds that the whole notion of mind-body interaction is incoherent. Moreover, it has been claimed that there is no intelligible way to individuate disembodied souls. More recently, theological critics have argued that dualism is a Greek import into Christian thought that is incompatible with the holistic account of humanity that is characteristic of Hebrew and biblical thought. Favoring a view they call "biblical monism," these theologians hold that dualism not only denigrates the physical dimension of who we are but also truncates the biblical picture of salvation. In addition, dualism has been charged with being at least partially responsible for a whole host of unsavory social and political consequences.

It is not my purpose here to engage in a lengthy defense of dualism, but a few words are in order because of the relevance of dualism to issues of identity. First, dualism comes in a number of varieties ranging from Platonic dualism to Cartesian dualism to Thomistic dualism to "emergent dualism." While some traditional forms of dualism may be vulnerable to the charges cited above, it can be formulated in ways that avoid those problems. In particular, dualism can be formulated in such a way that it respects the biblical picture of man as an integrated soul and body and that appreciates the holistic nature of salvation.[13] Such a biblical dualism will not denigrate the body or the social dimensions of who we are. When dualism is formulated along these lines, it can accommodate many of the concerns that motivate monism, while avoiding the drawbacks of that view.

One such difficulty is in accounting for those biblical texts that have traditionally been understood to teach an intermediate state of conscious survival between death and resurrection. Let us consider, for instance, Jesus' words to the thief on the cross: "Today you will be with me in paradise."[14] Apart from some sort of dualism, this must be interpreted to mean that the thief receives his resurrection body immediately after death, a notion that seems to conflict with the teaching that the resurrection will occur at the end of the age. This difficulty might be circumvented by suggesting that the experience of time is not identical for those who have died, on the one hand, and those who are still alive on the earth, on the other. Thus, the resurrection of the dead is still a future event for those on earth, but for those who have died, it is already past.

Other interpretations of Jesus' words are also possible,[15] but dualism allows us to interpret them straightforwardly and in a way that is compatible with other lines of New Testament thought. New Testament scholar Joel B. Green, a defender of monism, has warned against taking eschatology as a starting point in developing a biblical view of human nature and has suggested that eschatological considerations have been a major impetus toward dualism.[16] While Green is perhaps right that eschatology is not the proper place to start this discussion, surely it must be coherently accounted for in a Christian account of who we are.

Another New Testament text that appears to support both an intermediate state and some sort of dualism is 2 Corinthians 5:1–10. Verses 2–3 are especially suggestive in this regard: "For in this tent we groan, longing to be clothed with our heavenly dwelling—if indeed, when we have taken it off we will not be found naked" (NRSV). Paul's language is admittedly difficult, but he appears to anticipate survival of some sort between the time of his approaching death and his future resurrection. Ben Witherington III comments on this passage as follows: "Paul speaks of three states: the present condition in the tent-like frame, the intermediate state of nakedness, which he does not find desirable, and the future condition in which a further frame will have been put on, hopefully, over the present one."[17] Witherington's remarks reflect a balanced dualism that does not fall into the extreme of suggesting that separation of the soul is an unqualified good thing. Since we are integrated soul-bodies, the intermediate state involves a rupture of our nature. Persons who survive in this form are incomplete without their bodies.

But the important point is that survival of the person is possible if dualism is true. Interestingly, a modal argument of considerable force for dualism reverses this claim. That is, it is argued that if such survival is possible, this is a good reason to believe in dualism. The argument is typically advanced in terms of thought experiments that ask us to imagine the possibility that we might survive even if our body was replaced piece by piece with a new body or, more radically, that we might survive if we suddenly switched bodies with someone else. These lines can be extended to imagine our body being eliminated piece by piece and yet our surviving with our consciousness intact.

This line of argument is pertinent to our concern to show that personal identity can be maintained during the intermediate state between death and resurrection. Let us imagine further that apparent memories survive intact. Imagine that after Paul dies, he remains conscious and seems to remember writing the words to the Corinthians quoted above. He seems to recall other things he experienced such as being stoned, being beaten, traveling around to various cities preaching the gospel, and so on. Given what I argued about the need to trust memory, surely he would be justified in believing that he, Paul, had indeed survived and was still the same person, albeit in an incomplete form.

What this points up is that dualism provides both ontological and epistemic resources for personal identity. Ontologically, identity resides in the fact that the same substance, the very same soul, persists not only throughout one's embodied life until death but also continues to exist after death in disembodied form. Epistemically, mental life, particularly continuity of memory, persists and gives warrant for believing that one is the same person who lived on the earth for such and such a time and did such and such things.

It is important to emphasize that sameness of soul is an ontological criterion and not an epistemic one. Sameness of soul cannot be established in a way that is invulnerable to epistemic challenges and doubts. In his dialogue on the subject of personal identity and immortality, John Perry has one of his characters, Weirob, who is about to die, make this point. Weirob notes that there is no way directly to observe sameness of soul. For all we know, our soul could change regularly without our knowing it or being able to observe it. Perhaps every five years a soul that is psychologically similar to the one before takes on the beliefs and memories of the previous soul and takes over where it left off. Or maybe this happens every five minutes. Or more radically still, perhaps there is a constant flow of new souls taking over in this fashion.[18]

The proper response to this suggestion is essentially the same as that given to the notion that we might merely be a psychologically continuous series of person slices. While nothing in immediate experience can refute it decisively, it should not trouble us unduly if we recognize that Cartesian certainty on these matters is beyond our reach. Those who believe in a good God will think it unlikely that he would operate in this way and will be inclined to accept the more natural belief that we are individuals with a distinct identity who persist through time. And if we have souls that are the locus of consciousness and memory, then it is natural to believe these souls persist as unique individuals, both in this life and beyond.

Critics of dualism have often argued that there is no intelligible way to individuate disembodied souls. As immaterial objects, souls do not have the property of spatial apartness that readily distinguishes pieces of matter. Joshua Hoffman and Gary Rosenkrantz have suggested, however, that there is a relation existing between any two souls that is similar to spatial apartness in matter, namely, the "relation of being a soul x which is incapable of directly experiencing a mental state of soul y." It follows from this definition that souls are "epistemically apart" in a way that parallels spatial apartness in distinct pieces of matter.[19] This relation holds between disembodied souls as well as embodied ones.

Such a relation might be criticized as trivial or irrelevant. It is admittedly rather generic and abstract, but it is also reasonably clear and to the point since we are dealing with an entity that is mental and psychological by definition. There is surely more to a substantive account of personal identity than this, but it is one component of the uniqueness that is essential to identity.

Another way to individuate disembodied souls is by way of personal memory. Personal memory is memory of one's own acts and experiences. It is to be distinguished from memory of how to do things that are commonly known, from memory of facts that are widely known, and so on.[20] Each person's personal memory is distinctive and unique to some degree, and this distinct history is part of who one is.

Of course, memory is not infallible, and not all apparent memories are true to reality. In view of this, the critic can suggest scenarios in which more than one soul might claim the same memories and claim to be the same person on that basis. Insofar as these scenarios are inspired by the lurking presence of Cartesian demons, the theist can reply that such scenarios are not likely in a universe created by a good God. Moreover, he can distinguish between memories that are produced by actually having the experiences and doing the deeds in question, and apparent memories that are not. Thus, if two souls claim to be Michael Jordan and to have accomplished his extraordinary athletic feats, the real Michael Jordan is the one whose memories are caused by actually having performed the feats in question.

To conclude this discussion of dualism, let us note that it has profound affinities with a theistic worldview. I do not mean to say that dualism is entailed or required by theism, but I do want to insist that some of the stock objections against dualism, if valid, pose equivalent difficulties for theism. Take the notorious problem of interaction for a start. If this is a problem for dualism, it is no less a problem for traditional theism, which holds that God is a spirit who created a material world and sustains it by his activity and power. Moreover, God not infrequently has interacted with the material world by way of miraculous activity. If dualistic interaction is incoherent or unintelligible, the same must be said for these theistic claims. Moreover, the difficulties in individuating disembodied souls should hardly seem insuperable for a theist, particularly a

Christian theist. Recall that the doctrine of the Trinity is that God consists of three distinct persons, none of whom has physical properties, at least prior to the incarnation. Again, these considerations do not require a Christian to be a dualist, but they do show that dualism should be defended as a coherent position by Christians even if they do not think it is true.

One other point about dualism should be mentioned in this connection, namely, that it seems to cohere better with libertarian freedom than does monism. The basic reason for this is simple. If we are composed only of matter, then it is reasonable to think that all of our actions are determined by natural laws like everything else in the physical world. Advocates of materialist accounts of humanity have often noted this implication. John Searle, for instance, has noted that if libertarian freedom is true, it would require some fundamental changes in our beliefs about the world. In particular, "it looks as if we would have to postulate that inside each of us was a self that was capable of interfering with the causal order of nature."[21] While dualists may want to quarrel with how Searle has stated their position, especially his description of the self as "inside" us, they would grant the basic point. Dualists believe our self is composed of something more than the physical, and that part of us which is not physical does affect the physical. The material side of us is not determined solely by natural laws to act as it does. Rather, the physical and the mental interact, and in many instances, actions in the physical world are the result of free choices in the mental world.

I would not want to insist that one cannot be both a libertarian and a monist in terms of one's view of human nature. Perhaps it is possible to hold these positions together in a coherent fashion. All I am suggesting is that dualism has close affinities with libertarian accounts of freedom whereas materialism seems to flow naturally toward compatibilist accounts of freedom, as Searle notes. If one believes libertarian freedom is important to maintain for theological reasons, some of which I have sketched in an earlier chapter and some of which I will develop later in this chapter, then one has another reason to favor dualism.

IV

Let us suppose now, for the sake of argument, that monism is true. Or suppose some impressive new arguments against dualism have been formulated, arguments that do not threaten the integrity of theism itself. Is there a satisfactory account of identity that can explain how resurrected person B can be the same individual as person A even if person A does not survive in conscious form between death and resurrection? One obvious question here is whether personal identity can be sustained across a temporal and material gap, perhaps a very lengthy one. Another issue is whether this entails that the person in question has two beginnings, one when he was conceived and the other when he was resurrected. Can one thing have two beginnings? Or would this second beginning, which would include things like accumulated memories, not really be a beginning in the strict sense of the word?

The defender can argue that persons can be "gap inclusive" by pointing to other entities that include gaps in their existence. Take as an example a baseball game that has a lengthy rain delay. It is the same game when it resumes despite the gap in activity. Or take the World Series. We may view it as a single event despite the temporal gaps between the different games that compose the series.

Suppose a person is resurrected and has striking physical similarities to James M. Black. He claims to remember writing his famous song and other things from the life of James M. Black. Perhaps he even claims to recall some or all of the things to which no one but Black would be likely to be privy. Indeed, he claims he is James M. Black and believes he is living proof that the prediction of his song has come true. While we may doubt that he would represent decisive proof of his claim, surely he would be justified in believing himself to be the same person. And anyone meeting and interacting with him would be justified in believing him to be James M. Black.

What about the question of whether Mr. Black has two beginnings, a strongly counterintuitive notion? Here the defender of monism can reply that, strictly speaking, Mr. Black had only one beginning. His resurrection was a resumption of his existence, not a new beginning, numerically speaking. So monists also have a plausible response to this difficulty.

But another well-known problem is still lurking in the metaphysical woods, namely, that of duplication. Consider this scenario. Suppose at the resurrection there are two persons who appear and claim to be James M. Black. Or two dozen. It doesn't matter what the number is, for the problem is the same. Each of the persons is qualitatively indistinguishable from the others, and all seem to have Black's memories, personality, and so on. Would any of these persons be Black? Stephen T. Davis responds to this problem as follows.

> If the existence of multiple replicas of a given person in the afterlife in some cases threatens personal identity and thus survival of death, then, necessarily, if God intends that a given person should survive death, God will not allow there to be any replicas of that person in the afterlife. Christians would hold, however, that God has the power to create such persons, so it is perfectly fair for critics to ask how it would affect their advocacy of resurrection if God were to exercise this power.[22]

In such a case, Davis goes on to argue, it would place such a strain on our concept of person that we could not say that the person who lived on earth had survived. More strongly, he would argue that the person had not survived, since uniqueness is a criterion of personal identity.

I believe Davis provides the critic more of a response than he needs to. I believe the correct response is in the first sentence in the quote. There Davis notes that it is a matter of necessity that if God intends that a given person should survive death, and if replicas would threaten his personal identity, then he will not allow any replicas of that person to exist after death. In other words, there are no possible worlds in which such replicas exist. It is a clear part of Christian teaching that all persons will be raised from the dead and face the judgment of God. So there is no possible world in which anyone will face challenges to his personal identity in the form of replicas in the afterlife.

Davis's claim in the next sentence that God has the power to create such persons is misleading if not ambiguous. In what sense does God have such power? Is there a possible world in which he creates such persons? I would argue that there is not. There may be countless conceivable worlds, but, as I noted above, not all conceivable worlds are possible. Consider another example in the same neighborhood. Does God have the power to create a world populated exclusively by infants, all of whom are maintained in infancy and tormented with severe pain for one million years and then annihilated? At first glance, this seems like a description of a logically possible world. Moreover, it does not depend on the free choices of other beings to actualize it, so it may seem that God could create it.

I would argue, however, that this is not even a possible world. The main reason is that God is a necessary being who exists in all possible worlds. Moreover, he necessarily has all his essential properties in all possible worlds, including the properties of perfect wisdom and perfect goodness. It seems clear that the world described, though conceivable in some sense, is incompatible with God's perfect goodness, and therefore not really metaphysically possible. In the same vein, I doubt whether worlds in which replicas of persons appear in the afterlife, complete with the same apparent memories, personality and so on, are really possible. Such worlds are incompatible with God's perfect wisdom and goodness. God would neither himself have reason to create such replicas nor to allow others to do so.

Earlier in his discussion, Davis invokes the will of God to deal with the problem of duplication. He views the will of God, along with uniqueness, as the two necessary criteria for personal identity. A sufficient account must also include either striking psychological similarity and continuity between P_1 and P_2 or striking bodily similarity and material continuity between B_1 and B_2. In each of these latter criteria, Davis specifies that there must be the proper kind of causal relationship between the psychological properties of P_1 and P_2 and the material continuity or similarity between B_1 and B_2. Since only one of the latter two criteria must be met to provide a sufficient account of personal identity, Davis believes both dualism and monism can offer satisfactory accounts.

Three of Davis's criteria are commonly cited in discussions of personal identity, but his fourth, the will of God, is much less so. But, following R. T. Herbert, Davis defends it as an integral part of a theistic account. As just noted, he thinks it provides a resource for dealing with puzzling cases like duplication. He describes a case—which he doubts is really possible—in which Jones dies at T_1 and at T_2 two replicas of Jones appear, Jones1 and Jones2. Lacking some sort of recognized continuity between Jones and one of the two replicas, Davis suggests the will of God could decide the issue. If God wills for Jones1 to continue the life of Jones and does not will the same for Jones2, then Jones1 is in fact the continuation of the life of Jones.[23]

Davis does not tell us how the replicas of Jones are supposed to appear in the afterlife, and I strongly doubt, as he apparently does also in this case, that it even describes a possible state of affairs. But let us think of the scenario in terms, not of the afterlife, but of this life. In an age of cloning, it is perhaps not too far-fetched to think we may have to face the prospect of brain transplants, or partial brain transplants, in which questions of personal identity would become pressing and acute. What if half of Jones's brain was transplanted into B1 and the other half into B2? Which of these would be Jones?

Here I think the appeal to the will of God is quite appropriate. God is the creator who structured our world and all that is in it. It is he who determined which individuals would exist. Moreover, he created each thing with the powers and potentialities that it has. So if such brain transplants are possible, then God designed human beings with such potentialities. While God presumably does not will every such potentiality to be actualized, he must at least know of it and all of its implications. If he does will this particular potentiality to be actualized, then he knows which person would be Jones. It does not follow that we could see with any sort of clarity which would be Jones, but this does not make meaningless or threaten the coherence of the claim that God's will and intention is an essential criterion of personal identity.

Let us return now to the possibility that personal identity could be resumed after a temporal gap. In this case, the creative will of God is surely a legitimate criterion of personal identity. God's creative will and power brought Black and Jones into existence in the first place and sustained their existence and identity during their earthly lives. It seems to be a coherent possibility that he could choose to resume their lives after a temporal gap rather than sustain it in conscious disembodied form. This could be the case even if dualism is true and God chooses not to sustain the soul in life during the time between death and resurrection. This possibility also seems to hold for monism.

Let us summarize our discussion thus far. I have argued that Christians, both dualists and monists, have adequate resources to deal with the conceptual difficulties of personal identity posed by the doctrine of heaven.[24] Dualists can provide a ready explanation of how identity is sustained between death and resurrection since, according to their view, the soul can continue to exist in conscious form when separated from the body in death. The soul is reunited with its resurrected body, a body that, although transformed, bears striking likeness to one's body in this life. The model here is the resurrected body of Jesus. Although his body was changed and had powers and properties it did not have before, it was recognizable by his disciples, and even included scars from his crucifixion.

Monists will also rely on striking physical similarities in their account of identity across the temporal gap between death and resurrection.[25] They can appeal to the creative will of God to deal with problems posed by gaps in conscious existence. Both views also cite continuity of memory and personality as essential to identity. And both would stipulate that personal identity is unique and particular. By definition, it cannot be shared with another individual.

The criterion of uniqueness is rather abstract in itself. We might attempt to illumine it by referring to the medieval scholastics' notion of an individual's *haecceity*. This term refers to the "property of being that very object, or the property of being identical with that very object."[26] My haecceity is by definition unique to me. This notion is intuitively simple and beyond cavil. Its drawback, however, is that it is highly abstract and formal. As such, it does not begin to capture the substance of what we value in individuals that forms their unique personalities and makes them the distinctive persons they are. I want to turn now to explore in more detail just what our uniqueness in this sense consists in.

V

Let us begin to consider this by reflecting on the following words of Nicholas Wolterstorff, written about his son Eric, who was killed in a mountain climbing accident.

> A center, like no other, of memory and hope and knowledge and affection which once inhabited the earth is gone. Only a gap remains. A perspective on this world unique in this world which once moved about within this world has been rubbed out. Only a void is left. There's nobody now who saw just what he saw, knows what he knew, remembers what he remembered, loves what he loved. A person, an irreplaceable person, is gone. Never again will anyone apprehend the world quite the way he did.[27]

Wolterstorff's mention of his son's hopes and memories point up the fact that we are historical beings. We have a unique history with a particular past, and we have distinctive anticipations of the future, shaped by our past experiences and hopes of fulfillments we will yet enjoy. The particular contour of our own story is largely drawn by who and what we have loved and cared about.

These matters are obviously difficult to define with philosophical precision. Nevertheless, since our lives compose a kind of story, telling that story is perhaps the best way to convey what is distinctive about us. Indeed, it is this relatively amorphous reality we claim as our story that constitutes what is really distinctive about us and what we truly value about each other as individuals. Despite its lack of philosophical precision and its vulnerability to Cartesian doubts and Lockean puzzle cases, we have a clear enough grasp of this reality that it enables us readily to interact with other persons with secure and substantive knowledge of who they are. So long as we are confident of our grasp of this reality, we are not likely to be overly concerned with philosophically more precise accounts of personal identity.

It is worth asking now whether there are grounds in the Christian tradition for maintaining this confidence and especially if the doctrine of heaven is relevant in this regard. Consider in this light Alasdair MacIntyre's suggestion that the problem of personal identity is only generated and maybe can only be generated "in the aftermath of some tradition, when the shared beliefs which formerly underpinned the complex metaphysical conception of personal identity and continuity, such beliefs as that in life-long accountability and in the teleological ordering of each life, are no longer held."[28] When only a residual conception of personal identity remains, and it is isolated from the original context in which it made sense, then the philosophical problem is generated along with its various solutions. Among the solutions is that of Parfit, who sees identity as nothing more than a sort of connectedness between the stages and events of one's life.

MacIntyre thinks that this "dissolution of a whole into its parts is precisely what should be expected in a society in which the background beliefs that made it possible to identify and understand that whole are no longer shared."[29] He goes on to explain that the notion of accountability assumes a truth to be discovered about what makes for a good life. Moreover, such accountability to truth depends on a community that tests one's claims and one's life.

I would suggest that the Christian doctrine of heaven involves a profound and powerful conception of both lifelong accountability and the notion that our lives are ordered teleologically. It is worth remembering that the modern problem of personal identity as formulated and addressed by figures such as Locke and Butler was largely motivated by a concern to make sense of such accountability as assumed in the Christian doctrine of final judgment before God.[30] Indeed, the notion of heaven and its attendant doctrine of divine judgment represents the ultimate account of a human telos imaginable. The final aim of life is to share the life and fellowship of the Trinity. This requires a thorough moral and spiritual transformation that embraces all that we are. Thus, the hope of heaven entails lifelong accountability. Nothing is outside the pale of God's transforming grace. Our life as a whole must be reordered. Our past actions, including those that were wrong and self-centered, must be reevaluated in light of God's will and purpose for our lives, and much must be repented of. The future direction of our lives must be ordered by God's will as well. We are no longer our own, and all of our plans and aspirations must be sifted and weighed by our aim of being eternally united with God.

All of this involves the belief that there is a truth about what makes for a good life, a life of true happiness and flourishing that fulfills our divinely given nature and achieves the human telos. Heaven, fellowship with the Trinity, is thus not viewed as a mere personal preference that may be reasonably rejected in favor of another end. Rather, it is the end for which all human beings were created. We are all accountable to God for the gifts and grace he has given us. We cannot truthfully view our lives as our own. There is a truth about our past and how we should have lived. Likewise, there is a truth about how we should live in the future and what we should pursue. We cannot with integrity focus our future efforts on living a life of self-centered pleasure or other false ultimate goods. The hope of heaven requires a thoroughgoing reorientation that leaves nothing untouched. There is no other way to enter into the loving relationship with God for which we were created.

The fellowship of heaven is, moreover, a community experience. To enter the fellowship of the Trinity we must begin by entering the fellowship and community of those who love God in this life. In accountability to this community we are trained in the ways of love and prepared and equipped for the experience of perfect love that is communion with the Trinity.

The discussion of this section reveals that <u>our individual identity is finally a</u> <u>relational matter. Who we are is defined by our relationships with others.</u> Colin Gunton has articulated this point as follows.

> All particulars are formed by their relationship to God the creator and re-
> deemer and to each other. Their particular being is a being in relation, each
> distinct and unique and yet each inseparably bound up with the other,
> and ultimately all, particulars. Their reality consists, therefore—and this is the
> crucial difference from other theories of substance—not in the universals they
> instantiate, but in the shape of their relatedness with God and with other cre-
> ated hypostases.[31]

Gunton's larger thesis is that many of the problems of modern culture have stemmed from an inadequate account of the relationship between the one and the many, the ancient conflict between Parmenidean unity and Heraclitan flux. Western theology has been dominated by a Parmenidean view of God that tends to suppress particularity and individual significance. Much of mo-dernity can be interpreted, Gunton believes, as a legitimate revolt of the many, the particulars, against the stifling tendency toward oneness and homogeneity characteristic both of certain strands of ancient Greek thought and of tradi-tional theology. Ironically, late modernism and postmodernism have ended up undercutting and losing many of the positive values that motivated moder-nity. One such instance of this is the loss of individual identity and significance in the Heraclitan flux of postmodernity.

To cure these maladies, Gunton thinks we need a refurbished doctrine of creation rooted in a doctrine of the Trinity that does full justice to the particu-larity within the unity of God. Ultimate reality is such that the particularity within God is constituted by relationality. Gunton accordingly rejects the in-terpretation of the Trinity that sees the substance of God as some abstract thing underlying the three persons. Rather, he follows the Cappadocian theologians, who view the individual persons as substances. "By using hypostasis to refer to the concrete particulars—the persons—and then proceeding to say that the *ousia*—general being—of God is constituted without remainder by what the persons are to and from each other in eternal perichoresis, these theologians made it possible to conceive a priority of the particular over the universal."[32] The notion that particularity is at the heart of ultimate, uncreated reality es-tablishes the particularity of created beings.

Thus, the doctrine of creation, rooted in such Trinitarian theology, is most relevant to our question of personal identity. God has created us as particular individuals, and our substantive identity is to be located in our relationships, both to God and to other created particulars. Thus, our distinctive identity is not defined primarily over against others but rather in terms of our relationships to them. It is a mistake, then, as Gunton points out, to pit a relational understanding of identity against an ontological one. Rather, the two stand or fall together.

The substances in question are precisely who and what they are, and enjoy a rich sense of identity, because of the way they are related to other substances.

On the other hand, only substances with certain given powers and potentialities can relate to each other in the ways we have been considering. Thus, the
relational account of identity complements and provides depth and texture to
the ontological account of identity I discussed earlier in this chapter.

In view of the fact that we are both historical and relational beings, I would
suggest that our identity is forged largely in terms of the history of our relationships, primarily with God, and secondarily with other created beings. Our
relationship with God is primary because that is what we were ultimately created for. But this relationship cannot be achieved in isolation from other relationships. Indeed, the image of God that distinguishes human beings from other
creatures consists, according to Joel B. Green, "in the human capacity to relate to God as his partner in covenant, and to join in companionship within
the human family and in relation to the whole cosmos in ways which reflect
the covenant love of God."[33]

Let us consider further this conception of identity by examining a biblical
example, namely, that of the apostle Paul. In particular, let us look at the early
chapters of Galatians, a passage rich in autobiographical material that gives the
historical shape of Paul's identity. He describes there his early life in Judaism
and his zeal and advancement in that religion. This sets the context for his
account of how God revealed God's Son to Paul and called him to preach the
gospel. The contrast between his old way of life and his new life in Christ is
reflected in the report about him that reached the Christians in Jerusalem when
he went there to meet Peter for the first time: "The man who formerly perse-
cuted us is now preaching the faith he once tried to destroy."[34] It is worth
remarking that the force of this statement depends on continuity as well as
contrast between Paul's earlier and later way of life. A radical change has taken
place in his life, but this point loses its impact if Paul the Christian evangelist is
not in some important sense continuous with, indeed, the same person as, Saul
the persecutor of Christians. He now has a new relationship that has changed
the focus and orientation of his life. But the nature of the change depends on
his being in some sense the same man. In philosophical language, he is the
same metaphysical entity, the same substance.

Paul continues the narrative with another visit to Jerusalem fourteen years
later. The story expands to include the roles of Barnabas and Titus as well as
Peter. What is at issue now is the question of whether Christian converts must
be circumcised and follow other similar Jewish religious practices. It was Paul's
conviction that to require this would compromise and distort the very truth of
the gospel. Thus, Paul argues with Peter on this issue because he is convinced
that Peter is wrong. The point is that all of his other relationships are now
defined by his relationship to Christ.

Indeed, this relationship now defines who he is. Paul states this memorably
as follows: "I have been crucified with Christ and I no longer live, but Christ
lives in me. The life I live in the body, I live by faith in the Son of God, who
loved me and gave himself for me."[35] This somewhat paradoxical statement is,
I would argue, a vivid expression of personal identity from a Christian point of
view. Paul recognizes that Christ, who is the Son of God, loved him enough

to give himself in death for him. In response to this love, Paul now lives his life by utter faith in Christ. The resulting transformation is so thorough that Paul can describe it as having his old self and old way of life crucified. In place of his old self, Christ now lives.

At the very end of the book of Galatians, Paul comments, "I bear on my body the marks of Jesus."[36] He is likely referring here to scars that he received as a result of persecution for his faith. He was beaten several times as well as stoned, and these experiences surely left their physical marks. The point again is that Paul's identity is constituted by the history of his relationships. Even his body conveys the story of how he was transformed by Christ and how he henceforth lived his life by faith in the Son of God, who loved him enough to give his life for him.

Given that it is God's will to elicit such faith from all persons and to transform them in the same fashion that Paul was transformed, the core of who we are is defined by the history of our response to God's love and grace. Those who do not respond positively in faith and love are still identified by their response. They are identified in terms of their history of refusing grace and rejecting the gracious relationships that transform. Their relationship to God is not one of faith and love but of sinful mistrust and disobedience.

Heaven is the community of persons who have entered the fellowship of the Trinity by allowing themselves to be transformed by the perfect love made available to us in the incarnation of the Son of God and outpouring of the Holy Spirit. The Son of God gave his disciples the command that they should love each other as he had loved them. We cannot appreciate the meaning of this unless we recognize the Trinitarian implications involved. In particular, Jesus had told his disciples that he loved them as the Father had loved him, even before the world was created. The love of Christ for his disciples, then, is the same kind of love that eternally unites the members of the Trinity. In commanding his disciples to love each other as he loved them, he is telling them to reproduce, in their relationships, the same kind of love that unites the persons of the Trinity in perfect communion. When Jesus prays to the Father that his disciples will be one, "just as you are in me and I am in you," he prays for a unity that is like the eternal oneness of the Trinity.[37]

Just as the Trinity is a perfect unity in which individual distinctions are maintained, so individual identity is maintained in the merely human persons that come to share in the fellowship of the Trinity. As John Hick has noted, the Trinity provides a model that allows us to conceive of the community of perfected human selves such that "they just *are* so many different selves, each with its own unique character and history," all of whom "are so harmoniously interrelated as to form the immensely complex personal unity of mankind, a human unity which perhaps requires all these different unique contributions."[38] Note particularly Hick's point that each of us has a unique character and history and thus a distinctive contribution to the perfected human community.

Recall in this light the quote from Wolterstorff that began this section. He notes that his son was a unique person and that no one saw just what he saw, remembered what he remembered, and so on. Each of us is unique in this sense, and each of us brings such a distinctive perspective to the human community. Moreover, as free beings, we craft a distinctive history of relationships to God and each other. I noted earlier the importance of freedom and its consonance with dualism. Now I want to emphasize that our character, the shape of our soul, so to speak, is determined by the history of our free choices in relation to both God and other persons. Our character is shaped by the story of our response to God's grace and our interactions with other people. Some people respond readily to grace, others are more reluctant, and others still form their characters by steadfast refusal of grace.

By our free choices, moreover, we can influence other persons to enter into fellowship with God. We can encourage them to trust God and live by faith in the Son of God who gave himself for them. This too is part of the history of our relationships that we bring to the redeemed human community, and as such, it is part of our personal identity.

I would suggest that this is part of what is involved in the biblical notion that in heaven we will be rewarded according to our actions. Those who have loved much and influenced many persons to live a life of faith will enjoy this as part of their lasting history and identity. The reward is one that is intrinsic to loving relationships. The more such relationships we have cultivated and contributed to the human community, the greater will be our reward.

It is worth remarking here that the conception of identity I am sketching here depends upon substantial continuity of memory. John Hick has noted that the notion of eternal life poses distinctive problems for the role of memory in personal identity. In particular, the sheer time involved seems to stretch the notion of memory beyond anything we can imagine and accordingly to pose difficulties for our ordinary conception of how memory contributes to identity. "When I imagine myself thinking of one who was alive a million years ago, though objectively continuous with myself now, I find that the increasing attenuation of memory combined with the increasing inner distance, produced by continuous personal change, from an individual who lived so very long ago, amount to a real discontinuity."[39]

I am inclined to think that this problem is indeed largely conjured by imagination. We may find it difficult to picture how continuity of memory could hold over enormous stretches of time, not to mention eternity. This is especially true if we suppose that we will be continually growing, learning, and experiencing new things—in short, continually making new memories. In the first place, however, there is no reason to assume that our mental powers, including our memory, will be subject to the sort of conditions that render them frail and vulnerable in this life. Perhaps our glorified bodies will equip us with greater powers of concentration, understanding, and clarity of memory. Our distinctive humanity will thereby be preserved, redeemed, and enhanced.

It is worth noting in this connection that Hick is inclined to think that the final state of salvation will be disembodied as well as outside of time. If so, it seems our humanity has been obliterated rather than redeemed. Indeed, it is hard to know what sense can be made of Hick's notion that the final unitive state will be one in which we contribute our "unique character and history" to the ultimate human unity if we do not retain substantial continuity of memory.

The Christian hope of communion with the Trinity is one in which our identity is fully maintained. The heart of that identity is the personal memory of our history of being transformed by the love of God in Christ. Surely the memory of that history will be retained, along with the history of our relationships in Christ. Moreover, the Christian hope is that we shall enjoy this perfect communion in our bodies. Indeed, if Christ has retained his glorified body, with scars intact, there is no reason to doubt that the experience of perfect communion with the Trinity will be bodily for us as well. And if Paul's scars were part of his identity as a disciple of Christ in this life, there is no reason to doubt that they will be so in the next life.

Our defects are another matter, however. Given that heaven is a place of perfect wholeness and happiness, it is surely reasonable to believe that defects of mind and body will be repaired.[40] Physical deformities, diseases, maiming, crippling, mental deficiencies, and the like obviously represent obstacles to human satisfaction in the fullest sense of the word. Jesus' healing of various maladies and impairments during his earthly ministry is a foreshadowing of the wholeness that all of the redeemed will enjoy as the fruit of his incarnation. Blind men who are enabled to see and crippled persons who are empowered to jump for joy are images of the coming kingdom.

This is not to deny that such defects will continue as a part of human identity in heaven. Those who negotiated this life with the additional struggles of mental or physical deformities will retain the memories of doing so as well as the positive character traits they formed as a result. Indeed, such struggles may have been means of grace that taught lessons of humility and dependence upon God. This is as true for those who have cared for such persons as it is for the persons themselves. The extra sacrifices of kindness and patience given on behalf of handicapped persons also shape the identity of those who offer them in faith and love and will remain a part of their history.

All of these considerations are obviously relevant to the frequently asked question of whether we will know each other in heaven. The answer is that we will know each other truly and completely for the first time. When our true identity is fully disclosed in our mutual relations, we will know ourselves with honesty and perfect clarity.

In one of his more memorable epigraphs, Nietzsche wrote, "'I did this,' says my memory. 'I cannot have done this,' says my pride, remaining inexorable. Eventually my memory yields."[41] In heaven, pride will have yielded to memory. We will remember the story of our sin, our failed relationships, our forgiveness, and our transformation by grace. We will know how we have responded to God's grace and all the ways we were changed by that response. Thereby all of us will know who we are.

5

HEAVEN AND THE PROBLEM OF
"IRREDEEMABLE" EVIL

I

Richard "Dickie" Hoard was jolted awake one summer morning in his four-teenth year by what he first thought was a thunderclap. But the scream of his mother indicated it was something far worse. Following her outside, he saw flames leaping from the engine of his father's car with his father inside. The explosion that had awakened him not only demolished the car but took his father's life as well. Floyd Hoard, a forty-year-old solicitor general in a small town in Georgia, was in the process of prosecuting a prominent bootlegger who had thus far evaded the reach of the justice system.

Dickie's initial shock reached another level when his uncle arrived on the scene moments later.

> He pounded his fist into the palm of his hand, tears streaming down his face. "Who would have done this? God damn! Who would have done this?"
>   He stared at me as if expecting me to answer. I shook my head, my mouth hanging open in disbelief as I realized for the first time that someone had meant for this to happen.[1]

The ensuing investigation uncovered a loosely knit conspiracy headed by Cliff Park, the bootlegger whose illegal operation Floyd Hoard was working to close down. The man who actually planted the dynamite in the car was hired for the task for a few thousand dollars.

Writing several years afterward, Richard Hoard tells the story of how the tragic loss of his father profoundly altered the shape of his existence. Something irreplaceable was ripped from his life, and the resulting pain intensified the normal struggles of youth and young adulthood. Everything from athletic achievement to adolescent romance was tinged by the unrelieved grief that filled his heart. "My father's death was like someone had hammered a nail into my senses and the infection was spreading. I hated the whole world, hated myself, could not see any sense of worth unless someone were pinning a varsity letter on me or applauding me for some game-winning shot."[2]

Consider now the case of Suzy Holliman, a beautiful sixteen-year-old girl. Home from school alone one day with the flu, she was confronted by Ricky Lee Sanderson, who was breaking into her home to get money to buy drugs. Sanderson turned his crime into a tragedy as he proceeded to drag her from her home, lock her into the trunk of his car, stab her to death, and then bury her in a shallow grave in a farmer's field.

Evil of this magnitude is shocking even to the casual observer. At a deeper level, such evils exacerbate already difficult issues in theodicy, for these evils involve loss so profound that it is tempting to believe that nothing could ever compensate for it or redeem it. Such evils pose severe questions about God's goodness or power, if not his very existence.

As noted in chapter 1, the doctrine of heaven has played a key role in traditional discussions of theodicy. Recall that Demea, the orthodox believer in Hume's *Dialogues*, appealed to heaven to resolve the obvious difficulty posed by pervasive evil in this life. He claimed that this life is "but a moment in comparison of eternity. The present evil phenomena, therefore, are rectified in other regions, and in some future period of existence."[3] The belief in heaven represents a major parting of the ways between Demea and Philo, who readily agree that the evil in our world constitutes a major challenge to belief in a perfectly good God, for Philo rejected out of hand the appeal to heaven as a solution to the problem of evil.

The notion that heaven can rectify temporal tragedy is also rejected in eloquent fashion in one of the most famous passages on theodicy in modern literature, in *The Brothers Karamazov*. Through the lips of Ivan, Dostoyevsky brings the problem of evil into extremely sharp focus through the poignant reality of children who suffer. Ivan paints several graphic pictures of innocent children suffering unthinkable cruelty at the hands of heartless adults. One of these involves an aristocratic general who turned his hunting dogs loose on an eight-year-old boy who had hurt the paw of the general's favorite hound with a stone he had thrown in play. The boy was torn to pieces before his mother's eyes.

Ivan goes on to imagine a future in which God's justice is made clear and a harmony in which the mother embraces the fiend who threw her child to the hounds. Yet he finds himself unable to accept such a harmony and feels he must repudiate it here and now and insist that it is not worth the terrible price required to achieve it.

I don't want the mother to embrace the oppressor who threw her son to the dogs! . . . [S]he dare not forgive the torturer, even if the child were to forgive him! And if that is so, if they dare not forgive, what becomes of harmony? Is there in the whole world a being who would have the right to forgive and could forgive? I don't want harmony. From love of humanity I don't want it. I would rather be left with unavenged suffering. . . . Besides, too high a price is asked for harmony; it's beyond our means to pay so much to enter on it.[4]

The heart of Ivan's claim is that some evils are so horrendous that nothing can redeem them or compensate for them. Some evils cannot be forgiven, and this moral reality stands in the way of the ultimate reconciliation required for heaven. Indeed, a morally sensitive person must reject the hope of heaven if it requires affirming that God could be justified in allowing such severe evils to occur and even forgiving them in the end. Ivan's claim here appears to be a deontological one to the effect that some evils are intrinsically so bad that to allow them could never be morally justified.

Whatever the philosophical credentials of this claim, its emotional force is undeniable. Many sensitive persons are inclined to agree that they must, in good conscience, return to God their entrance ticket to heaven if such a price must be exacted from innocent persons. This is a serious problem indeed if the hope of heaven is blocked by legitimate moral concerns as well as emotional objections.

Let us pursue this further. Just why is it that some evils seem unforgivable? What is distinctive about such evils that it could seem plausible that they must remain forever as monuments that prevent the possibility of heaven ever being realized? Why are these evils such an outrage that it is tempting to believe they can never be redeemed? According to Marilyn Adams, "[W]hat makes horrendous evils so pernicious is their life-ruining potential, their power prima facie to degrade the individual by devouring the possibility of positive personal meaning in one swift gulp."[5]

Let us reflect on why these evils can threaten the very possibility of personal meaning in our lives. As a preliminary observation, it is obvious that such evils are violations of the most extreme sort and result in profound loss for the victims involved. Something of great, even incalculable, value is wrenched from them that rips apart the very fabric of their lives. The tear is so great that it seems nothing can repair it. Hugh Holliman, Suzi's father, freely admitted the difficulty of forgiveness in the case of his daughter's brutal murder, despite the fact that he is a practicing Christian and that Sanderson himself professed to have repented and have found forgiveness from Christ. "The hopes and dreams he took away from us and the world—I tried but I can't forgive him," Holliman said. "You know there is forgiveness there, but I can't see God totally forgiving him for something like that."[6]

Hopes and dreams are at the heart of meaningful existence. Tragedy always means that some of these are brought to bitter end. Commenting on his feelings after the death of his son in the mountain climbing accident mentioned in chapter 4, Nicholas Wolterstorff writes, "Something is *over*. In the deepest levels of my existence something is finished, done. . . . Sometimes I think that happiness is over for me. . . . But I can still laugh so I guess that isn't quite it. Perhaps what's over is happiness as the fundamental tone of my existence. Now sorrow is that."[7]

To have hopes and dreams destroyed by some natural disaster or accident is terrible enough. But the devastation involved can seem unbearable with the added realization, as it dawned on Dickie Hoard, that someone actually intended and deliberately caused the evil. This sickens the soul in a way that can seem terminal. Hoard, Holliman and Ivan in Dostoevsky's story speak for countless sufferers when they give vent to a depth of hurt that seems beyond the power of any conceivable healing.

Wolterstorff's remarks point to the essence of this hurt. It is fundamentally the destruction of happiness. As it has often been argued, nothing is more fundamental to rational beings than the desire for happiness. Apart from this, there is no plausible account of meaningful existence. This is not to say that happiness in its fullness should be expected in this life. To the contrary, Christian theology instructs us that whatever happiness we enjoy in this life is at best a foretaste of the joy to be anticipated in the world to come.

The devastation of tragic evil consists in its power to destroy the very things that make it possible even to hope for complete happiness. Tragic death, for instance, represents the ripping asunder of relationships that were the very fabric of hopes and dreams and thus of a meaningful life. Moreover, horrendous evil typically has devastating emotional and psychological effects. Its victims feel in the depths of their souls the loss they have sustained and wonder if things can ever again be made right in their lives.

Of course, human relationships inevitably come to an unhappy end. Every marriage ends in death or divorce. Every relationship between parents and children ends with death. Nevertheless, there are added layers of grief and pain when these are torn asunder by the deliberate or randomly accidental destruction that forcefully brings them to an unexpected and premature conclusion. In this case, something has been taken that was not only of incalculable personal worth but was also the substance of reasonably nurtured hopes and dreams. Cruelty and murder can be seen as the crushing of the psychological well-being as well as the hopes and dreams that constitute human happiness and meaning. This is what constitutes the profound sense of violation and outrage that is expressed in the face of extreme cruelty and evil. To strip one of his hope of happiness and meaning is to strip him of his very humanity. To forgive such an outrage is seemingly to accept the loss of our humanity as a negotiable or trivial thing. This is what makes the stance of unforgiveness in the face of tragic evil morally plausible.

II

I will argue in the remainder of this chapter that heaven is an essential resource for a satisfactory theodicy. Indeed, heaven is essential to make sense of the sort of evils sketched here. This is not to deny that some persons have managed to maintain faith in God, despite horrific evil, without either a hope of heaven or any sort of theodicy.[8] But it is to insist, as argued earlier, that any God truly worthy of our worship and faith must have both the ability and the desire to preserve and perfect his relationships with his human creatures.

My purpose here is not to engage in detail the various theodicies or to grapple with the numerous subtleties of this multifaceted debate. Rather, I want to focus on the particular case of those horrendous evils that seem beyond repair and to show that heaven is our only hope of resolving these and of providing an adequate theodicy for those who hold to a rich conception of God's goodness.

Let us approach this by reflecting on something that is absolutely fundamental to Christian theism, namely, the notion that human happiness can be found only in a right relationship with God. John Wesley puts this basic point as follows: "In this alone can you find the happiness you seek—in the union of your spirit with the Father of spirits; in the knowledge and love of him who is the fountain of happiness, sufficient for all the souls he has made."[9] Writers from Augustine to Pascal to C. S. Lewis have expounded upon this point and have shown how it naturally follows from God possessing the nature he does and human beings possessing the divinely created nature they do.

There is general agreement among these writers that the desire for happiness is endemic to rational creatures such as ourselves. Moreover, it is the human tendency to seek happiness in all kinds of worldly and creaturely pursuits, ranging from the sensual to the aesthetic to the intellectual. But the common testimony of human experience in every age is that the pursuit of happiness along these trails ends in futility, failure, and disappointment. This conclusion can be evaded for a considerable time with sufficiently ingenious and persistent diversions, but thoughtful seekers in all times and places have eventually conceded that even the best of natural pleasures do not fully satisfy.

Christian theology maintains that the deepest reason for this failure is because God has made us for a relationship with himself, and since we are so made, nothing finite can fill the void that cries out for relationship with an infinite God. Moreover, the very thing that is our fulfillment is also our obligation. As our creator and redeemer, God is such that we owe him our wholehearted love and worship. "To him therefore alone our heart is due. . . . And to give our heart to any other is plain idolatry. Accordingly, whatever takes our heart from him, or shares it with him, is an idol; or, in other words, whatever we seek happiness in, independent of God."[10]

This does not mean, of course, that we are not to love other persons or appreciate and enjoy other things. Christians are clearly commanded to love other persons, sincerely and deeply, especially family members and other believers. The point is that we are forbidden to seek happiness in any of these independent of God, or to seek elsewhere the happiness that can only be found in God. In other words, our love and devotion to God must define all of our other relationships and loves. Paradoxically, we can love other persons best when we clearly maintain the priority of our love for God. As C. S. Lewis has pointed out, to love others more than God is not an excess of love but rather a failure to love God enough. Such inordinate love for any creature inevitably tends to destroy itself, for it is turned against the source of love himself.

What this emphasizes is that God is not imposing an arbitrary requirement on us when he forbids us to love others more than himself. It is not that God jealously resents our finding happiness in loving others more than we love him. The point is that we cannot be truly and deeply happy if God is not our supreme love. We cannot, in the long run, sustain any of the natural loves without being rightly related to Love himself. Cut off from the love of God, the natural loves inevitably are distorted and finally wither and die.[11]

If our true happiness and satisfaction are found in a right relationship to God, and if all other loves are to be subordinated to this commitment and defined in terms of it, this has obvious implications for the problems of theodicy we have noted. First and most important, our true happiness is secure so long as our relationship to God is maintained. This means that no earthly loss can destroy the ultimate source of our happiness. This is central to Paul's assurance to his readers that nothing in all of creation can separate believers from the love of God.[12] If the love of God is the one necessary and sufficient condition for human happiness, then nothing that happens in this life can prevent our happiness.

But surely our happiness is not perfect in this life, as already noted. Indeed, it is often far from it. Surely the sort of tragedies described above prevent perfect happiness by introducing loss, grief, and sorrow into our lives. It would be unrealistic and insincere to pretend otherwise. In the very passage where Paul assures us that nothing can separate us from the love of God, he also reminds his readers that the Christian life is a life of hope, and hope involves what we do not yet have. He graphically describes our present situation as one of groaning in the pains of childbirth as we anticipate the fullness of redemption. We groan along with the rest of the created order as we await the full liberation of our world from the effects of the fall.

In the same vein, Wolterstorff comments movingly on Jesus' pronouncement that the mourners are blessed. He describes them as "aching visionaries" who have a poignant awareness of the profound difference between the state of our present world and the coming kingdom when God's will is perfectly achieved. To such mourners, Wolterstorff tells us that Jesus says, "Be open to the wounds of the world. Mourn humanity's mourning, weep over humanity's weeping, be wounded by humanity's wounds, be in agony over humanity's agony. But do so in the good cheer that a day of peace is coming."[13]

The Christian stance toward evil, even in its tragic dimensions, is the somewhat paradoxical one of cheerful mourning. Mourning because evil still touches our lives and tears at the fabric of what gives them meaning; cheer because of our hope that evil will be fully defeated and that even the worst tragedies can be redeemed in the end. This is why heaven is essential to any satisfactory theodicy. It is what sustains our hope in the present and gives us reason to believe our hope is not an empty delusion. It is what gives sense to the notion that the mourners are truly blessed.

III

But the question persists, Can any future really resolve the sort of pain and suffering that cloud our past and present experience? Could anything compensate for the losses some have sustained and heal the hurts some have felt?

The answer to this question is a corollary of the basic point that our true happiness is ultimately found only in a right relationship with God. Marilyn Adams has developed this point by arguing that divine beauty is an incomparable good and that intimacy with God is a good that is incommensurate with any and all created goods and evils. The intimate vision of God that heaven promises is thus an immeasurable good for any who behold it. "It would follow that any such contemplation of Divine Beauty not only balances off but engulfs participation in horrendous evils."[14]

Adams's claim that the beatific vision is a good that is incommensurate with the goods and evils of this life is part of her larger strategy to recast how Christians respond to the problem of evil. She wants to provide an alternative to the traditional approach of attempting to specify a morally sufficient reason for why God allows evil. Thus, she thinks it is misguided to answer Ivan's challenge, cited earlier in this chapter, by arguing that such horrendous evils might find a moral justification at the end of the day.[15] Her preferred method is to argue that evil, even of the horrendous variety, can be shown to be compatible with the existence of God if that evil can be defeated in the life of each person. This will be the case if there is some scenario in which the life of each person, as a whole, can be recognized as a great good.[16] The beatific vision, with its status as an incommensurate good, is a crucial resource to give substance to this scenario. It is of such immeasurable value that anyone who experienced it would consider their life a good thing and have no quarrel with God. Accordingly, God will be recognized as justified even if the evils he allows can never be.

This claim involves a retrospective judgment that, of course, no persons presently suffering are in a position to make. It is noteworthy, however, that some have expressed this judgment in prospect. Paul makes this claim, significantly, in Romans 8. While reminding believers that this life is marked by suffering, he assures them that "the sufferings of this present time are not worth comparing with the glory that is to be revealed to us."[17] Elsewhere, but in the same vein, he writes, "For our light and momentary troubles are achieving for us an eternal glory that far outweighs them all."[18]

Paul's description of suffering in this life as "light and momentary troubles" is one of the most remarkable phrases in the New Testament. Taken by itself, the phrase would suggest trivial difficulties hardly worth mentioning. That is just how Paul seems to view earthly suffering in light of the glory of eternal salvation. Coming from the pen of another writer, it would be tempting to dismiss the phrase as a bit of sunny rhetoric reflecting insensitive blindness to the devastating force of real suffering. But Paul's profound familiarity with human adversity and suffering will not allow him to be dismissed in this fashion. In 2 Corinthians, he produces a litany of his own experience that vividly shows he had firsthand knowledge of the full range of human suffering, from human cruelty to natural disasters to deprivation to emotional stress.[19] Indeed, his words in 2 Corinthians 4:17 even suggest that there is a connection between suffering and the glory that Christian believers anticipate.

The nature of this connection is construed in various ways, most commonly perhaps in terms of personal transformation. That is, evil is recognized as an instrument that God may use to transform us morally and spiritually and thereby make us fit for the glory of eternal life in the presence of God and other saints.

Perhaps, however, there is an even more direct connection between evil and good here. In particular, Marilyn Adams has ventured the bold suggestion that there is a direct correlation between severe suffering and the great good of insight into the very inner life of God. In contrast to the view, common in much traditional theology, that God is impassible and thus beyond suffering of any kind, Adams inclines toward the notion that the inner life of God includes not only ecstatic joy but deep agony as well. Thus, the experience of severe suffering may afford the sufferer the opportunity of a glimpse into the divine agony. This is not to say that suffering is itself a good but only that it has a good aspect as well as an obvious evil one. In view of this, a believer "might be led to reason that the good aspect of an experience of deep suffering is great enough that, from the standpoint of the beatific vision, the victim would not wish the experience away from his life history, but would, on the contrary, count it as an extremely valuable part of his life."[20]

This claim obviously raises some very pointed questions. If terrible suffering can in the end be counted as an extremely valuable part of one's life, then it might be judged a good thing to lose a child or a parent in a tragic fashion. Perhaps tragedy should be courted as some of the early Christians courted martyrdom. Indeed, perhaps tragedy is wrongly named and should rather be recognized as one of the truly exquisite blessings of life. But can the cruel murder of a child really be seen in any meaningful sense as a blessing to be embraced with gratitude?

Nicholas Wolterstorff wrestled with the ambiguities involved in these questions in the aftermath of his son's death. He readily acknowledged that he had learned some profound and important truths through his personal experience of tragedy. The reality of the suffering of others entered him in a way it never had before. He gained a sensitivity to dimensions of suffering he had hardly suspected before. Among the sufferers he saw in a new light was God himself, about whom Wolterstorff writes, "[S]trangely, his suffering I never saw before."[21]

But in recognizing these gains, he observes that things began to "slip and slide around." It was no longer easy to tell what to celebrate and what to lament. "And how do I sustain my 'No' to my son's early death while accepting with gratitude the opportunity offered of becoming what otherwise I could never be?"[22] Earlier in his reflections, Wolterstorff had written, "I have changed, yes. For the better, I do not doubt. But without a moment's hesitation I would exchange those changes for Eric back."[23]

Here is the question. Can Adams be right that even severe suffering is such that we would not wish it away from our life history from the vantage point of the beatific vision, while Wolterstorff is also right in being gladly willing to exchange the positive changes in his character for Eric back? Or are these positions simply incompatible?

Despite appearances, these positions are not necessarily incompatible. Let us begin with Wolterstorff's remark. One way to construe it is as a counterfactual statement to the effect: "If the world were so constituted that the dead could be restored in this life if we so chose, then I would so choose, even if it meant giving up the positive changes that have taken place in me." In a similar vein, it might be understood as follows: "Given the choice beforehand, I believe I would have preferred a world in which my son did not die a tragic death and in which I did not experience the changes I have, to the present world."

Presumably one could so choose and still aspire to achieve heaven and the beatific vision. In other words, one would not consider the experience of tragedy necessary to prepare one for heaven but would believe the necessary transformation could occur some other way. After all, many persons do not have such tragedies touch their lives so immediately, so there is good reason to think they are not essential means to such moral and spiritual changes.

It might be objected at this point that perhaps not all persons need such tragedies for moral transformation but that some do, and that those who experience such tragedies are precisely those persons who need them. C. S. Lewis, for instance, seemed to believe that his wife was taken from him because God needed to expose his faith as a "house of cards."[24] Thus, tragedies specifically target those who need to have their faith tested or perhaps exposed as an illusion.

It may be allowed that God sometimes employs suffering and tragedy in this fashion without drawing the general conclusion that evil is normally sent by God for such specific purposes. Certainly it seems implausible to believe that tragedies generally indicate the need for spiritual testing that those exempt from such adversity do not need. It surely appears that many genuinely mature Christians experience great trouble while many persons with a superficial "house of cards" type of faith are spared similar difficulty.

This would suggest that tragedies generally occur through the contingencies of free human choice and genuine accident. In a world of free agents who interact regularly with each other as well as with the world of natural law, tragedy can be seen as a normal, albeit contingent, part of the fabric of life. On this view, all of us are vulnerable to tragedy and all of us can learn from it whenever and wherever it occurs. But there is no reason to think the victims of tragedy are particularly in need of the lessons that it teaches.

This account of the distribution of tragedy makes it possible to wish a tragedy reversed if the world were constituted so that they could be, even if one has learned important lessons from its tutelage. It would also be coherent to have preferred a world in which the tragedy did not occur. Of course, it is this world we live in and not another. In this world, Eric Wolterstorff died prematurely in an accident and Floyd Hoard and Suzi Holliman were cruelly murdered. In this world, no one can exercise the option to have their tragically killed loved ones returned to life in exchange for other things. So our question returns: Is it coherent to wish things away from one's life in *this* world while also believing we will not wish such things away from our life history in heaven?

I would suggest that it is not. The main reason is very simple. It is incoherent to wish that the past were different. This is evident from two fairly uncontroversial observations. First, one cannot properly wish for something unless he thinks it is at least possible. Second, once something has happened, it will always be true, from that time forward, that it happened. Indeed, there is a sense in which such truths are now necessary truths.[25] The upshot of these points is that there is no intelligible sense to the notion of wishing things away from our life history.

Of course, in everyday language, we often speak of wishing something had not happened. Indeed, so common is this language that we may be inclined to insist that something must be awry with the above argument. Our common language is not to be dismissed lightly, but it is often imprecise and sometimes misleading. This is one of those cases. While we may easily enough speak of wishing the past were different, strictly speaking, this is not a proper object of wishing since it concerns the impossible. Properly speaking, wishing can apply only to what we recognize as possible. To be sure, what is possible is sometimes highly improbable and against all odds. It is surely legitimate to wish for the improbable, and indeed, such wishing may be a paradigmatic instance of what the notion involves. But what is simply impossible is another matter altogether. To recognize that something is impossible is to rule it out of court as an object of our wishes.

Note that this point applies to both our own evil actions as well as evil actions performed against us that have caused us great suffering. To be sure, we can regret our actions as well as those of others, although this involves more complexities than we may suspect, as we shall see later in this chapter. To regret the past is to be sorry that it happened, and this feeling can mislead us to say we wish it had never happened. But again, strictly speaking, we can no more coherently wish we had acted differently than we in fact did than we can wish others had not hurt us or our loved ones as they did.

Indeed, the very fixity of the past is part of what constitutes evil as we experience it. As Elizabeth Templeton has remarked, "[M[uch of what *is* evil in the world—much, that is, which frustrates the convergence of freedom and love in our existence—is rooted in the past and in the fact that we are stuck with it."[26] In view of this, Templeton argues that theology must tackle the question of undoing the past if it ever hopes to articulate a satisfactory theodicy.

IV

Any realistic theodicy, then, must proceed from clear recognition of this hard truth: God thought it good to create our world even though terrible things happen in it, things that, necessarily, once they have happened, are such that it will always be true that they happened. In this sense, the past is unalterable, and this reality is surely a large part of what makes the problem of evil seem so intractable. Not even God can change the fact that once an event has occurred, it will always be the case that it occurred. Theodicy must face the challenge of showing how God's perfect goodness can be fully compatible with this fact.

In order for theodicy to succeed in this project, it must be true that God has the ability to loosen the grip of the past on our lives and defeat its power to spoil our happiness. This, I take it, is what Adams has in mind when she argues that from the vantage point of the beatific vision, no one would be inclined to wish away from his life history even the worst sort of suffering. But still, questions remain. Even if we grant that the vision of God's beauty is an immeasurable good, the question persists of just how this great good can resolve the pain of the past. And what of the problem of those actions that seem unforgivable? Can we flesh out in more detail how the incomparable goodness of heaven can address these difficulties?

Let us move in this direction by considering Templeton's suggestion that theology must tackle the problem of undoing the past. Is there an intelligible sense in which this can be pursued, or is this an incoherent notion like wishing the past were different?

These issues have been fruitfully explored by Patrick Sherry, who prefers to speak of redeeming the past rather than of undoing it. What does such redemption consist of? Sherry proposes that two fundamental things are involved. First, something must be salvaged from the past by removing or mitigating the evil consequences of the action, or even finding some good that comes out of it. Second, the evil must be put in a wider context that alters our view of it in such a way that we change the significance of that evil.[27]

Let us consider the first of these. Suppose that Cliff Park wanted to redeem the evil he caused to Richard Hoard and his family by removing as much as possible the effects of his action. He could begin by restoring or replacing the car that was demolished by the dynamite. The new car might be even better than the one that was destroyed. This would salvage something from the past and would remove some of the evil consequences of his action. But the real question is how could he redeem the evil of killing Floyd Hoard? Obviously, he cannot literally restore or replace Dickie's father. But he might try in some sense to do this by offering Dickie fatherly support and helping him in other ways a father typically helps a son.

Good can also come from such terrible situations, and this also contributes to redeeming them. Recall that Ricky Sanderson repented in prison and embraced Christ as his savior. Perhaps his cruel actions finally showed him the state of his life and character and moved him to be open to accepting the Christian gospel. As a Christian, he asked forgiveness for his slaying of Suzi Holliman.

But obviously these actions, though good, still fall far short of completely redeeming the situations in question. Persons and relationships cannot be replaced in the way material objects can. What this points up is that only God has the power fully to redeem evils of this magnitude. Only he can restore

persons to life and renew relationships that otherwise must remain forever sev-
ered. This places any possibility of complete redemption squarely in a future
context. Without the resource of life beyond the grave, there simply is no hope
of full redemption for some evils.

What about the notion of changing the significance of past events by putting them in a wider context? What does this involve? Sherry cites several
analogies from various authors to illustrate this concept. Some of the most il-
luminating examples are works of music or literature. William Temple, for
instance, gives the analogy of a play, the full meaning of which is not apparent
until the end. The same point could be made about movies or novels. An isolated chapter or scene is not fully grasped without the larger context of what
comes before as well as after. Temple draws the following general lesson: "The
value . . . of any event in time is not fixed until the series of which it is a member is over, perhaps, therefore, not to all eternity."[28] In a similar vein, Adams
also employs aesthetic insights and analogies to describe how God can overcome evil with good. She argues that for God to accomplish this, he must be
"a modern artist, ready, willing and able to turn horror-torn individual careers
into *Guernica's*, to house distortion within a unifying framework to produce
wholes of outstanding merits, at least some of which can eventually be appreciated by the individual him/herself."[29]

These are deeply suggestive proposals with far-reaching implications. The
Christian vision of reality stretches from eternity to eternity. This vision is the
context in which we must interpret all events if we are to understand them
rightly. Since we are in the midst of an eternity that is still unfolding, our
understanding of things is obviously provisional and open to revision. New
events are constantly occurring and new insights being born, and many of these
shed new light on past events. As this happens, our understanding of our life
and that of others changes. As Sherry puts it, "We seem to be confronted with
the possibility of a kind of continuous sequence of: living—evaluating and restructuring our lives—living—re-evaluating and restructuring, and so on, with
an interplay between events, our actions and how we reinterpret the past."[30]

Let us consider a particular example of this. As the years passed and Richard Hoard continued to reflect on his father's death and the events surrounding it, as well as other events in his life, he came to see many things in a different light. For one thing, he came to see the complexity of human motivation
in the plot to kill his father. Even though Cliff Park had received the stiffest
sentence, four other men had been involved, in various degrees, in the conspiracy to kill Floyd Hoard. Thus, Hoard concluded, "to say that Cliff Park
was responsible for the death of my father is a little bit like saying that Pontius
Pilate was responsible for the death of Jesus." The murder took a whole team
of men "pressuring and threatening and bragging and bullying. . . . Remove
any one of them from the plot, and it may have never happened."[31]

As Hoard tells the story of his own life, it becomes apparent that his in-
volvement in his own smaller-scaled evils illumined this truth for him. In particular, he tells about his relationship with an old man called T. C. who was
the target of ridicule because he cheered for Georgia Tech in a town where

almost everybody else sided with the Georgia "Bulldawgs." The local high school football players took great delight in provoking T. C. into arguments and then mocking him when he became angry.

Ever since Dickie had been a baby, T. C. had claimed him as a fellow Georgia Tech fan, and whenever they met they had a ritual in which T. C. would say, "Me and you, Georgia Tech," and Dickie would respond by raising his hand and saying, "Me and you." As he grew older, Dickie came to support Georgia but also retained some sense of loyalty to Tech because of his feelings for T. C., and he continued to follow the ritual whenever the old man greeted him.

One day Dickie was at the soda fountain in the local drugstore with several of his friends, including some of the football players, when T. C. walked in. As always, the football players began to ridicule him for his support of Tech. Attempting to brush them off, the old man approached Dickie with his usual greeting. His friends told T. C. that Dickie now supported Georgia and urged Dickie to admit this to the old man. T. C. persisted in tapping on Dickie's shoulder and waited for his normal response. Finally, under pressure from his friends, Dickie pushed T. C.'s hand away and shouted in his face, "Go Dawgs," to his friends' snickering approval. Reflecting on the event in retrospect, Hoard writes, "I knew at the time that had none of them been present I simply would have raised my hand to T. C. and said, 'Me and you.' But to save face with them I hurt an innocent man, whose only crime was to choose a different team."[32]

This description of his own actions is consciously parallel to the actions of his father's killers. He saw himself as a coward in this instance, not unlike some of the men who had conspired to kill his father under pressure from their peers.[33] This is not to trivialize their treachery in murdering his father, but it is to point up that what goes on in our hearts when we commit smaller-scaled evils may not be radically different from what is present in more spectacular crimes. C. S. Lewis makes the point as follows: "One man may be so placed that his anger sheds the blood of thousands, and another so placed that however angry he gets he will only be laughed at. But the little mark on the soul may be much the same."[34] Hoard's growing understanding of this reality was one of the things that enabled him eventually to be willing to forgive Cliff Park.

Another crucial event was his coming to grasp for the first time the reality of Christ's death for his sins. One evening in a church youth meeting he found himself attending against his wishes, his thoughts were arrested by a recently erected cross that someone had made from a small pine tree with the bark still intact, a cross very much in contrast to the beautiful brass crosses that typically adorn churches. "'A hell of a way to die,' I thought, staring at the tree. 'Nailed up like that.' And suddenly a thought I had never before considered struck me clearly, like a sword piercing my heart: It was real. As real as my own father's murder."[35]

As he reflected on these thoughts, he became vividly aware of Christ's presence in the room. The event profoundly changed his life and began healing him of the deadly infection that had for years produced in him a pervasive numbness of spirit. For the first time in years, he felt life return to his soul, and he immediately began to see things in a new light.

Later, in a college composition class, he was given the assignment to interview someone who had deeply affected his life. Hoard made the decision to interview Cliff Park, who was at the time in the hospital recovering from surgery. As he approached Park's room, he put these questions to himself: "Would I spend the rest of my life with emotions controlled by another? Or would I take charge of my life, even if no one understood why I was doing it, and release my hatred for a human being who, like myself on many occasions, pulled by the manipulations of others, had done what maybe he thought himself incapable of doing?"[36]

As he interviewed Park, he realized he no longer wanted to kill him, and he came to see him as an object of God's love. Recalling his own failures, Hoard reflected, "For I, too, knew something about conspiracies, and about hurting others to either look big or to save face. And this old man needed forgiveness every bit as much as I."[37]

This recognition obviously represented a profound reevaluation and restructuring of his life. Seeing the significance of Christ's death recast the significance of many of his own actions as well as Cliff Park's. He came to see himself alongside Park as a sinner in need of forgiveness. This surely puts the past in a wider context that in some sense undoes its horrible effects. What was done is no less terrible, but now it is seen as part of the common evil of humanity that requires the power of Christ to forgive and transform. The realization that Christ is our only hope of healing and redemption has large implications for the willingness to forgive. Christ alone is without sin. As a perfect innocent, he willingly suffered to provide atonement, and he offers forgiveness to all who repent and plead that atonement. He further requires that all who receive forgiveness be willing to forgive other sinners.

It is important to emphasize here that what is required is the willingness to forgive. Otherwise, forgiveness is trivialized into a morally vacuous concept that condones or winks at evil. Forgiveness, properly speaking, is contingent upon repentance. It is not, therefore, unconditional. We are called to unconditional love, even of our enemies. Such love entails wanting what is best for our enemies. What is best for all sinners is that they repent of their sins and accept the grace of Christ that can transform them. So love for a person who has done a great evil toward oneself consists essentially in the wish that that person would repent and enter a relationship with God that would transform that person. Such love involves a sincere willingness that the person be forgiven.

Consequently, those who have this attitude are not locked into a state of unforgiveness. Because of their love for the persons who have wronged them, they have released the hatred and anger they may have previously held onto, and they truly desire that those who have hurt them will be forgiven. Such offenders remain unforgiven, but it is not because of the attitude of those they have hurt. Rather, it is because they have refused sincerely to repent and to accept the forgiveness that their victims wish to extend to them. So the withholding of forgiveness is not a matter of unwillingness to forgive on the part of the victim but simply a recognition of the moral reality of the situation, namely, that the offender has chosen to hold on to his evil rather than repent.

Failure to distinguish between unconditional love and unconditional forgiveness complicates unnecessarily the understandable struggles many have with forgiveness. Recall again the father of Suzi Holliman, who freely admits the difficulty of forgiving Ricky Sanderson, the slayer of his daughter, despite Sanderson's profession of repentance and faith in Christ. Holliman confesses that he is skeptical about the sincerity of "jailhouse conversions" such as Sanderson's. He says he is hopeful that Sanderson was forgiven and recognizes the issue is finally between Sanderson and God.

Either Sanderson was sincere in his conversion or he was not. Let us consider the implications of each of these possibilities. Suppose first that he was insincere. If so, then his profession of faith was both foolish and futile. It was foolish because we can never deceive God, who always clearly sees through our insincerity. The attempt to deceive in such a matter as our relationship to God himself is a particularly striking example of human folly. It is possible to deceive other human beings in this matter, but such a project is doomed eventually to failure and futility. God will expose it, and it will be one more thing for which any who attempt it will be accountable to him. We need not worry that God will be conned by clever criminals who make insincere professions of faith.

If Sanderson was insincere, a Christian believer should hope that he will be forgiven even for his foolish attempt to use religion for his selfish and distorted purposes. But prior to this, he should hope Sanderson was sincere in his repentance and be truly willing that he should be forgiven.

Let us explore this possibility. If Sanderson's repentance was sincere, it represents the beginning of a process that will eventually transform him into a thoroughly new person, like Christ himself. This is the key to the remarkable Christian vision of full forgiveness and reconciliation. John Hick develops this point in a discussion of Dostoyevsky's story of the mother whose son was thrown to the dogs by the heartless general. As Hick notes, genuine transformation keeps the Christian notion of forgiveness from being morally superficial or psychologically incredible.

The Christian vision of heaven does not hold out for this mother the repulsive prospect of being spiritually united with a man who is still a heartless fiend, and winking at his treacherous evil. Rather, it offers the remarkable possibility of embracing a man who was previously a fiend but who has been perfected by the grace of Christ. "His perfecting will have involved his utter revulsion against his own cruelty and a deep shame and sorrow at the memory of it."[38] In an important sense, he is identical with the man who committed the atrocity. It remains in his memory bank as an act he committed and for which he was responsible. But in another sense, he is now a new person. As I argued earlier, the heart of personal identity is the history of our response to God as revealed to us in Christ. Even this cruel general could eventually have a personal history that includes sincere repentance and faith in Christ. This possibility makes it a matter of profound hope that the victimized mother could genuinely embrace her son's killer with true forgiveness.

In the Christian vision of things, this is not a romantic escape but a sober facing of the deepest truths of reality. To bring this point into focus, let us come back to the story of Suzi Holliman and Ricky Sanderson. As he faced his death, Sanderson reflected on the relationships he would have to negotiate in eternity. "I think about facing Suzi Holliman when I'm executed. What's that going to be like? I'm ready to do it."[39] Again, this may strike us as cavalier insensitivity. But if the Christian account of life after death is not a fantasy, then Sanderson's comments may well reflect a steely resolve to come to terms in the deepest way with the reality of his sin and its terrible consequences. His comments may reflect a stage in the perfection of his character that will lead ultimately to his becoming the sort of person who views his past actions just as Christ views them. To so view them would be to view them with perfect moral clarity. It would be to see with full honesty the evil involved as well as the human infirmities that contributed to his actions. It would consist of perfect repentance and complete sanctification.

Such clarity is perhaps only achieved in its completeness as an aspect of the beatific vision. Perhaps this explains how viewing the immeasurable beauty of God fully resolves the pain of the past and makes possible the forgiveness of those deeds that seem unforgivable. This is what makes genuinely possible the perfect reconciliation of profoundly estranged persons that heaven requires. What seems impossible in this life may be merely natural in light of incomparable beauty.

V

Our discussion thus far has shown that Christians have some powerful resources to deal hopefully with tragedies of the past. But even if we maintain hope that such tragedies can be redeemed, it is natural to have a sense of regret that they ever occurred in the first place. As natural as this feeling is, however, it raises serious difficulties, as William Hasker has shown in a fascinating discussion of the complexities involved in such regret. Before concluding this chapter, let us turn now to consider some of these issues.

Hasker has analyzed a number of these complexities by way of some rather precise definitions of what it means to regret something on the whole, on the one hand, and to be glad on the whole that something is the case, on the other. As he notes, being glad on the whole is a rather strong attitude of preference. It is a matter of taking all relevant factors into account and still preferring the present state of affairs. Being glad on the whole is thus distinct from merely being circumstantially glad.

Consider an example Hasker supplies. Suppose I am glad that Indiana won the NCAA championship in basketball, defeating North Carolina in the final game. I might nevertheless prefer no tournament at all because I regret the existence of the NCAA with its vulnerability to corruption, its tendency to detract from academics, and so on. If I am only glad that Indiana won *given the existence of the NCAA*, then I am only circumstantially glad of that fact. By contrast with this attitude, suppose I am glad Indiana won the championship and I prefer this state of affairs to no tournament at all, despite whatever drawbacks the NCAA represents. In this case, I am glad on the whole for Indiana's championship.[40]

The question Hasker wants to pose to his readers is whether they are glad that they and their loved ones are alive. This is a "person-relative" question that each person must answer for himself. While some may return a negative answer because of severe suffering, most would readily agree that they are glad that they and their loved ones are alive.

This question is philosophically interesting for several reasons, but Hasker is particularly concerned with the issues that arise from the fact that our very existence—at least for many persons—is inextricably connected with tragic events in the past. Hasker illustrates this point with the contingencies involved in his own birth. His parents came from widely separated parts of the country and met through a series of events that involved several other people as well. The most significant of these events was the First World War, which sent his father to France and led his mother to move to Washington to work for the government. In short, Hasker believes that had there been no war, he would not be here. Moreover, there are no doubt similar complexities in the lives of many of his progenitors of earlier generations. From these considerations, Hasker formulates the following general principle: "Had major or significant events in the world's past history been different than they were, then in all probability neither I nor the persons whom I love would ever have existed."[41]

Hasker's argument hinges on a certain thesis about personal identity, namely, that each of us is initially individuated by his body. Thus, if that particular body had not been conceived and born, neither would that person ever have existed. On this view, one's soul is correlated to his body in a manner like that suggested by Aquinas, who held that the soul is the form of the body. That is, the soul is individuated by the particular body that it informs. Consequently, if the man who is Hasker's father had married a different woman, then Hasker would not be here formulating arguments along this line.

What follows from Hasker's view of personal identity, along with his definition of what it means to be glad on the whole, is quite interesting. In the first place, consider the following implication of what it means to be glad on the whole that something is the case: "If I am glad on the whole that P, and I know that if Q did not obtain neither would P, than I rationally must be glad that Q." When this implication is combined with his thesis about personal identity, we get this striking result: "If I am glad on the whole about my own existence and that of those whom I love, then I must be glad that the history of the world, in its major aspects, has been as it is."[42]

This consequence is not only striking but also disconcerting. In view of it, we may even be inclined to retract our previous claim about being glad of our existence. Hasker finds this reaction understandable. "Perhaps, indeed, your reaction is one of bewilderment—you may feel, as a colleague suggested, that when you lump your life together with the whole past history of the world, you don't know *what* to say about it."[43] In this case, one has no "on the whole" attitude about his existence and simply finds himself perplexed. As Hasker argues, the person who is merely bewildered is not situated to press the problem of evil as an objection against the existence of God. To make that argument effectively, one must positively regret his existence and that of those he loves.

My concern here is neither to defend nor to criticize Hasker's central argument, although I am inclined to think it is sound. What I want to point out is that the doctrine of heaven is a powerful resource to relieve the perplexity engendered by Hasker's argument. Let us proceed by spelling out more fully the nature of this perplexity. It is due, I think, to a sense that we have no right to be glad for our existence if our existence depends in any way on events that have brought terrible suffering and misery to other persons. To be glad in such circumstances can seem obliviously self-centered and insensitive. It is as if those who have suffered before us, and with whom our existence is inextricably connected, have a moral claim against us and our happiness. To be rightly happy, it may seem almost as if we need their blessing or approval, or even their forgiveness.

Lacking this, we may feel that we have a moral obligation to regret our existence. But this is at best a rather vague feeling. What could it mean to regret one's existence in this sense? Would it be a matter of actually preferring that one, as well as those one loves, did not exist? To be truly sincere and not merely a matter of empty hand wringing and guilt mongering, should such a preference lead to suicide or even murder? Or should it involve a choice not to be happy, a choice to bear the suffering of others in one's heart in such a way that one never experiences any real joy in life?

One thing regretting cannot mean is wishing one had never been born or wishing that past tragedies had not occurred. As argued previously, it is not coherent to wish, strictly speaking, that the past were different from the way it is. Our only real hope is that the past might be redeemed. And this is the key to relieving the bewilderment Hasker identifies. Specifically, the doctrine of heaven represents the only substantive hope that the past might be redeemed in such a way that we can be fully glad for our existence even if our existence is somehow implicated in the worst tragedies of human history. Heaven holds out the promise that persons who have suffered in terrible ways and died premature deaths—such as the many victims of the countless wars in human history—have not been consigned to oblivion. That is, they are not merely the waste product of human history who had to be sacrificed so that later generations could enjoy lives for which they are truly grateful.

Earlier I defended the notion of optimal grace, the notion that God will do everything he can, short of overriding freedom, to save all persons. Indeed, God will compensate for lack of opportunity to receive salvation in this life and make sure that all persons have a full and fair opportunity to receive the eternal life for which all persons were created. If this is so, then all persons will have the opportunity to experience full satisfaction and happiness. The only ones who will not actually do so will be those who freely and decisively refuse the offer of grace.

This is the final issue for all persons who have ever lived, whatever their fate in this life. The only hope for true happiness and satisfaction for those who have suffered greatly and tragically is precisely the same as that of persons whose temporal lives have been marked by joy and pleasure.

In view of this, I do not think anyone has reason to regret his existence or refuse the joy of life. This is not to say that believers in heaven should not mourn in the fashion Wolterstorff describes, as noted earlier in this chapter. But the mourning of the believer in heaven is set in the larger context of hope for a day of redemption that will dry all tears and heal all hurts. This is what relieves the perplexity and bewilderment of being glad of our existence while recognizing that our existence is contingent on tragedies that would otherwise be unspeakable.

VI

Let us conclude this chapter with a summary of the central argument. I have been examining the issue of how God can be perfectly good even though he has created a world in which terrible things happen, things that have a permanent place in the history of our world. I have been contending that none of these evils are in principle irredeemable. The fixity of such evils is indeed a formidable problem. However, Christians are encouraged to hope that not even evils having deep roots in the permanence of the past are beyond the resolution of God's amazingly creative grace. One of the most emotionally appealing promises about heaven is that God will wipe every tear from the eyes of the redeemed.[44] No human tears are beyond the reach of God's infinite goodness.

At the heart of my case is the basic Christian notion that our true happiness is found in a relationship with God and nothing that happens to us can separate us from God or destroy this relationship. Moreover, for us to enter this relationship, we must accept the grace of Christ. This requires accepting forgiveness from the only perfect person who ever lived and allowing him to transform us into persons who will eventually be perfect as well.

These truths provide the framework that makes it possible for us to forgive the things that have been done against us, even things of extreme wickedness or cruelty. We must recognize that the One who forgave us desires also to forgive the worst of sinners and asks us to be willing to do the same. Such willingness to forgive is not a matter of trivializing evil, for true forgiveness requires repentance and final reconciliation is ultimately dependent upon the moral and spiritual transformation that will unite believers in a bond of genuine mutual love. Those who refuse the offer of transforming grace continue to suffer the consequences of their evil choices. In view of this, the doctrine of heaven satisfies our deepest moral convictions about both forgiveness and accountability.

The doctrine of heaven holds out the hope that all persons can experience the perfect happiness for which we were created, regardless of what they have suffered in this life. Indeed, heaven is the only realistic hope not only for loved ones who have suffered tragically but also for countless anonymous persons whose suffering may have contributed significantly to our very existence. To give up the hope of heaven is to consign such persons to oblivion and to render the verdict that their suffering is irredeemable and finally meaningless in an indifferent universe. To hold on to one's anger, hatred, and indignation, more-over, destroys one's happiness. Thus, the only hopeful alternative for both the victims of cruel suffering and for their advocates is forgiveness and redemption.

The doctrine of heaven, with its resource of eternal transforming grace, offers the only realistic way of restructuring our lives and reinterpreting all our past histories in such a way that there is a truly hopeful future for any of us. Only belief in a God who is powerful enough and good enough to make eternal salvation fully available to all his children can relieve the sharpest barbs of the problem of evil. Only a salvation that represents the satisfaction of our deepest longings for happiness and peace holds promise that any earthly suffering will finally pale in comparison.

6

HEAVEN AND VISIONS OF
LIFE AFTER LIFE

I

The Reverend John Littlejohn, a prominent clergyman of the eighteenth and early nineteenth century, records in his journal the remarkable story that was told him of a boy who lay in a trance for twenty-four hours. During the time he was in the trance, his brother tried to rouse him by bleeding his arm and pouring water into his mouth, among other things, but to no avail. When he awoke, the boy told how Christ took him by the hand and led him to heaven and then to hell. He saw several people who had previously died who gave him messages for living persons, urging them to repent so they would not go to hell. The last person he mentioned, however, was believed to be still alive. Littlejohn continues the account as follows.

The boy said well if he is alive, I have told a lie but if he is dead I have spoke the truth, he told his Br [brother] he shd[should] not stay wth [with] him long he shd die soon. About a week after, news arrived that the Man he spoke of was dead & the boy is now expected to die. those things do not move me, I state the fact as I heard them—they may be of God—or of Satan I cant tell, be this as it may, I pray good may come out of it &c.[1]

Consider now the experience of a person who encountered death in a modern operating room. From his own perspective, he was sure he was dying because he knew he was outside of his body, which he could see on the operating room table. At first, he found this unpleasant, but then a bright light came to him. The light gave off a warm sensation and covered everything around him, yet not in such a way that it prevented him from clearly seeing the doctors, nurses, and operating table. The person elaborates on the encounter with the light.

> At first, when the light came, I wasn't sure what was happening, but then, it asked, it kind of asked me if I was ready to die. It was like talking to a person, but a person wasn't there. The light's what was talking to me, but in a *voice*.
>
> Now, I think that the voice that was talking to me actually realized that I wasn't ready to die. You know, it was just kind of testing me more than anything else. Yet, from the moment the light spoke to me, I felt really good— secure and loved. The love which came from it is just unimaginable, indescribable. It was a fun person to be with! And it had a sense of humor, too—definitely![2]

This experience was recounted to Dr. Raymond Moody, Jr., and appears in his best-selling book *Life after Life*. This book, more than any other work, has been responsible for a renewed fascination with life beyond the grave in contemporary Western culture. As a result of its popularity and related media coverage, the basic features of life-after-life experiences have become widely known.

While Moody's book and others like it have been eagerly seized upon by many believers as confirmation for their views, they do not simply reiterate traditional views of the afterlife. Indeed, the front cover of the book informs readers that the experiences described by it are "so similar, so vivid, so overwhelmingly positive that they may change mankind's view of life, death and spiritual survival forever." Editorial hyperbole duly noted, it is still clear that the book intends to offer a significantly different picture of life after death from the one dominating the popular imagination.

Some of the books that followed in the wake of Moody's, however, offered accounts that explicitly reflected traditional Christian concepts and imagery. One such account is by Betty Malz, who had a brush with death after an attack of appendicitis. Although her condition was correctly diagnosed by the first physician who examined her, she delayed surgery when another physician gave her a different diagnosis. Gangrene set in and she was given little hope of surviving. Six weeks after the initial attack of appendicitis, she had been through four rounds of surgery and her weight was down to eighty pounds. To complicate matters further, she contracted pneumonia. One afternoon, in this condition, she came to the door of death when her pulse stopped. After intensive efforts, her vital signs returned to normal, but the attending physician expressed doubts that she could ever live a normal life again, even if she survived.

The next morning, at around five o'clock, she apparently died, and the night nurse called her mother to inform her that Betty had just passed away a few moments earlier. Remarkably, her father had awakened at three-thirty and driven to the hospital. He arrived just as the call was being made and went up to Betty's room unaware of the bad news. When he walked in, a sheet had been pulled over her face. Realizing she had died, he stood there for several minutes in silence and then began to repeat the name of Jesus. Then, to his amazement, he thought he saw movement under the sheet. Next, and even more amazingly, Betty pushed the sheet away and sat up in bed. She had been "dead" for twenty-eight minutes.

Her account of what she experienced during this time is extraordinary. She describes a serene transition in which she wondered if she had died. She felt no uncertainty, however, but only a strong sense of well-being. As she walked up a hill of vivid green grass, she was aware that she was not alone, that she was accompanied by an angel. At the top of the hill, she heard her father's voice calling, "Jesus, Jesus, Jesus." Then they approached a magnificent structure and she heard a melodious chorus. The only words she could remember were "Jesus" and "redeemed." The angel put his hand on the gate of the structure and she glimpsed a dazzling light inside. She said she felt ecstatic joy at the thought of going inside. She continues her account as follows.

> I saw no figure, yet I was conscious of a Person. Suddenly I knew that the light was Jesus, the Person was Jesus.
>
> I did not have to move. The light was all about me. There seemed to be some heat in it as if I were standing in sunlight; my body began to glow. Every part of me was absorbing the light. I felt bathed by the rays of a powerful, penetrating, loving energy.
>
> The angel looked at me and communicated the thought: "Would you like to go in and join them?"
>
> I longed with all my being to go inside, yet I hesitated. Did I have a choice? Then I remembered my father's voice. Perhaps I should go and find him.[3]

She says that she made the decision to go back down the hill and that as she did so, she saw the hospital and then her room with a sheet pulled over a figure. Shortly after that she sat up in bed and saw her father staring at her in a state of shock.

We could go on indefinitely relating similar and equally fascinating stories of persons who believe they have come to the door of death and have been given a glimpse of what lies beyond. But our question is what to make of such stories. To ask this question immediately puts us in a world of considerable complexity. These accounts raise fundamental issues for a number of disciplines, and the literature on these experiences is accordingly multifaceted. Near-death experiences have been examined from the standpoint of religion, philosophy, medicine, psychology, biology, neuroscience, and sociology.

From a cultural and sociological perspective, there can be little doubt about the significance of these accounts. They have been widely and frequently reported in the popular media, and few persons in contemporary culture have not had their views of the afterlife challenged by these accounts. Indeed, as sociologist Allan Kellehear notes, the media reaction "has been nothing short of spectacular."[4] As a result of this extensive coverage, images of being out of the body, passing through a dark tunnel, encountering a being of light and viewing an instantaneous replay of one's life have become part and parcel of our common cultural consciousness.

According to Kellehear's analysis, there are several significant changes in social conditions that account for the popular appeal of near-death experiences (NDEs) in our culture. Of particular interest is his suggestion that reports of NDEs began to receive attention at a time in Western society when many persons had lost confidence in traditional religion and its ability to make sense of pressing issues and problems.

NDEs appealed to persons in alternative religious and spiritual circles because they did not typically emphasize traditional components of spirituality such as doctrine, church attendance, and the like. Moreover, NDEs were attractive to many more traditional adherents of religious faith who believed in the afterlife but had only the vaguest notions of what it might entail. Some of the well-known aspects of NDEs blended easily with biblical imagery and teaching. The encounter with the being of light, for instance, is obviously reminiscent of biblical language that describes God as light and Christ as the light of the world.

Clearly then the adaptability of NDEs to a variety of worldviews is a large part of their attraction in a time of ideological diversity and fragmentation. As Kellehear sums it up, "The NDE is the quintessential postmodern idea of death—eclectic in imagery; philosophically accessible to a wide range of beliefs without being particularly harmful to any of them; and critical of broad, singular, and simplistic ideas, whether materialist or religious."[5]

Underlying these social factors, however, is a more basic reality endemic to human nature that accounts for the eager fascination with which NDEs have been received in contemporary culture. As Carol Zaleski suggests, near-death literature is appealing for the same fundamental reason that spiritualism and psychic research gained such a following in the second half of the nineteenth century. Now, as then, people aspire to eternal life and immortality. The contemporary life-after-life movement originated largely in medical and psychiatric circles and brings the prestige of those disciplines to its claims. Consequently, it enjoys more credibility and plausibility than the claims of earlier psychical researchers. As Zaleski puts it, "experiential reports of life after death are popularly considered to be practical evidence which, when verified in the lab, will yield scientific confirmation of religious hopes."[6]

What is perennially human, I am suggesting, is the desire for assurance of eternal life and immortality. Throughout most of human history, this hope was undergirded by religious worldviews and authoritative texts that gave assurance of immortality. For several generations in the West now, the religious view of reality has been under fire, and the certainty previously afforded by authoritative texts has been eroded. Science remains the new authority for much of Western culture, and it is only natural that many people look to it to provide grounding and confirmation for their deepest hopes and aspirations.

II

Let us turn now to a more careful examination of NDEs to see why they seem to provide support for belief in life after death. Susan Blackmore, a critic of NDEs who believes they can be fully explained in naturalistic terms, cites four main arguments advanced by proponents of NDEs who believe they support, if not prove, life after death: the consistency argument, the reality argument, the paranormal argument, and the transformation argument.[7] I will summarize each of these, beginning with the consistency argument, which will require more space than the other three.

The essence of the consistency argument is the fact that accounts of NDEs have reflected a remarkable similarity from person to person, a similarity which suggests that something objective and real is being experienced and encountered. This point is underlined from the outset in Moody's groundbreaking book in the foreword, written by Elizabeth Kubler-Ross, another pioneer in near-death research. Kubler-Ross attempted to undercut the inevitable skepticism Moody's book would face by noting that his discoveries are "corroborated by my own research and by the findings of other very serious-minded scientists, scholars and members of the clergy who have had the courage to investigate in this new field of research in the hope of helping those who need to know, rather than to believe."[8] Note the claim that science can enable us to move beyond mere belief to the stronger foundation of knowledge on this matter of vital human concern.

Moody's description of the experience of dying begins with a famous generalized account of a near-death experience that includes sixteen distinct features which recurred in the numerous firsthand accounts that had been recounted to him in his research. Though no single account typically included all, or even most, of these sixteen features, there was enough overlap and repetition of these features to warrant at least the tentative conclusion that the similarity was best explained by encounters with objective reality.

Subsequent research has lent support to the initial claim of significant similarity put forth by Moody. Studies by Kenneth Ring, Michael Sabom, and Bruce Greyson, among others, have analyzed NDEs more formally and scientifically than Moody, but their findings have been broadly consistent with his and have supported his main contentions. Perhaps the most rigorous of these studies are those of Greyson. He developed a quantitative NDE scale composed of sixteen items. The scale enables researchers to explore the relation between NDEs and hypothesized causes and to distinguish NDEs from other reactions to near-death encounters. The scale can also be used to categorize NDEs into four discrete types: cognitive, affective, paranormal, and transcendental. The classification is based on which of the components are most prominent in a reported experience.[9]

More recently, Greyson conducted a study in which he contrasted the near-death encounters of 183 persons who reported NDES and 63 persons who did not. He found a statistically significant difference between those who had NDEs and those who did not on all sixteen items of the scale. Most interesting for our purposes are Greyson's transcendental NDEs, which involve the following four features: (1) entering some other unearthly realm, (2) seeming to encounter a mystical presence or being, (3) seeing deceased spirits or religious figures, and (4) coming to a border or point of no return. Forty-three of Greyson's 183 subjects, or 24% of them, had experiences he classified as transcendental.[10]

The argument from the similarity of NDEs has been further strengthened by studies of cross-cultural NDEs and NDEs from earlier ages. Kellehear summarizes data from the following cultures: China, India, Western New Britain, Guam, Native America, Australian Aborigine, and New Zealand Maori. Except for China and India, the number of cases studied is no more than a handful, so conclusions must be tentative at best at this point. Kellehear compares the cases on five features: (1) entering a tunnel, (2) being out of body, (3) the life review, (4) encountering other beings, and (5) entering another world. Features 4 and 5 were reported in all cultures; feature 2 was reported in all but two of them.

The transcultural features of NDEs are also documented in Zaleski's detailed comparison between near-death accounts in medieval and modern times. While basic similarities are impressive, Zaleski believes close examination shows significant differences as well. "The most glaring difference is the prominence in medieval accounts of obstacles and tests, purificatory torments, and outright doom."[11] While exceptions have been noted, the prevailing picture in modern accounts is one of bliss, peace, and acceptance by the being of light who even displays a sense of humor as he helps persons grow in self-realization.

Zaleski warns against the notion that any near-death accounts are free of cultural bias and influences. It may be tempting for modern persons to think contemporary accounts, delivered to us by medical and scientific investigators, are stripped clean of cultural coloring. But, Zaleski urges, contemporary accounts are shaped by cultural coloring no less than medieval ones. This observation, along with obvious cultural factors in the accounts summarized by Kellehear, point up the need for careful qualification of the consistency argument. But even when such qualifications are duly noted, the consistency argument is not without force.

Let us turn now to the reality argument. The claim here is that NDEs are so vivid and feel so real that they must be what they seem to be, namely, encounters with a loving being in a real world beyond this one. The feeling of certainty is expressed by one of Moody's subjects: "I'm not trying to make a big explosion in your life, and I'm not trying to brag. It's just that after this, I don't have doubts anymore. I know there is life after death."[12]

Consider now the experience of Richard John Neuhaus, one of the most distinguished Christian intellectuals and statesmen of our time. Neuhaus nearly died several years ago from complications arising from emergency surgery, and part of his story includes what could be described as an NDE. While lying in bed, he reports that he was suddenly jerked into a state of lucid awareness. Although his body was still lying flat, he was sitting up and intently staring into the darkness. As he was staring, he saw a color like blue and purple that looked like drapery. Near the drapery were two "presences" who spoke distinctly, although not in an ordinary way, this message: "Everything is ready now." After a couple of moments they were gone and Neuhaus was lying flat on his back again, his mind racing wildly as he made a determined effort to understand what had happened to him. To rule out the possibility of dreaming, he pinched himself hard, went through the multiplication tables and recalled the birthdays of his seven siblings. Throughout this time, he says he was as lucid and awake as he has ever been.

For present purposes, the point I want to stress is the profound sense of certainty that Neuhaus retains about the reality and significance of the experience years after it occurred. Given his skeptical tendencies, he admits he thought he would later come to doubt it. As a matter of fact, however, he reports, "Since then I have not had a moment in which I was seriously tempted to think it did not happen. It happened—as surely, as simply, as undeniably as it happened that I tied my shoelaces this morning. I could as well deny the one as deny the other, and were I to deny either I would surely be mad."[13]

Third, there is the paranormal argument. One of the impressive things about NDEs that is hard to account for naturalistically is that those who have had them have often accurately reported on things that happened while they were "dead." For instance, persons with no medical knowledge have described in detail how they were resuscitated, claiming they observed the whole process from above while out of their bodies. Another intriguing aspect of this evidence comes from cases in which persons claim to have met people in the afterlife who they did not previously know had died. Recall that in the vignette at the beginning of this chapter, the young boy who had the vision cited this as proof of the reality of his vision.

Finally, the transformation argument points to the positive moral and spiritual changes that those who have them frequently undergo. Such persons typically become less interested in material things and more concerned with people. They return from their brushes with death with a new passion to be more loving to other persons and with a renewed awareness of the importance of learning and the life of the mind. Betty Malz reports that one of the first things she saw outside her window when she returned was a black man carrying on his shoulder a case of soft drinks into the building. Before, she admits, she was guilty of racial prejudice. But her immediate feeling then was great love for the man. Such changes, it is maintained, are best explained by real encounters with an actual divine being in the next life.

Blackmore's project is to provide a full explanation of these lines of evidence in an exclusively naturalistic framework. In particular, she defends, with elaboration, the dying-brain hypothesis. That is, she argues that NDEs are visions of a dying brain that do not correspond to anything objective or supernatural. I will not engage the details of Blackmore's position at this point. What I want to emphasize now is that something like Blackmore's account is the only option for making sense of NDEs within the confines of naturalism.

Things are much different, however, for supernaturalists. They have more interpretive options. For a start, they might well agree with Blackmore that NDEs are indeed the product of a dying brain with little further significance. Of course, their reasons for thinking this will not be altogether the same as Blackmore's, given their belief in supernatural reality. But my point is that their belief in supernatural reality certainly does not require that all such matters be understood or explained supernaturalistically. Indeed, one's very beliefs about supernaturalism might incline one to interpret NDEs naturalistically. For instance, one might embrace a theology that held that God does not want us to know much about the particulars of heaven in this life. In view of this sort of belief, one would have reason to be doubtful about NDEs because such experiences might be thought to encourage unhealthy speculation about the details of the afterlife.

But even if a supernatural explanation of some sort seems preferable, it is surely not obvious just what that explanation should be. For instance, some supernaturalists have been inclined to explain NDEs in terms of satanic or demonic activity. Recall that Littlejohn, in the incident cited at the beginning of this chapter, mentioned this as a possibility. In particular, critics have offered the explanation that they are satanic deceptions designed to assure people that everything will be fine for them no matter what they believe or how they have lived. A number of traditional Christian believers have noted the easy assimilation of NDEs into New Age thought, as well as the occult tendencies of some prominent figures in near-death studies, and have seen this as good reason to be skeptical about the source of NDEs.[14]

While skepticism toward NDEs is certainly a defensible position for Christians to take, I want to argue that it is not incumbent upon thoughtful believers to take such a stance. Indeed, other interpretations, including supernatural ones that construe NDEs positively, are also worthy of serious consideration.

III

What is the best way to interpret NDEs if one views them positively and is open to alternatives other than the reductionistic program advanced by Blackmore and her naturalistic colleagues? This is the issue I want to pursue in the remainder of this chapter. In particular, I want to examine the question of whether NDEs provide support for the Christian doctrine of heaven. I will begin to approach this question by considering the views of Zaleski, who has offered a sympathetic account of NDEs, which she intends as an alternative to naturalistic approaches. After looking at Zaleski's approach to NDEs, I will examine them in light of the work of two leading Christian epistemologists, namely, Alvin Plantinga and William Alston.

Let us turn now to Zaleski. It is important to emphasize at the outset that her preferred approach is not offered as support for those who see NDEs as evidence or proof for life after death. Indeed, she aims to steer a course between "the self-defeating extremes of shallow relativism and naive affirmation."[15] So what view of NDEs can avoid these extremes and achieve a properly critical yet sympathetic balance? Zaleski's proposal is that they should be understood as "works of the religious imagination, whose function is to communicate meaning through symbolic forms rather than to copy external facts."[16] The question this raises is how she understands symbol and imagination. In the first place, she wants to distinguish these from metaphor and literary motif that merely illustrate some psychological or moral truth. To see an NDE this way is to "render it harmless."[17] Obviously, Zaleski wants to understand NDEs in a way that will avoid this result.

As she understands a religious symbol, it not only represents something beyond itself but also participates in some way in the reality it symbolizes. It represents the reality in such a way that it communicates some of the power of that reality. Such symbols, accordingly, are not to be judged in terms of truth or falsity but rather in terms of vitality or weakness. Indeed, Zaleski doubts that any of our concepts of God, the soul, or the world to come are true, at least in any ordinary sense of the word. Nevertheless, she does not think we need to abandon the notion that there is an ultimate truth of the matter. But since we have "no direct sensory or conceptual access to the reality for which we aim," we must employ pragmatic criteria for truth.[18] That is, we must ask which symbols have a healing power and assist us in the quest for truth.

Zaleski's position seems deeply ambivalent. Clearly she wants to say something substantive about the significance of NDEs and resist the tendency to trivialize them. On the one hand, she does not want to fall into the skeptical dead end of denying that there is an ultimate reality in these matters, but on the other hand, she has no confidence that we have access to that reality.

Her ambivalence is further evident in her explanation of how NDEs should be seen as works of religious imagination. Again, it is apparent that she is motivated in this regard by a desire to salvage as much as she can of near-death testimony and its significance. She tells of a colleague who admitted fascination with NDEs but could not embrace them because they seem to imply body-soul dualism. He felt he had to reject either the empirical data in favor of NDEs or give up his philosophical sophistication.

> Fortunately, however, a third alternative becomes available if we enact what I have called the Copernican revolution of regarding the other world as the domain of imagination and interpret its features accordingly. Without requiring adherence to any particular school of philosophical or psychological idealism, this revolution or change of perspective allows us to reclaim a whole range of imagery and experiential testimony that we might otherwise have to reject on theoretical grounds. Not only dualism and somatomorphism but also personification imagery . . . can be understood and valued as imaginative forms rather than descriptive models. They provide coherent patterns for dramatizing inner experience, yet they entail no particular metaphysics.[19]

Notice particularly the last sentence, where Zaleski sees it as a virtue of her approach that it allows NDEs to be affirmed as valuable ways to dramatize inner experience, without committing one to any particular metaphysic. She goes on to suggest on the next page that the "other world is the inner world projected on the stage of the imagined cosmos."

It is hard to know what to make of this. Just what is the ontological status of the other world according to Zaleski? Her desire to avoid any sort of meta-physical commitment leaves this entirely unclear. A few pages later, she reiter-ates the rightness of seeing NDEs as "socially conditioned, imaginative, and yet real and revelatory experiences." But in what sense they are real and just what they reveal remains vague. She continues that this approach allows us to respect the visionary's claim to have experienced death, even if that remains controversial by medical criteria. The important thing is that the experience "opened to him a discovery of what death means to him at the core of his being. When he stepped onto the stage of the other world—which is the inner world, turned inside out—he confronted his own deeply held image and pre-sentiment of death, perhaps just as he will at the time of his actual death."[20]

So what does Zaleski believe is revealed in NDEs? Apparently they are real encounters with what death means at the core of their being to those who have them. Their own deeply held views of what death will be like are dis-closed with revelatory vividness. They come face to face with what they be-lieve about death in their heart of hearts. And this insight has great value for living this life. It can bring vividness and life to our ideas of the other world and thereby open up new worlds for us to live in now. NDEs are like conver-sion experiences in this respect. By giving focus and color to ideas of the next world, they provide orientation and a sense of direction for living meaning-fully in this one.

This is no small gain to be lightly discarded. But in the end, the question re-mains whether we actually encounter anything beyond ourselves, or connect with any objective reality, or learn anything about that reality. On this score, Zaleski still leaves us with relatively modest claims about the significance of NDEs and continues to resist those who want to make stronger truth claims on their behalf. Nevertheless, she continues to hold that her approach is the best way to maintain proper appreciation for near-death witness: "Paradoxically, the very method that permits us to respect visionary testimony prohibits us from using it to make a case for survival. To this extent, we must frustrate the truth claims of near death literature. . . . Even if we grant that near death visions convey some-thing real, there is no reliable way to formulate what that something is."[21]

In a subsequent work, however, Zaleski seems to move somewhat beyond the constraints of her earlier book on NDEs. In the latter book, she discusses NDEs around the framework of the three great hours of the divine office, the cycle of prayers that is the heart of monastic life in the Christian tradition. This approach, along with the title of her book, suggests Zaleski's aim to offer her account of NDEs as a religiously significant source of genuine insight about the Christian hope of eternal life. She continues, however, to reiterate essen-tially the same view of NDEs she defended earlier. She holds that those who have NDEs meet their death and encounter the other world only in the sense that they enter "the domain of the imagination, the inner world turned inside out and projected on the stage of imagination."[22]

Despite her continued insistence that NDEs remain enclosed in the inner world, never making contact with a reality external to the self, she maintains that they are revelatory. "Only a lively appreciation for the revelatory potential of the religious imagination can keep us from falling over that edge into the fold of the skeptics and debunkers."[23] As in her previous work, it is clear that Zaleski wants to avoid falling over the edge. But again, it is far from clear whether she does or not.

She acknowledges that she is frequently asked what she *really* thinks is going on in NDEs and that her approach seems to leave her open to reductionism. In response to this challenge, she offers further reflections on the nature of revelation, beginning with the paradoxical observation that the God of the Bible wishes to be known, yet has declared that no one can see him and live. Her resolution of this paradox is to follow the Kierkegaardian suggestion that God reveals himself indirectly: "If God, the unknowable, wishes to be known, what other recourse does God have but to avail himself of our images and symbols, just as he has availed himself of our flesh?"[24]

This is an interesting proposal, but it is hard to understand it in view of her claim that those who have NDEs encounter nothing more than the inner world turned inside out. Her appeal to the incarnation is especially significant in this connection. God came to us in the medium of human flesh, but those who encountered Jesus still encountered the real Son of God and not merely a product of their own imagination. Traditional Christianity holds that what God reveals in the incarnation is himself, not merely our own most deeply held views of who he is. Indeed, his actual revelation of himself conflicts, sometimes sharply, with our ideas of who he is.

If we take seriously Zaleski's comments about revelation, they suggest that more is disclosed in NDEs than our own most deeply held views of death "projected on the stage of the imagination." As before, her views reflect ambivalence about the status of NDEs. She continues to hold that they are both imaginative and real, but the sense in which they are real remains deeply ambiguous. She insists on the right to believe in actual life after death in connection with NDEs, as well as the right to imagine what such life might be like. But her continued restriction of NDEs to the inner world of imagination leaves it entirely unclear how such experiences can in any way warrant such belief. To put the point another way, NDEs apparently provide no epistemic contact with the reality they attempt to describe. They do not in any way provide epistemic warrant for belief in life after death. The claim of her earlier book that she must frustrate the truth claims of those who appeal to NDEs to warrant belief in survival seems to remain intact despite the apparent advances of her subsequent book.

To bring this discussion into focus, it is worth comparing Zaleski's views with those of Blackmore, who offers an explicitly naturalistic and reductionistic account of NDEs. In a chapter discussing the fact that NDEs seem so vividly real to those who have them, Blackmore distinguishes three senses in which the experiences could be real. First, there is the question of whether those who claim such experiences really have them. Second, there is the question of whether they were experienced as real by those who report them. Third, there is the issue of whether things seen and events experienced are part of an objective world or "whether they were products of the individual and private to them. This means contrasting 'real' with 'imaginary.' It is this that causes all the problems."[25]

Blackmore readily concedes that NDEs are real in the first two senses. But in the third sense, she believes they are unreal, although they seem as real, if not more so, than any other experience. Indeed, she grants that they can be life changing. But they are not in fact encounters with a world beyond that of the inner world of the imagination. Whereas Blackmore wants to distinguish and contrast the real and the imaginary, Zaleski resists the contrast and wants to insist that NDEs are both imaginary and real. The sense in which NDEs are imaginary is clear in both writers, and the sense in which they are not real is clear in Blackmore. It is unclear, however, whether Blackmore would have any real quarrel with Zaleski's account of how NDEs are real, so long as she maintains that they are artifacts of the religious imagination projected on the screen of one's inner mental life. She can cheerfully allow that NDEs reveal what death means to those who have them so long as no claims are made that NDEs are encounters with a world of external reality and that such experiences warrant belief in that world.

There is a major point of difference between Zaleski and Blackmore on the question of whether there is a world of reality beyond that of our own mental constructions. Blackmore doubts that there is any such world of reality. She rejects the idea that the heart of mystical experience is seeing through the world of illusion to the underlying world of reality. As she sees it, there is nothing but our constructed models of reality, and the great illusion is to believe there is more. Real mystical insight is seeing that there is nothing but our mental constructions.[26] As noted earlier, Zaleski apparently believes there is an ultimate reality and truth about things, including God and the afterlife. Indeed, she believes Christianity is the ultimate truth about these matters. This is a major difference indeed. Yet Zaleski's doubt as to whether we can have any real access to the realities involved beyond that afforded to us by symbol leaves her few resources to make substantive truth claims about them.

This is not to deny that symbolic access can be a means of real access. Symbolic access, properly construed, could well be a means of achieving access to something real beyond the symbol, and there is reason to believe Zaleski intends symbolic access in this way. But the problem, again, is that her account of this access does not succeed in making this connection. Rather, it leaves us trapped in the world of inner experience and imagination. The fact that we may gain insight in this world that is personally and spiritually meaningful does not alter in any way the nature of what is experienced.

Zaleski's stated intention was not to render accounts of NDEs harmless. Despite the sophistication of her account, its religious sensitivity, and the obvious sympathy with which she views NDEs, I think in the end her account is epistemically harmless to Blackmore and others who prefer a reductionist explanation of those experiences. The metaphysical neutrality of her account does not provide a serious challenge to naturalistic descriptions of NDEs.[27]

Given that Zaleski's views on religious epistemology constrain her conclusions on what can justifiably be believed on the basis of NDEs, it is worth asking whether different accounts of epistemology might suggest different conclusions in this regard. Recall in particular that Zaleski believes that we can have no direct access to theological or postmortem reality. In this connection, it is particularly noteworthy that some of the most important work in contemporary religious epistemology is much more optimistic about the prospects for knowledge of God. I have in mind especially the work of Alvin Plantinga and William Alston. In what follows, I consider what implications their work has for the epistemic significance of NDEs.

Before proceeding, let us sharpen our focus by giving attention particularly to what Greyson calls transcendental experiences. As noted, these are especially interesting for our purposes since they involve seeming to enter some unearthly realm and encountering a mystical presence or being as well as the spirits of deceased persons. Clearly if these experiences are veridical, they lend at least a measure of support to belief in the Christian doctrine of heaven. With our focus accordingly sharpened, I turn now to sketch the views of Plantinga.

IV

The essence of Plantinga's position, now spelled out in detail in a three-volume work, is that epistemic warrant is a matter of the proper function of our epistemic capacities. More fully, Plantinga proposes that

> to a first approximation, we may say that a belief B has warrant for S if and only if the relevant segments (the segments involved in the production of B) are functioning properly in a cognitive environment sufficiently similar to that for which S's faculties are designed; and the modules of the design plan governing the production of B are (1) aimed at truth, and (2) such that there is a high objective probability that a belief formed in accordance with those modules (in that sort of cognitive environment) is true; and the more firmly S believes B the more warrant B has for S.[28]

Several components of this definition are worth emphasizing. First, proper function depends on an appropriate environment. Just as a car is designed to function well in a certain range of temperature and weather conditions, our epistemic faculties are designed to function properly in certain contexts and situations but may malfunction and produce misleading results in others. Second, some of the modules of our design plan are aimed at goals other than truth. For instance, we may be designed with an optimism function that inclines us to believe our chances of surviving a disease are better than objective evidence would warrant, but this belief may actually enhance our prospects for survival. Consequently, some of our faculties may be aimed at survival rather than truth. Third, notice that warrant comes in degrees. The more firmly S is inclined to believe B, the more warrant the belief has.

Plantinga's position is a version of what is called externalism in epistemology. That is, warrant depends on factors that are not immediately accessible to the subject by way of introspection. One cannot tell by introspection that his epistemic faculties are functioning properly. Proper function is required for warrant, but we are in no position to know it obtains from any sort of immediate awareness. But we are aware of different degrees of certainty we feel for different beliefs. The design plan bestows different degrees of warrant on different beliefs, depending on how firmly we are inclined to accept various beliefs.

The notion of a design plan is not just a metaphor for Plantinga. He believes we have actually been designed by a real designer, namely God, and placed by God in an environment appropriately designed for our epistemic and other faculties. Indeed, Plantinga musters a theistic argument against naturalism on the basis of the notion of design and its importance for an adequate account of warrant. In view of this, Plantinga's epistemology can be broadly construed as Cartesian in the sense that God is the ultimate guarantor of the reliability of our beliefs. Broadly, I say, for there is surely much about Descartes's project that Plantinga rejects, including his unrealistically rigid account of what it means to know something. Plantinga insists that we know many things for which we do not have anything like Cartesian certainty. But the belief that we and our world have been designed by a wise and perfectly good Creator gives us reason to trust the deliverances of our epistemic faculties.

Among the beliefs we have a right to take as true are our beliefs about God himself. Following Calvin and other "Reformed Epistemologists," Plantinga believes God has created us in such a way that we naturally find ourselves believing certain things about God in response to certain experiences. Such beliefs do not require evidence, strictly speaking, in order to be justified. Rather, these beliefs can be properly basic, like basic sensory beliefs, basic memory beliefs, belief in other minds, and so on. Take a basic sensory belief, for instance, such as the belief that "I see a tree." This belief is immediately formed in me upon being appeared to in a certain way. Similarly, I may find myself believing that "God is speaking to me" or "God forgives me" in certain circumstances in which it seems to me that God *is* speaking to me or that he does indeed forgive me.[29]

There is, of course, much more that could be said in spelling out Plantinga's position. But his work is well-known and there is no need for further details, given our purposes. Enough has been said to give us grounds to propose what his epistemology implies can justifiably be believed by those who have NDEs. I would offer the preliminary suggestion that Plantinga's epistemology should give a favorable reading to the epistemic status of NDEs, for those experiences often involve persons being appeared to in such a way that they believe they are being encountered by God, that God is communicating with them, giving them assurance of his love, and so on. Of course, sometimes the being who is encountered is understood as a being of light with no further identity. But at other times the being is thought to be Jesus or some other religious figure. Moreover, it is often characteristic of such experiences that they produce a strong sense of certainty in those who have them. They are profoundly and unshakably convinced that it was indeed God who encountered them, assured them of his love, allowed them to return to this life, and the like.

Unless there is some reason to think God could not or would not appear to people in this fashion or give them a glimpse of the afterlife, those who have NDEs are warranted in believing they have really experienced what it seems to them they have experienced. Indeed, it appears they have a high degree of warrant for this belief if warrant comes in degrees and increases or decreases according to the level of confidence one has with respect to a given belief, as Plantinga holds.

But perhaps this conclusion is much too hasty. In particular, the question might be raised of whether NDEs are produced by segments of the design plan that are aimed not at truth but at something else, such as survival. That is, NDEs are produced not to give us true beliefs about God and the afterlife but rather to help us cope during the stress of facing death and having near brushes with it.

It is hard to know how to assess this suggestion. The question is whether this is the sort of thing a perfectly good and wise God would do. At first glance, it seems he would not, for it would involve God in producing misleading beliefs about himself and the next life. Why would God design us in such a way that many people would form strong convictions that they had encountered him, had experienced his love and the like, when in fact they had not really done so? Would the positive psychological benefits outweigh the apparent deception required to achieve this? I am inclined to think they would not, so I judge it unlikely that God would deceive us in this fashion.

But there are other complications involving the design plan that could account for NDEs without implying that they provide warrant for beliefs about God and the afterlife. For instance, Plantinga points out that the design plan does not specify how we should respond in any and all circumstances. For instance, the design plan will specify that when I am "appeared to redly," I will naturally be inclined to believe there is a red object in my field of vision. However, it "says nothing about how I will respond when appeared to redly, but am also suffering a massive heart attack, or have just ingested huge quantities of strychnine, or have just hit the ground after a 300-foot fall."[30] In such circumstances, it is hard to imagine how one should respond to visual stimulation or any other sort of appearances. Moreover, Plantinga also points out that our design plan may involve certain unintended by-products as well as trade-offs and compromises. He illustrates with the example of a refrigerator that may make loud squawks when a screwdriver touches a particular wire. This is not intended but is simply a by-product of sound electrical design. Likewise, certain trade-offs may be inevitable in any sort of material object. What is gained in an automobile's speed must be sacrificed in mileage.

Is it plausible to think NDEs are best explained as, say, unintended by-products in human design? That is, God did not intend human beings to have such experiences in their brushes with death, but might they naturally result in certain circumstances in any well-designed human creature? Or is the experience of coming near death but not actually dying one in which we should simply have no idea how to assess beliefs formed therein, like Plantinga's examples of being appeared to redly after ingesting a large amount of strychnine? Or could such experiences, although illusory, be a necessary trade-off in beings designed to have mostly true beliefs in most other circumstances?

Surely it would be presumptuous to answer these questions with a high degree of confidence, for we must admit a large amount of ignorance concerning the human design plan, especially with respect to something as mysterious as our epistemic faculties. However, I do not believe we are entirely without recourse in offering plausible responses to such queries. In the first place, it seems highly unlikely that such experiences could be unintended by-products when the designer involved is perfectly wise and good. Even if one does not accept the traditional view of omniscience according to which God knows all future events with perfect certainty, a perfectly wise God would be aware that his creatures would have such experiences in given experiences. To deny this is to suggest that God does not understand his human creatures very well, that he did not anticipate these experiences or expect them to occur. Surely this could not be the case with a perfectly wise designer.

In this vein, it is hard to see how such experiences could be necessary trade-offs for persons with well-designed epistemic faculties. This is especially so since orthodox Christian belief holds that persons will encounter God after death and that our ultimate well-being is to spend eternity in his presence. It seems very unlikely that illusory experiences which seem to align with these cherished hopes could be a necessary trade-off in excellent epistemic design. For similar reasons, it is not easy to dismiss NDEs on the grounds that we simply have no idea how to assess beliefs formed in the extreme experience of coming close to death. Christian doctrine gives us at least some hints about what lies on the other side of death, and NDEs confirm these expectations, at least to a significant degree. Taking this into account, being "appeared to heavenly" in such situations surely gives one more warrant to believe one saw a glimpse of the afterlife than being "appeared to redly" after ingesting a large amount of strychnine gives one warrant to believe there is a red object in front of him.

There are other Plantingian subtleties and distinctions we could explore in this connection, but I do not believe they would change the thrust of our discussion. I conclude then that on Plantinga's account of warrant, particularly when God's role in our design plan is taken into consideration, those who have NDEs are justified in believing that they have indeed experienced what they believe they have.

V

Let us turn now to the work of William Alston, who has explored in detail the issue of the epistemological significance of religious experience. At the outset of his book, Alston identifies as his main thesis the claim that the experience of perception of God contributes significantly to grounds for religious belief. "More specifically, a person can be justified in holding certain beliefs about

God by virtue of perceiving God as being or doing so-and-so."[31] Focusing on the Christian tradition, Alston dubs the widespread experience of perceiving God and forming beliefs in response to that experience "Christian mystical practice" (CMP), and sometimes simply "Christian practice" (CP). Much of his argument consists of showing that CMP is analogous in important respects to the nearly universally accepted practice of forming beliefs in response to ordinary sensory perception (SP). Given these crucial similarities, there is no good reason to accept the latter but reject the former.

As important as this analogy is to his argument, Alston emphasizes that it is not the heart of his case. Rather, his positive case for CMP depends on his theory of doxastic practices, ways of forming and evaluating beliefs. As he puts it, his central contention is "that it is prima facie rational to engage in CMP, not because it is analogous to SP in one or another respect, but because it is a socially established doxastic practice; and that it is unqualifiedly rational to engage in it . . . because we lack sufficient reason for regarding it as unreliable or otherwise disqualified for rational participation."[32] Alston follows Thomas Reid and Ludwig Wittgenstein in developing his notion of doxastic practices. These practices are fundamentals that play a role similar to Wittgenstein's "language games" insofar as "there is no appeal beyond the doxastic practices to which we find ourselves firmly committed."[33]

Alston's description of these practices as ones to which we find ourselves firmly committed is significant. It points up the fact that basic doxastic practices are not simply a matter of choice or personal preference. We find ourselves with certain perceptual beliefs when we are "appeared to" in certain ways just as we find ourselves believing the conclusion of a simple syllogism follows when we reflect on its premises. There is no meaningful sense in which we choose to accept these beliefs or the doxastic practices that generate them, nor is it the case that we have a better alternative to these doxastic practices. If we are going to have beliefs at all, we must rely on these practices and their outputs.

It important to emphasize that there is only prima facie justification for taking as true the deliverances of our basic doxastic practices. The prima facie rationality of such beliefs can be overridden by other considerations. For instance, perceptual beliefs must be consistent with each other. In the case of a clear inconsistency, at least one of the beliefs must be false. Likewise, if there is "massive and persistent inconsistency" between the outputs of different practices, there is good reason to regard one of them as unreliable.[34] Of course, questions arise about which practice to trust in such a case, and perhaps the best we can do is give the nod to the more firmly established practice. But the point for emphasis is that although we have reason to take our doxastic practices as innocent until proven guilty, in some cases the guilty verdict is appropriate, even if the evidence is complex.

There is, however, one way in which the prima facie claims of our doxastic practices can be strengthened, namely, by what Alston calls "significant self-support." For instance, the claims of SP can be supported by pointing out that by engaging in SP we can make predictions that turn out to be correct, we can anticipate and control events in our environment, and so on. Of course, such appeals do not escape circularity, for we must engage in SP in order to muster the evidence in support of it. But such support is not trivial, for it is conceivable that such support might not be forthcoming; moreover, not all practices support themselves in such a fashion. For example, Alston cites the example of crystal ball gazing as an instance of a practice that lacks such self-support.

It is also important to emphasize that Alston's view is a version of direct realism. That is, it is his view that we perceive things directly as they appear to us as so-and-so. This relationship is taken to be fundamental and unanalyzable. What this means is that it is not the case that our experience gives us grounds to infer that so-and-so exists and is somewhere in the neighborhood. Rather, we have immediate awareness of things as they appear to us. "For S to perceive X is simply for X to appear to S as so-and-so."[35] That is, it must be the case that X really is the entity appearing to S and X must be appropriately involved as one of the causes of S's experience if it is really X that S is perceiving.

Many people through the ages have had experiences in which it appeared to them that God was speaking to them, forgiving them, assuring them of his love, guiding them, and so on. The prevalence and persistence of this experience is what grounds the claim that CMP is a socially established doxastic practice. In Alston's view, such persons are justified in believing that God really is appearing to them unless there are overriders for these beliefs. Two of the potential overriders Alston considers are particularly worth noting for our concerns.

First, there is the claim that mystical experiences can be explained naturalistically. Such naturalistic explanations come in two broad varieties, namely, psychological and neurophysiological. The latter, which is especially pertinent, maintains that mystical experiences, like all other conscious experiences, can be accounted for by neurophysiological happenings in the brain. As Alston points out, we can readily grant that such changes in the brain are the proximate cause of mystical experiences, for it is also the case that neurophysiological happenings in the brain are the proximate cause of ordinary perceptual experiences. But this hardly inclines us to doubt that ordinary perceptual experience is reliable. Likewise, the "mere fact that mystical experience can be explained in terms of causally sufficient, proximate natural factors has no tendency to show that it does not constitute veridical perception of God."[36]

The second potential overrider I want to mention arises from the obvious reality of religious diversity. This difficulty, which Alston considers the most serious problem for his view, is due particularly to the fact that there are several incompatible religious perceptual practices. More specifically still, the problem is generated by the fact that these different perceptual practices produce beliefs that are logically incompatible. Since not all these beliefs can be true, this undermines our confidence in religious experience as a source of reliable belief.

Alston discusses this challenge in detail and concludes that the problem cannot be resolved by eliminating the contradictory truth claims advanced by the various world religions. It may be tempting to minimize or excise these contradictory beliefs and to emphasize only those beliefs held in common by the major religions. But as Alston points out, these very truth claims are derived from purported revelation, and they accordingly have a normative status. These normative truth claims are necessary to provide an overrider system for evaluating the prima facie reliability of any claims based on religious experience. Without such an overrider system, truth claims from religious experience are vulnerable to the charge of lacking any sort of criteria for checking and testing such claims.

How does Alston deal with the nettlesome problem of religious diversity? The essence of his response is drawn from an imaginary scenario he constructs in which there are competing sense perceptual doxastic practices with no neutral means of deciding between them. In such a situation, one would be perfectly rational to "sit tight" with the practice with which one was familiar and that had served one well in negotiating interaction with the material world, rather than switch to another. This is exactly parallel to the actual situation we face with respect to competing religious doxastic practices. "Hence, by parity of reasoning, the rational thing for a practitioner of CP to do is to continue to form Christian beliefs, and more generally, to continue to accept, and operate in accordance with, the system of Christian belief."[37]

It is also important to stress in this connection that Alston thinks CMP, like SP, enjoys significant self-support. Indeed, Alston goes so far as to say that this consideration is "the capstone of the entire edifice."[38] In particular, he considers it the final test of the Christian scheme to try it out in one's life and to see if one is changed as the tradition promises and predicts. There is substantial evidence to back up the claim that countless persons through the ages have had their lives changed as they have opened their lives to the Holy Spirit and cooperated with his transforming work. In the end, Alston considers this the most basic contribution provided by experience in support of Christian belief.

With this sketch before us, let us ask how NDEs fare in light of Alston's epistemology of religious experience. Two observations need to be made right away. First, NDEs often include sensory content, particularly in descriptions of the being of light and heavenly environs. Alston, by contrast, focuses on nonsensory experiences of God. However, he notes examples of encounters with God that have sensory content and argues that there is no reason why God could not or would not appear in such a fashion.[39] Consequently, I see no reason why the sensory content of NDEs pose a problem for assessing them in term of Alston's epistemology.

Second, it is not clear whether NDEs qualify as a socially established doxastic practice that deserves the status of innocent until proven guilty. It is a disputed question how common NDEs are, and given that they occur near death by definition, it is hardly to be expected that a large percentage of the population would even be situated to have them.[40] But it is beyond dispute that a significant number of persons who have come near death and lived to tell about it report such experiences. Moreover, these experiences have been reported for centuries, although they are probably more common today due to modern medical technology that has made advances in resuscitation techniques and the like. It is part of Alston's case for CMP that a doxastic practice should not be rejected as unreliable simply because it is engaged by only a minority of the population, even a small minority. Indeed, some doxastic practices that we consider highly reliable are practiced by a tiny minority. Therefore, NDEs should not be disqualified on the grounds that relatively few people have had them.

But it is further doubtful whether NDEs count as a "practice" in any meaningful sense of the word. Such experiences are not typically sought or deliberately engaged in, nor is there an ongoing practice of nurturing the experience as there is in the case of normal Christian devotion. Such experiences are by nature brief, episodic, and typically occur only once in a lifetime.

This point can be blunted, however, by noting that the same is true of a certain class of more typical religious experiences. For instance, conversion experiences, along with other intense encounters with God, may be brief episodic events that are never repeated in a believer's life. Nevertheless, the experience may profoundly alter his life and open him to an awareness of God that he experiences as an ongoing reality. As noted earlier, NDEs may function like conversion experiences in terms of their impact on those who have them. Indeed, in some instances, persons have been converted to Christian belief by NDEs or have had their belief strengthened or revitalized. In view of this, it might be suggested that at least some NDEs could be properly understood as a proper subclass within the larger class of experiences that constitute Christian perceptual doxastic practice. So whether NDEs are understood in this fashion or as a distinct minority practice similar in interesting respects to more typical Christian mystical practice, it is worth asking how they should be assessed on Alston's epistemology.

I want to argue that Alston's epistemology, like Plantinga's, should render a favorable verdict on the epistemic significance of NDEs. Indeed, Alston provides the detailed apparatus to defend what Zaleski says we cannot have, namely, direct access to the realities described in NDEs. As he notes in making his case for direct experience of God, there are no "general a priori constraints on what can appear to our experience."[41] Nor, he argues, are there any theological reasons why God could not or would not appear to us. So if it is possible for mystical experience to be genuine perception of God, the issue in the face of such experience "is just a question of whether it is what it seems to its subject to be."[42]

These points are quite pertinent to an assessment of NDEs. As suggested earlier, I see no good reasons why God could not or would not allow persons who come near death to have a glimpse of what lies on the other side of death. Indeed, it is even arguable that such glimpses of the afterlife are to be expected. In the New Testament, Paul describes certain "visions and revelations from the Lord," including one when he was "caught up to the third heaven" and "heard inexpressible things." Some have speculated that this may have occurred when he was stoned by his opponents and left for dead.[43] If Paul had such an experience, there is no reason in principle why others could not have similar experiences as well.

These comments point up the fact that purported experiences of God and the afterlife are taken as such at least partly because the subjects in such encounters have at least some idea what an encounter with God would be like. As Alston makes the point, "[I]f the object presents itself as being or doing what it would be natural or reasonable to expect God to be or do, and/or if one reacts as one would expect to react to the presence of God, that supports the claim that it is indeed God Who is perceptually presented."[44] In some cases, there are rather explicit indicators that the being is God, or Jesus, as in the experience of Betty Malz cited earlier. But in other instances, the being of light is perceived as God because of what the being communicates to the subject or how the subject feels in the being's presence.

However, it is important to note in this context that some critics of NDEs have rejected them as genuine encounters with God precisely because of their expectations of what is involved in meeting God after death. As they see it, NDEs do not meet those expectations. In particular, as previously observed, it has been a point of emphasis in much near-death literature that encounters with the being of light are positive experiences in which the subjects feel loved and accepted, regardless of their religious beliefs or lifestyle. In short, modern accounts of NDEs are conspicuously lacking in descriptions of judgment and wrath. This is at odds not only with medieval accounts of NDEs as noted by Zaleski but also with what traditional Christian doctrine might lead one to expect. Moreover, persons in other cultures who have NDEs typically report encountering religious figures from their tradition. Hindus, for instance, report encounters with Shiva or Krishna. Christian teaching might not lead one to expect this either but for the being to identify himself clearly in something like Trinitarian terms.

Do these considerations constitute overriders that rule out NDEs as evidence for life after death for those committed to orthodox Christian doctrine? First, with respect to the missing element of judgment, it must be pointed out that NDEs including hell and judgment have been reported in recent literature, although these accounts are not as well known as the more positive ones.[45] But more to the point, it is not necessarily to be expected that those who have NDEs would see hell. As J. P. Moreland and Gary Habermas point out, those who have NDEs have not finally died, at least not irreversibly. It is after death in this sense that judgment is to be expected. In view of this, Moreland and Habermas do not see a substantive theological problem in the fact that hell is largely absent from near-death literature.[46]

Two particular feature of NDEs are perhaps significant in this regard, namely, the limit or border that represents a point of no return, and the life review. Subjects of NDEs often say they instinctively know that if they pass this limit, they cannot return to this life. This suggests that NDEs are at most glimpses of the afterlife "from a distance." Perhaps NDEs are a glimpse only of the intermediate stage before the final judgment, when heaven and hell are realized in their fullness. The intermediate stage may be one in which all persons continue to encounter God's love and have opportunity to respond to it. The life review, often reported by subjects of NDEs, is typically taken as an occasion to evaluate one's life and how one has lived. This could be understood as God's call to accountability, along with encouragement to accept his transforming grace in those areas of one's life that need reformation and renewal. To accept such transformation is to draw closer to God and the life of heaven in all of its fullness.

What about the problem posed by the fact that what is perceived in NDEs varies significantly from culture to culture, particularly in how the "being of light" is perceived? The first thing I want to say in reply to this problem is that it is exactly analogous to the problem posed for Alston's epistemology by the phenomenon of religious diversity. Accordingly, Alston's solution could be borrowed and applied to the case of NDEs with little effort. Thus, a Christian believer who has an NDE and perceives the being of light in Christian terms has every right to do since Christian beliefs and practice have served him well in making sense of spiritual reality and interacting with it.

Alston's solution, however, faces a rather serious difficulty, as he readily recognizes, namely, that it has the consequence that incompatible beliefs in other religious mystical practices are equally justified. It is important to note in this regard that he has also sketched a backup position that could deal with this difficulty. Specifically, he proposes that Christian believers could make the case that there are independent reasons for preferring CMP over other mystical practices. For instance, it might be argued that there are better historical grounds for accepting Christianity than its rivals. Although he does not defend the claim in detail, Alston registers his belief that the project of arguing for Christianity from neutral starting points is worthy of more serious attention than it often receives.[47]

It would take us too far afield to make the case here, but I would contend that Alston's suggestion is on the right track and that such a case needs to be made if beliefs formed on the basis of CMP are to be justified in a strong sense. In his final chapter, Alston defends the notion that there are various interrelated grounds for Christian belief and that these grounds mutually support each other in a cumulative fashion. CMP serves as one of these grounds but not as an isolated or exclusive ground. It is more than noteworthy that Christian revelation is one of these grounds when we recall that the data of revelation also plays the crucial role of providing an overrider system for checking purported encounters with God.

Given these very significant roles played by revelation, it is surely important to have good grounds to believe that the claims of revelation are true. This is important if one is to have good reasons to believe that one's overrider system is a reliable measure of purported experiences of God. If one has such justified beliefs about one's overrider system, then one likewise has good reasons to think his beliefs formed on the basis of CMP are strongly justified even in the face of competing claims from other religious traditions.

It does not follow from the claim that the Christian revelation is the true account of God that there is nothing true in other religious traditions, nor does it follow that mystical practices in other traditions must yield only false beliefs. To be sure, where logically incompatible claims are made, both cannot be true. But surely some of these incompatible claims could involve details that may be due to prior beliefs and cultural conditioning. If the Christian revelation is true, those persons whose prior beliefs and cultural conditioning are shaped by it will have the best categories for interpreting and conceptualizing their experience. Likewise, those persons whose prior beliefs and cultural conditioning are least informed by Christian categories, or most at odds with it, will naturally be least prepared to interpret and describe accurately an encounter with God, even if it is a genuine encounter.

The fact that there is significant broad agreement, as well as disagreement about the details of religious experience, suggests something real and objective is being encountered but that cultural conditioning colors and shapes the perception as well. I think the same analysis applies to NDEs. There is good evidence that such experiences are significantly similar across various cultures, but significant difference in detail must also be recognized. In short, with respect to the issue of diversity, I think the case for belief in heaven based on NDEs is no better or no worse off than the case for belief in God on religious experience more broadly construed. If CMP can provide support for Christian belief despite religious diversity, then NDEs can provide support for the Christian doctrine of heaven despite the diversity of reports in various cultures.

What about the other potential overrider for religious experience I noted as particularly relevant for our concerns, namely, the claim that such experiences can be perfectly explained in terms of neurophysiology? Does Alston's answer to this challenge also apply to NDEs? Recall that his response to this argument is to point out that it poses no problem for the veridicality of an experience to acknowledge that happenings in the brain are its proximate cause. Recall too that Blackmore's naturalistic account of NDEs is essentially in terms of events in a dying brain. Can her challenge to NDEs be answered by allowing that events in a dying brain are the proximate cause of NDEs, while insisting that they could still be veridical experiences if God is an approximate cause of them? Of course, on theistic premises, God is the approximate cause of everything that happens in some sense. So the sense in which God is the approximate cause of NDEs would have to involve something more specific. That is, it would have to be the case that God intentionally causes the experience by appearing to the subjects of NDEs and causing them to perceive the afterlife. I see no reason in principle why this could not be the case, so the fact that proximate causes are involved in NDEs does not show that they are not veridical.

VI

There is an important and potentially problematic class of assumptions that must be made if religious experience is to be judged veridical in this fashion, namely, what Alston calls "normality assumptions." These assumptions are clearly relevant for assessing any purported experience of God, including NDEs. "Any reasons for suspecting the experiences to be artificially induced, or the work of the Devil, or due to nervous or mental imbalance, would, arguably, reduce or cancel their justificatory force."[48] This obviously raises questions about the veridicality of NDEs for the simple reason that it is most difficult to say what is normal when it comes to close brushes with death. Indeed, Blackmore's thesis is built around the assumption that NDEs occur in conditions of abnormality and that it is precisely this abnormality which accounts for their occurrence.

Consider, for instance, her explanation of what causes the sense of being out of one's body, which often happens in NDEs. Essentially, these occur when our normal model of reality breaks down. Our normal model is a "conglomerate of the body image and a model of the outside world."[49] The former depends upon sensory information from inside our body, while the latter depends on sensory information from outside. During NDEs, we lack sufficient sensory information to sustain our normal model of reality. But if we are to survive, we must keep some sort of hold on reality. We do so, Blackmore hypothesizes, by building a new model of reality from memory and imagination. An out-of-body experience occurs if our new model is constructed from a bird's-eye view, the sort of view we might imagine if we try to recall a time we were walking on the beach. We see ourselves from above in this sort of imaginary recall, Blackmore suggests.[50]

If these out-of-body experiences (OBEs) are veridical, then it is hard to see how they could have brain activity as even a proximate cause. They seem to be experiences in which one is literally out of one's body and existing consciously apart from it. For such experiences to be veridical, it appears that some version of mind-body or soul-body dualism must be true. Not surprisingly, Blackmore finds totally implausible the whole notion of dualism, with its implication that the soul could leave the body and still be able to perceive things in this world. In particular, she insists that if this is true, it must be detectable somehow. "If whatever leaves is undetectable it follows that it cannot interact with the world. If it cannot interact with the world it could not be seeing it because taking information from the world entails interacting with it."[51]

This is an interesting and important claim. It is also highly questionable, for it is far from clear that it follows from the soul's being undetectable that it cannot interact with the world, particularly if taking information from the world counts as interaction. Indeed, one of the most impressive aspects of OBEs and NDEs is the fact that those who have them have often accurately reported information about what was happening in the world while they were "dead." These accounts surely provide at least prima facie confirmation for OBEs and the claim that those who have them can interact with the world. Indeed, they provide a way to make detectable the departure of a soul, the very sort of evidence Blackmore demands.

Of course, Blackmore believes there are perfectly plausible explanations of how persons can describe what happened to them while they were near death even though their OBEs are not at all what they appear to be. To be more specific, she thinks all such accounts can be adequately explained by means of relatively mundane factors including prior knowledge, lucky guesses, fantasy, and remaining operations of the senses of hearing and touch. If the brain is functioning, even very poorly, it can sustain some sort of imagery, she hypothesizes. Moreover, persons who are thought to be totally unconscious may not actually be so and may hear things that allow them to form images of what is going on around them.[52]

While Blackmore's account of how persons near death can know about events in the surrounding area is broadly plausible, it is also strained at points, especially when she has to appeal to lucky guesses to explain some of the more remarkable instances of such knowledge.[53] But the point for emphasis is that such knowledge claims provide counterevidence for her view that there is no way to detect a departed soul's interaction with the world.

Of course, the very idea of such interaction has been the stock objection to mind–body dualism for centuries, as noted in a previous chapter. While dualists must affirm interaction, they have typically admitted that it is a mystery which may forever be inexplicable. However, it is also worth reiterating the point, also made previously, that such interaction should not be viewed as an absurdity on theistic premises in the same way it appears on naturalistic assumptions. If God is a Spirit who created the world, sustains it by his power, and so on, then ultimate reality is a mind who interacts with matter. If one believes theism is a plausible worldview, then mind–body dualism at the human level is a slight matter indeed. On the other hand, if dualism is simply incredible because of the sheer impossibility of interaction, then theism is equally incredible. Not surprisingly, Blackmore makes the connection. Just after the passage cited earlier in which she argues that an undetectable soul cannot interact with the world, she attempts to make the point less abstract by offering an observation of her seven-year-old son on God's powers. "'It's silly,' he declared. 'If God's transparent then he can't see and feel things. So how can he lift up trees and stuff to put them there?'"[54]

If Blackmore were genuinely interested in instructing her son on the logic of theism, she might have replied that God moves things like trees in something like the way we move our limbs. While there is only one piece of matter that we can move immediately, namely, our own bodies, God has power to move all matter immediately. Our free actions are a small image of God's action and give us some analogy to make sense of how God can act on the physical world. But the point for emphasis is that she is correct to make the connection between dualism and theism. Whereas she sees the absurdity of dualism as a reason to reject theism, I would argue that the power of the theistic worldview gives us good reason to find dualism plausible.

Let us bring this to bear on Alston's point about the importance of "normality assumptions." What one believes about theism and dualism makes a great difference in one's "normality assumptions." If theism and dualism are absurd or even implausible, then there is good reason to think OBEs should be explained in terms that will undercut their justificatory force. However, if one believes theism and dualism are credible accounts of reality, then OBEs may be viewed as normal, at least in some sense of the word. That is, the dualist believes that all persons who die have OBEs and experience life after death. NDEs would be brief OBEs that allow their subjects to have glimpses of what all persons will experience between death and resurrection.

All of this is surely relevant to the issue of how we should evaluate claims of persons who have had NDEs and who claim to have been aware of things happening in the world even while they were out of their bodies. As noted above, these claims provide prima facie evidence of the very sort of interaction Blackmore finds impossible, and she must explain them in terms of brain activity. However, if one is at least open to the possibility of dualism, then these claims can be more readily accepted as confirming evidence. Of course, one's prior beliefs always shape how one evaluates any putative evidence for a given claim, and this case is no different in this regard.

It is important to note in this connection that Blackmore's reductionistic commitments also lead her to embrace other positions, which clash with some of our most deeply rooted intuitive convictions. I am thinking especially of her view that our belief that we have a self is an illusion. Indeed, Blackmore believes this insight is what accounts for the moral and spiritual transformation that often follows NDEs. She thinks it is particularly important for any satisfactory theory of NDEs to explain why those who have them come to believe their deaths are not important and reject the notion that they must "Get as much as I can for myself 'cos I haven't got long."[55]

Blackmore asks how this can be if we are nothing more than biological creatures and there is no higher realm of life.

> It is because the NDE breaks down, if only for a brief moment, the self-model which was the root of all our greed, confusion and suffering. There never was any real persistent self; a self that makes conscious choices, a self that observes the objective world at a distance, a self that takes responsibility or is the centre of experience. There never was a separate self who lived through all those experiences, who had all those memories or made all those decisions. There never was any permanent self and there is no permanent self to survive when the body is gone. There was only a mental model that there was one.[56]

This claim that the self is only a mental model is integral to Blackmore's broad view that reality is nothing more than mental constructions. Real spiritual insight for her is not a matter of seeing through illusion to the world of reality but rather seeing through the illusion that there is a reality beyond our various mental constructions.

The notion that there is no real enduring self is popular in both analytic philosophy and continental philosophy, as noted in earlier. It also has affinities with Buddhist philosophy, as Blackmore notes. Indeed, it is a major theme of her book that Buddhism has the resources we need for genuine spiritual transformation and peace in the face of death. The notion that there is no real permanent self underwrites the claim that there is no self to survive the death of the body.

Note that for Blackmore the denial of a real self involves dispensing with the profoundly commonsensical notion that we make conscious choices for which we can take responsibility as free agents. I argued earlier that our free choices, especially in relation to others and in particular to God, give shape to our character and personal identity. It is the self so shaped by free choices that constitutes our distinctive identity and that gives meaning to the hope that we will survive death and live forever. For Blackmore, there are no such choices and there are no such selves.

Consequently, the transformation involved in NDEs is not what it seems to be to those who have them. This is an important claim, for it undercuts a potential source of what Alston calls "significant self-support" for NDEs. Recall that for Alston the moral and spiritual transformation associated with CMP is a powerful consideration in its epistemic favor. Likewise, in near-death literature, the transformation argument has been an impressive consideration in support of the epistemic claims made by those who have had NDEs. But as Blackmore sees it, subjects of NDEs are not only radically mistaken about what they have experienced but are likewise mistaken about why the experience affected them as it did. Of course, the two issues are closely connected, so if one is radically misguided about the former, it is only to be expected that he would draw wrong conclusions about the latter as well. If one thinks both that he encountered God in a glimpse of the afterlife and that he was changed by the encounter, then surely if he is fundamentally wrong about what he encountered, he is also mistaken about why he was changed.

But Blackmore's claim goes far beyond this obvious point. In particular, she holds that the transformation is really due to coming to see that we have no enduring self and thus that there is nothing about us which could meaningfully survive death. It is one thing to say that subjects of NDEs are objectively wrong about what they believe they experience, that what they believe they experience they do not really experience since it does not objectively exist. But it is another thing altogether to advance the further claim that the real reason they no longer fear death is because they have come to see they have no enduring self. If that were the case, they would surely know they had come to that insight and readily own it.

If one thing is clear from the public reaction to NDEs, it is that they have given many people fresh reason to hope for life after death. This more than anything else explains the fascination with which these accounts have been studied, analyzed, and debated. The fascination surely does not derive from the claim that NDEs bring the insight that we have no enduring self and that therefore death is not to be feared. Moreover, this is not due to the fact that the public has misunderstood the claims made by subjects of NDEs. They clearly have not told us that they learned from the experience that they have no enduring self. Rather, they have assured us that they now know that there is life beyond death and that is why they no longer fear it. They say that their encounter with the "being of light" and their newfound certainty about life beyond the grave has transformed their values.

Blackmore's account not only requires us to give a naturalistic explanation of what really caused an NDE but also to deconstruct its very content and to reconstruct it in terms most subjects of NDEs would surely reject. That is not to deny that some subjects of NDEs would accept Blackmore's reconstruction of the insights to be gleaned from their experience, but it is to say that her account of the transformation caused by NDEs does not match the testimony of most subjects of NDEs. There is little reason to think subjects of NDEs are transformed by coming to believe they have no enduring self. Blackmore's attempt to hoist this "insight" on them is singularly unconvincing.

In view of this, I think a case can be made for "significant self-support" for NDEs along the lines Alston suggests for CMP. This is especially so if NDEs are taken as similar to conversion experiences or other particularly vivid encounters with God that are crucial turning points in a longer process of spiritual and moral transformation. If we take the subjects of NDEs at their word, they believe they have been transformed by a real encounter with a personal being in another world beyond this one. If their lives are truly transformed by the experience, it adds credibility to their claims.

VII

Let us draw this discussion to a close now and summarize our conclusions. I have been examining the fascinating data of NDEs and asking what support they provide for life after death in general and whether this evidence is also compatible with the Christian doctrine of heaven. In particular, I have examined NDEs in light of the work of two leading Christian epistemologists. I have argued that the work of both of these philosophers give us ground to take NDEs as at least prima facie evidence for life after death. Moreover, I have argued that there are no convincing overriders from either Christian theology or other sources to warrant rejecting the beliefs produced by NDEs. This is not to accept uncritically all claims made by subjects of NDEs or to deny that NDEs raise questions similar to those raised by the reality of religious diversity, but I would argue that the problems raised by NDEs are no more difficult than those posed by religious diversity.

I do not deny the possibility that NDEs may some day be convincingly explained in naturalistic terms advanced by Blackmore and her colleagues. Scientific investigation of NDEs is still a relatively new field of research. I have not attempted to engage the scientific details of this research or to defend NDEs on empirical or scientific grounds. My concern has been to evaluate them theologically and philosophically. But given the current state of the discussion, I think it is safe to say that Blackmore's view is far from established.

I would not claim that NDEs are an essential support for the Christian doctrine of heaven or that the Christian doctrine is seriously threatened if it turns out that something like Blackmore's view is correct. Moreover, I would not claim that NDEs are a source of specific information about afterlife that affords us a more detailed knowledge than we can gain from Scripture. But perhaps they provide experiential knowledge—even if it is only a glimpse—of realities we know about from the revelation of Scripture and Christian tradition. In other words, unless and until the naturalistic account of NDEs is proven to be true, they deserve serious consideration as positive evidence for the Christian doctrine of heaven.

7

HEAVEN, MORALITY, AND
THE MEANING OF LIFE

I

In one of the most memorable and climactic scenes of Victor Hugo's *Les Miserables*, the central character, Jean Valjean, performs an act of striking self-sacrifice. He had been a criminal, but at the time of the scene he is the mayor of a city and a privileged man. Through the grace of others, particularly a Roman Catholic priest, along with his own efforts, he has risen above his previous life of crime to a position of distinction. He now goes by the name M. Madeleine, and his past is unsuspected by those who currently know him. But now he must look it squarely in the face as he observes a trial where an innocent peasant has been mistaken for Jean Valjean and is being accused of crimes he had committed. Sitting among the other privileged spectators, he watches as witness after witness confidently identify the peasant as the notorious criminal Valjean.

Finally, when it seems evident that the man is hopelessly lost, Valjean hesitantly rises from his seat and proceeds to the center of the hall where the witnesses of the accused stood. He asks them if they recognize him and they all shake their heads in bewildered denial. Then turning toward the jurors and the court, he speaks the riveting words: "Gentleman of the jury, release the accused. Your honor, order my arrest. He is not the man whom you seek; it is I. I am Jean Valjean."[1]

Thinking he has gone mad, the judge and prosecuting attorney ask if there is a physician in the house. But Valjean assures them that he is fully aware of what he is doing. "I am accomplishing a duty. . . . I am the only one who sees clearly here, and I tell you the truth. What I do at this moment God beholds from on high and that is sufficient."[2] As he continues his speech, explaining his past and convincing the witnesses of his identity, clarity descends on the audience as well. What they previously viewed as a pitiful act by a deluded man they now see as a wonderful act by a man of extraordinary goodness. In his elaboration of the scene, Hugo remarks that while nobody consciously "said to himself that he there beheld the effulgence of a great light, yet all felt dazzled at heart. . . . [T]he multitude, as by a sort of electric revelation, comprehended instantly, and at a single glance, this simple and magnificent story of a man giving himself up that another might not be condemned in his place."[3]

Hugo's description of this "simple and magnificent story" and the effect it had on those who witnessed it is a vivid picture of the power of altruistic actions. They have an electric quality about them that dazzles our hearts, stretches our minds, and strengthens our resolve. They enrich our lives with depth and meaning. If such actions never occurred, life would be a pitiful affair. What is striking is not merely the fact that individual persons from time to time perform such notable actions but also that those actions elicit profound respect from those who observe them. We instinctively admire such actions and are often deeply moved by them. Most people in the greater part of human history would resonate with Hugo's story and immediately identify with the feelings he describes in his account.

There is no more telling indicator of how times have changed than the fact that we can no longer take this for granted as a matter of cultural consensus. Remarkably, one of the great debates of our time concerns not only the nature but the very possibility of altruistic actions. As we shall see, such actions are now construed by some influential naturalistic philosophers in terms that would be unthinkable to moral philosophers of previous generations, not to mention "ordinary people."

In what follows, I shall argue that naturalistic views of reality undermine both morality and meaning. Naturalism has difficulty not only making sense of altruism but also providing us with deeply persuasive moral motivation. Deeply persuasive moral motivation, I maintain, is motivation that is not only sustained in the face of reflective awareness but even strengthened by it. Reflective awareness in this sense requires understanding morality in relation to one's basic ontological commitments, ranging from cosmology to what one believes about the ultimate origin and nature of moral feelings. To sustain deeply persuasive motivation in light of reflective awareness requires, I shall argue, a rationally convincing account of obligation. Without this sort of moral motivation, life loses much of its depth of meaning. Conversely, without depth of meaning, moral motivation suffers.

By contrast with naturalism, I shall show how orthodox Christian faith, particularly in its doctrine of heaven, both underwrites morality and charges our lives with depth of meaning. It provides resources that allow us to be fully rationally reflective in our commitment to the moral life. It explains why we are genuinely obligated to do what is right and why any rational person should be moral. The argument that unfolds shall show a natural connection between three things: the priority of mind, the objectivity of morality, and the depth of meaning.

II

Moral obligation is not easily accounted for in a naturalistic universe. This is not to deny that most naturalists are committed to morality and feel the force of moral demands, nor is it to deny that naturalists have offered theories of moral obligation and accounts of why we should be moral. But as many naturalists themselves concede, morality, at least as traditionally understood, is an odd thing in a naturalistic universe. To get a sense of why this is so, we can do no better than to ruminate on the moving and often quoted portrait of naturalism by one its most devoted adherents, Bertrand Russell. This famous passage will do double duty for us since it is also most relevant to the whole issue of the meaning of life.

> That man is the product of causes which had no prevision of the end they were achieving; that his origin, his growth, his hopes and fears, his loves and his beliefs, are but the outcome of accidental collocations of atoms; that no fire, no heroism, no intensity of thought and feeling, can preserve an individual life beyond the grave; that all the labors of the ages, all the devotion, all the inspiration, all the noonday brightness of human genius, are destined to extinction in the vast death of the solar system, and that the whole temple of man's achievement must inevitably be buried beneath the debris of a universe in ruins—all these things, if not quite beyond dispute, are yet so nearly certain that no philosophy which rejects them can hope to stand.[4]

Before drawing out the moral implications of this passage, let us consider for a moment the relationship between meaning and morality. The close connection between these matters may seem obvious with a little reflection, but it can hardly be taken for granted in contemporary moral philosophy. As Charles Taylor has observed, much modern and contemporary moral philosophy has been concerned primarily with defining what is *right* in terms of permissible actions and has given relatively little attention to the larger issue of the nature of the *good*. That is, the question of what makes for a meaningful or fulfilling life has been neglected, and philosophers have been notably reticent to discuss moral sources or to identify the good that gives significance to the rules that define the right. "This is what has been suppressed by these strange cramped theories of modern moral philosophy, which have the paradoxical effect of making us inarticulate on some of the most important issues of morality."[5]

By contrast, Taylor insists that questions of meaning are at the very heart of moral philosophy and must be squarely addressed if we are to regain our moral "articulacy." I will argue that the doctrine of heaven is an essential resource to relieve us of the strangely cramped feeling produced by swallowing modern moral philosophy and to make us morally articulate again.

Let us come back to Russell's picture of our predicament and its moral implications. In the first place, notice that he explicitly denies the priority of mind. As he sees it, both we and our world are the product of blind natural forces that had no "prevision of the end they were achieving." No one intended our existence or planned for it in any way. No intelligent mind created us for a purpose or provided direction or guidance for how we should live. Conscious minds, rationality, and the very notions of purpose and meaning emerged from "accidental collocations of atoms." There is no blueprint for how we should live that precedes our existence.

Moreover, there are no guarantees that our moral efforts will succeed, at least in any ultimate sense of the word. Indeed, our moral efforts seem destined, along with all our other achievements, however magnificent, to meet a bad end. Just as no mind intended our existence in the first place, so there is no mind with a large-scale plan for the ultimate well-being of our world. Impersonal laws blindly brought us into existence and will just as blindly destroy us in the end.

The moral consequences of such a picture are not hard to detect. For one thing, this picture does not provide us with nearly as strong a conception of human dignity as does the notion that we were created by a God who has a purpose not only for us but for his whole creation as well. In this latter view, human beings have a special place in the created order since we were created in God's very image. This conception of human nature and dignity is obviously a potent moral source since so much of morality has to do with valuing our fellow human beings and treating them with appropriate respect. To give it up is no small loss, as James Rachels points out: "The abandonment of lofty conceptions of human nature, and grandiose ideas about the place of humans in the scheme of things, inevitably diminishes our moral status. God and nature are powerful allies; losing them does mean losing something."[6] As a naturalist, Rachels is prepared to soldier ahead without these powerful allies and to forge an alternative account of human dignity and morality.

But the difficulties for naturalistic morality go much deeper than the loss of a lofty conception of human dignity. One philosopher who has exposed these with some force is George Mavrodes. Working from the sketch of naturalism that I have already quoted, Mavrodes begins his critique by defining what he calls a "Russellian benefit." Such a benefit is any good thing that could accrue to a person in a Russellian world. That is, it is any sort of benefit or advantage we may receive or enjoy if the world were as Russell describes. Instances of these would be contentment in old age, sexual pleasure, a good reputation, and so on. Going to heaven and enjoying eternal life, on the other hand, would not be a Russellian benefit.[7]

If the only sort of benefits that may accrue to us are of the Russellian variety, we can easily see why morality seems odd in such a world. As Mavrodes points out, it is clear in many cases that fulfilling moral obligations would result in a net loss for ourselves of the only goods that exist. Fulfilling moral obligations may be highly inconvenient, it may put us at a financial disadvantage, it may even cost us our health or our very lives. Soldiers who die on the battlefield rather than flee or turn traitor are the classic case of such moral sacrifice. But even when morality does not involve such dramatic sacrifice, it is undeniably difficult and personally costly on many occasions. It often demands more of a price in Russellian currency than it returns. Mavrodes argues that it is strange to think that we could have overriding obligations in a Russellian world. In his view, "[W]ere it a fact that we had such obligations, then the world that included such a fact would be absurd—we would be living in a crazy world."[8]

But there is another reason as well why Mavrodes believes morality would be absurd if things are as Russell described, namely, it would be superficial in such a world. The truly deep things in a Russellian world are things such as matter and energy, natural law, or even chance or chaos. They are the prime-val realities, and they will persist when all things distinctively human have been buried beneath the debris of a universe in ruins. Mind, purpose, and the values that guide them are relative newcomers on the stage of the world's history. They are neither original nor ultimate in the scheme of things. It is hard to see how morality can make overriding demands on us if it is superficial in this sense. If these demands are to make rational sense, morality must somehow be pro-foundly grounded and rooted in the very nature of reality. As Mavrodes puts it, morality cannot make a reasonable demand on me "unless reality itself is committed to morality in some deep way."[9]

The sort of commitment required would assure a correspondence between virtue and happiness. That is, morality would never require us to sacrifice our own ultimate happiness and well-being for the sake of doing what is right. Mavrodes sees in Kant a classic recognition of this point. For all his talk about doing what is right for the sake of duty, and for all his concern to protect moral motivation from the contamination of self-interest, in the end he realized that happiness and virtue must correspond if the moral enterprise is to make sense. That is why he said that we must postulate God and immortality in order to ensure this ultimate correspondence.

If reality is not "committed to morality in some deep way" such as this, then the bottom line is that there simply is no overriding reason to be moral. At the very least, there is no decisive reason to do so when it will require us to sustain a net loss in the goods of this life. In saying this, I do not mean to deny that there are often good reasons of the prudential variety to behave in a gen-erally moral way. It is often the case that moral behavior will assist us in gain-ing Russellian goods. Life may well be better overall for all of us if we coop-erate for the mutual good in terms of some sort of a social contract. And for the mutual good, it is necessary to follow the terms of the contract at least most of the time.

However, there is a large difference between merely behaving morally most of the time for prudential reasons on the one hand, and being genuinely com-mitted to *being* moral in a consistent fashion on the other. Truly being moral is more than a matter of overt behavior. It is also a matter of internal motivation, of character, and the like. A genuine commitment to being moral holds even when it is not prudentially advantageous. By contrast, if prudential considerations are paramount, there is no convincing reason not to cheat on the contract when one can get away with it. Indeed, the ultimate prudential position would encourage others to keep the terms of the contract, deceive them into believing that one was also keeping it, while exploiting one's advantage gained by the deception. If there are no moral sanctions other than human and naturalistic ones, there is no persuasive reason to dissuade those who are inclined to cheat from doing so.

Of course, not all are inclined to cheat. They are offended by the very idea and, moreover, they find it objectionable that any considerations beyond those of the intrinsic appeal of the moral life should be required to elicit moral commitments and behavior. This attitude may be coupled with the view that morality needs no grounding beyond its self-evident appeal. Those who hold this attitude may reject the request for a further account of why morality should be respected and obeyed. Why morality has the force it does in our world is admittedly hard to understand, they may concede, but clearly it does. You either feel the force of it or you don't, you either see it or you don't.

Indeed, the list of Russellian goods could be expanded to include a good conscience, and some may value this sufficiently that they are willing to sacrifice other goods to avoid guilt feelings and to preserve intact their personal integrity. Why conscience should have such authority in a Russellian world, again, may not be clear, but those who do not press this question, or simply take the authority of conscience as self-evident, may well be committed to a life of consistent moral behavior.

Such a line may be adequate to explain why given individuals are committed to a moral life and may even suffice to persuade selected others. However, such a view seems profoundly inadequate to address a central aspect of morality as traditionally construed, namely, its claim to universality. To accept a demand as moral is typically understood to involve the claim that everyone should do so as well. A moral demand is not merely a matter of personal preference, taste, or judgment. Rather, it is understood to be binding on all persons, whether they own it or not. In other words, it is a matter of real objective obligation.

The stark reality is that many people are not inclined to own these demands. It is hard to see how the line I have just sketched has much force with those who do not readily share the moral point of view and persist in asking why they should do so. Those who are morally skeptical may perhaps be forgiven if they are not prepared to make the sacrifices necessary to lead a moral life if nothing else can be said in its behalf than this.

It is important for the sake of clarity to highlight the underlying assumption informing this position, namely, that a commitment to the moral life requires a serious effort that is often very difficult to put forth, at the very least in the early phases of moral growth and formation. Acknowledgment of this reality is a major part of what gives urgency as well as cogency to the question "Why should I be moral?" This is true even if it is held that morality becomes easier with practice and returns a great sense of satisfaction in the long run. Most traditional moralists have recognized the difficulty of living a genuinely moral life. In fact, many moral philosophers in Western thought have gone further and have held that the moral life is beyond human capacity. As John E. Hare has noted, particularly with respect to the enormously influential Kantian tradition, morality typically has a three-part structure. It is "first, something I ought to be practicing; second, something for which my natural capacities are inadequate (except by approximation); and third, something that I should treat as the command of some other at least possible being who is practicing it."[10]

In traditional Christianity, this threefold structure is set in the context of doctrines that explain how God enables us to do his will and meet the moral demand. Apart from God's assistance, the recognition of our inadequacy for morality, along with its binding character, produces what Hare calls the "moral gap." That is, there is a gap between our ability and the demands laid upon us. As Hare notes, this gap is a somewhat curious feature of morality, and he ventures the tentative suggestion that without the influence of Christianity, morality would not have been construed in this fashion. Instead, it would have been understood as something that human beings could achieve in a full-fledged manner, relying only on our own resources. Moreover, this threefold structure produces in us a constant sense of failure and shortcoming. This means that guilt and the desire to avoid the pain it causes becomes a major part of our moral motivation. Without divine aid, we are stuck in the moral gap with a sense of guilt and failure as our steady companion.

Hare points out, barring God's gracious assistance, that there are three strategies for closing the gap and achieving some moral relief. First, we can find some naturalistic substitute for divine grace, some other account of how we can be inspired and enabled to accomplish our moral duty. Second, we can exaggerate the human capacity for moral achievement so that it measures up to the moral demand. Third, we can lower the standard to a level that fits our natural capacities. It is central to Hare's case for the relevance of Christianity to morality that none of these strategies finally succeed.

The first of these three strategies will be of particular relevance to us. As Hare shows, an essential part of divine assistance in the Kantian scheme is the hope of an afterlife. Without such a hope, it is hard to sustain moral faith, that is, the confidence that things are so ordered that my future happiness is compatible with living a moral life. As Hare himself defines the notion of moral faith, it does not necessarily require heaven and the afterlife. It is consistent with much more modest accounts of what kinds of happiness may be available. For instance, consider the notion that Kant ascribed to the Stoics, namely, that we can be self-sufficient so that happiness depends upon nothing more than our virtue and our awareness of our virtue. This conception of happiness requires no afterlife and is compatible with a life of suffering that ends in a terrible death. Indeed, such moral faith does not require a moral orderer, only a moral order.[11]

A truly robust moral faith requires both belief in a moral orderer and a reasonable hope for deep and lasting happiness. In other words, moral faith is best sustained by a worldview that includes a doctrine of heaven. I will continue my argument for this claim by turning now to consider some of the central issues in recent and contemporary moral philosophy and the relevance of heaven to resolving them.

III

Although the problem I first want to focus on emerged much earlier,[12] let us begin our examination of it with a landmark in moral philosophy from the nineteenth century, *The Methods of Ethics* by Henry Sidgwick, a work that went through seven editions between 1874 and 1907. Sidgwick identified as the greatest moral problem of his time what he called "Dualism of the Practical Reason."[13] This dualism arises because of a possible conflict between what may serve the happiness of a given individual on the one hand, and what would serve the happiness of the larger universe of sentient beings on the other. As a utilitarian, Sidgwick believes the ultimate good is happiness, or what he also calls desirable consciousness for sentient beings.

Consider the case of an individual who is called upon to sacrifice his own happiness, perhaps even his life, for the happiness of others. If we judge it to be a reasonable thing for him to do so, then it might be argued that we are assigning a different ultimate good for the individual than for the rest of sentient beings; whereas their good is happiness, his ultimate good is conformity to reason. While Sidgwick admits the force of this argument, he nevertheless maintains that it may actually be reasonable for an individual to sacrifice his own good for the greater happiness of others. It is at this point that Sidgwick identifies the dualism of practical reason in his footnote. There he acknowledges that it is "no less reasonable for an individual to take his own happiness as his ultimate end."

Sidgwick goes on to observe that in earlier moral philosophy, particularly the Greeks, it was believed that it is good for the individual to act sacrificially even when the consequences as a whole are painful to him. While Sidgwick attributes this belief partly to certain confusions, it is also important to recognize that he also recognizes it is partly due to a "faith deeply rooted in the moral consciousness of mankind, that there cannot be really and ultimately any conflict between the two kinds of reasonableness."[14]

Sidgwick returns to this unresolved difficulty in the final pages of his book. Significantly, he identifies one clear way of resolving it that he rejects, namely, by assuming the existence of God and divine sanctions that would be sufficient to ensure it was always in our best interests to be moral. He rejects this assumption because he does not believe it is strictly required to ground "ethical science." In his view, the fundamental intuitions of moral philosophy are as independently self-evident as the axioms of geometry and therefore need no grounding from theology or other sources. But while our moral duty is intuitively obvious, it is not equally evident that the performance of our duty will be suitably rewarded. Admittedly, we feel a desire that this be the case not only for ourselves but for all other people as well. However, our wish for this to be so has no bearing on whether it is probable, "considering the large proportion of human desires that experience shows to be doomed to disappointment."[15]

Even if this desire is doomed to disappointment, this gives us no reason to abandon morality, according to Sidgwick, but it does mean we must give up the hope of making full rational sense of it. Our moral duty is still binding on us despite the fact that it makes no rational sense how this can be so when duty conflicts with self-interest. In his final paragraph, Sidgwick tentatively offers some brief epistemological reflections on whether we might be rationally justified in believing in the ultimate convergence of morality and self-interest even if this belief cannot claim philosophic certainty. But what is still clear at the end of the day is that the issue remains unresolved for him.

What Sidgwick recognized as the profoundest problem of moral philosophy in his day has only intensified in later generations. In much twentieth-century moral philosophy, the conflict was stated in terms of egoism versus altruism, and morality was often defined in terms that exclude egoism. Moreover, this view remains widespread as moral philosophy advances into the twenty-first century. As a representative of twentieth-century moral philosophers, consider the words of John Rawls in his widely influential work *A Theory of Justice*: "Although egoism is logically consistent and in this sense not irrational, it is incompatible with what we intuitively regard as the moral point of view. The significance of egoism philosophically is not as an alternative conception of right but as a challenge to any such conception."[16]

While this conflict has been taken for granted for some time now, it is important to reiterate that it is sharply at odds with how morality has been conceived by most moral philosophers in the greater part of human history. As David Lutz has observed, it was the view of "the multitude" or "the many" that virtuous living might be in conflict with self-love, but moral philosophers forcefully argued just the opposite. But now, the view of "the multitude" has become the view of most moral philosophers. As Lutz sees it, "this change in how we think about our lives is both significant and regrettable."[17]

Surely the consequences for how we live our lives and for society at large are significant indeed. The issues here are too pressing to be confined to the halls of academic debate, because they touch on all aspects of our common life. It is no surprise that these debates have worked their way into popular culture and conversation. A vivid instance of this occurred in the late 1980s, a tumultuous time in American cultural history, during which a series of highly publicized scandals rocked a number of American institutions, including government, business, the military, and the church. *Time* magazine did a cover story on ethics, the title of which was simply, "What's Wrong." In the concluding paragraph of the article, the author noted a profound ambivalence in the American soul, even as the nation aspired to restore some sense of moral integrity: "[T]he longing for moral regeneration must constantly vie with an equally strong aspect of America's national character, self indulgence. It is an inner tension that may animate political life for years to come."[18] The tension that the author notes is, of course, another variation on the unresolved problem Sidgwick bequeathed to his successors. Moreover, events since that time, only the most notorious of which involve the Clinton administration, have certainly vindicated the prediction that this tension would continue to animate political life for years to come.

In an accompanying essay, *Time* probed the roots of our moral disarray. Again, it is interesting that the essay ends by grappling with the familiar issue of the relationship between morality and self-interest. After citing ethicists who believe that it is possible both to be ethical and to get what we want at least most of the time, the essay observes that this is an optimistic solution which only lays bare the heart of the problem, namely, the nature of human desires. The final sentences of the essay leave us with this prospect for moral renewal.

> If Americans wish to strike a truer ethical balance, they may need to re-examine the values that society so seductively parades before them: a top job, political power, sexual allure, a penthouse or lakefront spread, a killing on the market. The real challenge would then become a redefinition of wants so that they serve society as well as self, defining a single ethic that guides means while it also achieves rightful ends.[19]

The question this obviously raises is what could motivate such a redefinition of wants. Some convincing account needs to be given of goods that clearly surpass things like top jobs, political power, sexual allure, and so on. Notice that the goods just listed are all of the Russellian variety. The question is what sort of goods would not only be of surpassing value but would also be such that in choosing them one is not forced to decide between one's own ultimate interest and that of others.

When this choice is forced upon us, that is, when altruism is pried apart from self-interest, it is revealing to note that it is inevitably distorted in the process. Consider two extreme claims about the nature of self-sacrifice that are current in contemporary thought. On the one side are those who maintain that the only real gift is one that expects nothing in return. Thinkers such as Emmanuel Levinas and Jacques Derrida hold that the highest gift is a sacrifice of one's life for others, a sacrifice that is ultimate and uncompensated. Indeed, it is the very finality of death that endows morality with seriousness and makes it truly possible. The hope of life after death on this view is problematic for ethics. As John Milbank concisely describes this view, "Death in its unmitigated reality permits the ethical, while the notion of resurrection contaminates it with self-interest."[20]

On this view, altruism has been stripped of any vestige of human self-interest and raised to truly heroic proportions. This account of altruism takes moral sacrifice far beyond anything that traditional moralists imagined could be required or reasonably expected of human beings. These thinkers demand that humans be prepared to make the ultimate sacrifice without the support of the sort of moral faith that Kant thought necessary to make sense of morality.

By sharp contrast, there is another very different view of altruism current in contemporary thought, which I alluded to in the beginning of this chapter, namely, that of some influential sociobiologists and evolutionary theorists. These thinkers attempt to account for altruism in terms of naturalistic evolution, where it poses an obvious problem. The problem stems from the notion of natural selection, which maintains that traits that reduce reproductive advantages will be eliminated. Altruism is a double-edged sword in this regard, for not only is it a disadvantage to those who practice it, but it is also an advantage for those who are on the receiving end of it. So it seems that those who are altruistic would sacrifice themselves out of existence in the unforgiving competition for survival and reproductive advantage. Yet altruistic behavior of various kinds continues to be exhibited and highly admired in the human race. The question of how to account for this fact remains.

Sociobiologists have developed a number of different theories to meet this challenge, some of which can explain at least certain forms of altruistic behavior with a fair degree of plausibility.[21] It would take us too far afield to discuss these in detail, but one thing in particular is striking about some of these theories, namely, the role that deception plays in them. One such theory focuses on the recipients of altruistic behavior and suggests that behavior of that sort is produced by the skillful manipulation of those recipients. Altruistic actions such as adoption, organ donation, and even radical human sacrifice have been explained in terms of manipulation of various social instincts by those who benefit from such activity.

In a similar vein, altruism is also explained as a matter of elaborate self-deception. This account begins with the recognition that reciprocity is central to human society and the further observation that the optimal position is to cheat the system for personal advantage when one can get away with it. Successful cheaters, however, must obviously avoid detection. One way they can do this is to engage in impressive displays of sacrificial behavior. When cheaters are detected, ever more creative and costly exhibitions of altruism must be invented to persuade others of one's sincerity. Here is where self-deception enters the picture. If we are to be successful in our self-serving manipulations, we first need to deceive ourselves into believing that we really do care about others and that morality rightly obligates us to do so. Otherwise, we would never treat others well enough to accomplish our purpose of manipulating them. Moreover, we will be most persuasive in this regard if our real intentions never enter our minds as conscious thoughts. Thus, our altruistic displays mask our real purposes not only from others but even from ourselves.

Writing from a similar perspective, Michael Ruse and Edward O. Wilson maintain that nature has made us believe in a disinterested moral code according to which we are obligated to help others. "In short, to make us altruistic in the adaptive biological sense, our biology makes us altruistic in the more conventionally understood sense of acting on deeply held beliefs about right and wrong."[22] Since we have been wired by evolution to believe in moral obligation, we are not being insincere or hypocritical when we endorse it. It is because we consciously believe in morality in this sense that it works as well as it does and serves its reproductive purposes. But the element of deception remains, as Ruse and Wilson indicate.

> In an important sense, ethics as we understand it is an illusion fobbed off on us by our genes to get us to cooperate. It is without external grounding. Ethics is produced by evolution but not justified by it, because, like Macbeth's dagger, it serves a powerful purpose without existing in substance.[23]

The illusion lies in the fact that we are naturally inclined to believe morality has an objective grounding and this illusion is what makes morality effective. The illusion also explains why ordinary people do not view morality merely as a means of survival, or the promotion of our genes, or worse, as an elaborate form of manipulation and self-advancement.

This point deserves emphasis. Ruse and Wilson believe that our commitment to morality depends upon our natural belief that we are actually under a real objective obligation to be moral. Without this illusion, we would not defer to morality and its authority, and thus it could not serve the socially useful function that it does. To put the point another way, they believe that moral realism is an illusion, but a beneficial one.

Before moving on from this point, let us come back for a moment to Hare's analysis of the "moral gap" and the attempt to close this gap by use of substitutes for God's assistance. It is quite interesting in view of our current discussion to note that one of his central criticisms of those ethicists who follow this strategy is that they deploy accounts of morality that involve deception. To take just one of his examples, consider the views of Donald Campbell, a naturalist who sees religious belief as a positive moral influence. Specifically, he believes the "preachments" of religion play the important social role of counteracting the natural biological bias toward "egotism." Since the preachments tend toward absolute altruism, their actual social effect is to achieve a productive balance between egotism and altruism.

Campbell's positive view of the social utility of religion produces an obvious tension for him since it follows from his naturalism that religious beliefs must be mistaken. His solution to this difficulty is to translate religious beliefs into terms naturalists would find acceptable while retaining their social role of promoting worship. But as Hare points out, this strategy inevitably involves dishonesty, for while the translation might do among his fellow naturalists, it would not accomplish any useful purpose among the larger public; indeed, it would have the effect of diminishing the very beliefs that promote the behavior he finds valuable. Thus, Campbell cannot be forthright about his true beliefs but must engage in sleight of hand in order to promote the socially beneficial results of religious commitment.[24]

This brings us to another issue in contemporary moral philosophy I want to bring into focus, one that underlies those we have been discussing, namely, the ultimate origin of ethics. According to Wilson, centuries of debate come down to these two options: Either moral principles exist outside the human mind and are independent of human experience, or they are inventions of human minds. Wilson labels those who hold the former position "transcendentalists," and those who hold the latter he calls "empiricists." Transcendentalists believe that morality is grounded in the eternal nature or will of God, or at the very least in self-evident moral principles that any rational person can see as true. Empiricists see moral principles as products of biology and culture. Moral demands are nothing more than the principles of the social contract that have been transformed over time into requirements and obligations. As Wilson puts it, an "ought" statement is just shorthand for what society first chose to do and later hardened into moral codes.

The question of which one of these two fundamentally different views is true has far-reaching implications. Indeed, Wilson sees the choice between these two views as "the coming century's version of the struggle for men's souls." How this issue is settled "will depend on which world view is proved correct, or at least which is more widely *perceived* to be correct."[25]

One aspect of this issue is particularly relevant to our concerns. The perception of the world in empiricist terms involves much more than how morality is construed. As Wilson notes, the empiricist view also has implications for how one understands religion and the quest for meaning. Human beings, he concedes, are incurably religious. They seek immortality and eternal significance, they hunger for communion and everlasting union with God. Without such hope, they feel lost in a universe devoid of ultimate meaning. Of course, Wilson believes that religion, like morality, is ultimately explicable in terms of biology and evolutionary survival. This claim, obviously, is at odds with traditional religious accounts of reality, so in the end, the two views are finally incompatible.

In Wilson's view, then, those who desire both intellectual and religious truth face unsettling choices. "The essence of humanity's spiritual dilemma is that we evolved genetically to accept one truth and discovered another."[26] We must choose between the hope for transcendent meaning that traditional religion offers and the intellectual honesty of recognizing that science and biology are ultimate.

Let us summarize our survey of some of the central issues in recent moral philosophy. What we have seen are a series of dilemmas, beginning with Sidgwick's "Dualism of Practical Reason." This poses the dilemma of choosing between what is good for others on the one hand, and what is good for oneself on the other. This essential dilemma has been sharpened in the twentieth century as the conflict between egoism and altruism, and it has been taken as virtually axiomatic that the way of morality is at odds with self-interest. And with altruism split completely apart from egoism, it has been twisted and recast into badly distorted forms. Underlying these issues is the more fundamental question of the ultimate origin of ethics, an issue that promises to be the coming century's version of the battle for men's souls. As Wilson sees it, this battle poses a dilemma of choosing between intellectual truth and religious hope.

The choice of naturalism, now as in the nineteenth century when Sidgwick wrote, requires us to abandon deeply rooted human desires. Just as it led him to conclude that our wish that moral effort will be suitably rewarded may be "doomed to disappointment," so it leads contemporary naturalists to resign to futility our aspirations for transcendent meaning. Let us turn now to explore more fully the question of meaning.

IV

Naturalism poses difficulties for meaning just as it does for morality. The difficulties for meaning are suggested by Bertrand Russell's moving description of the naturalist's long-term outlook, cited earlier. What is troubling about Russell's picture and what requires "unyielding despair" is the certainty that everything we deeply cherish, everything that has made life worth living, will come to ruins in the end. The specter of everything coming to such an end forms a dark, foreboding cloud hovering over all of life and raises inevitable questions about its very meaning and purpose, and indeed, of whether it has any at all.

Widespread doubt and anxiety about the very meaning of life is a distinctly modern and postmodern phenomenon. This is not to say that the ancient world was totally devoid of such questioning. The Old Testament book of Ecclesiastes anticipates modern existentialism with its recurring refrain that all we do is finally meaningless. But by and large, until modern times, it was never suspected that everything we do might be pointless. To be sure, individuals could fail to achieve the meaning that life offers, and the prospect of such failure could precipitate great anxiety. But a crisis brought on by this sort of fear is profoundly different from the despair generated by a pervasive sense of meaninglessness. Charles Taylor points to Luther's spiritual struggles to illustrate the difference. While he wrestled in the depths of his soul with spiritual uncertainty and fears of eternal damnation, he never doubted that life has a meaning or questioned whether anything is really worth doing.

The most fundamental difference between earlier ages and modern and postmodern times has to do with their belief in what Taylor calls "frameworks" of meaning. These frameworks, which provide the structure and shape of "moral space," are defined by the belief that some goods are of incomparable value and make unconditional demands upon us. To be properly oriented in moral space is to know where we are in relation to these goods. Indeed, our very identity is constituted in terms of knowing where we stand with respect to such goods. Consequently, the contemporary naturalistic belief that there are no such frameworks, or that all such frameworks are merely matters of personal interpretation or preference, produces a sense of disorientation, a loss of identity and a fear of meaninglessness.[27]

Robert W. Jensen has made much the same point with his contention that the postmodern world has "lost its story." As Jensen observes, it was supposed by modernity that we inhabit a narratable world, a world that is really out there in such a way that stories can be told that are true to it. This was possible because of the further assumption that the world as a whole has its own true story, and this is what enables us to situate our individual stories in relation to this larger story. It is no secret, moreover, where this assumption derives from. It is a secularization of the Judeo-Christian practice of telling the archetypal realistic narrative, that is, the biblical narrative. As Jensen puts it, "Modernity was defined by the attempt to live in a universal story without a universal storyteller."[28]

But modernism's confidence that it could retain a secularized version of realistic narrative has been shattered by postmodern developments. Fragmentary competing narratives hold sway in place of the biblical story and the secularist version that succeeded it. The Enlightenment project inevitably failed because the universe cannot have a universal story if it has no universal storyteller. "Neither you nor I nor all of us together can so shape the world that it can make narrative sense; if God does not invent the world's story, then it has none, then the world has no narrative that is its own."[29]

One source that might be relied upon to provide a universal story to make sense of our world is science, a main wellspring of modern and postmodern perspectives. Unfortunately for this hope, however, contemporary science largely reiterates the sort of despair that Russell commended in the early part of the twentieth century. An often quoted remark of Nobel laureate Steven Weinberg underscores the futility of finding a meaningful narrative in scientific accounts of the world: "The more the universe seems comprehensible, the more it also seems pointless. . . . The effort to understand the universe is one of the very few things that lifts human life a little above the level of farce, and gives it some of the grace of tragedy."[30]

If there is a story to be told about the universe, it is finally one of tragedy. Contemporary naturalistic scientists see our emergence as due to chance, the extraordinary result of the accidental concurrence of a number of factors. Moreover, our ultimate fate is tied inextricably to that of the universe as a whole, which seems destined for a dismal end. The data from cosmology suggests that the final outcome for the physical universe is that it will go on expanding forever, dissolving in entropy.[31] The better we understand such scientific claims, the more futile everything seems. If the universe will conclude in this fashion, everything can finally seem pointless.

This is a widely shared feeling, but it is hard to say just what the insight or truth is that evokes it. Here is a preliminary stab at it. The feeling is due, I think, to the sense that the ultimate end of something casts its shadow over it and gives it final definition. The point here is similar to that of our earlier chapter on the problem of evil, where I argued that the significance of events often changes when put into a wider context. Recall William Temple's analogy of a play whose meaning may not be apparent until the final scene. Indeed, the broader point is that the meaning or value of any event is uncertain until the series of which it is a member has run its course. The point of the earlier chapter was that even horrendous evils could be redeemed and reinterpreted if our lives come to a happy end. The point now is the opposite one. Even wonderful goods may lose their meaning, or at the very least they may have their meaning significantly diminished, if they come to a negative end.

Consider another example. A few years ago the Phoenix Suns were playing the Seattle Supersonics in playoffs of the National Basketball Association. With Seattle leading by three points and less than two seconds left in the game, Phoenix guard Rex Chapman made an improbable, running, off-balance, three-point basket to tie the game and send it into overtime. But in the overtime period, Seattle regained the lead and eventually won the game. Afterward,

Chapman commented on his spectacular shot as follows: "It was great at the time, but we let the opportunity it gave us get away. I'm sure it was exciting to watch, but it's just a basket in a loss."[32] Obviously the shot would have taken on much greater and more positive significance if his team had won the game. So here is the question we can pose: If everything will end in death and disintegration, is it the case that everything we value and enjoy is like baskets in a losing game? It may be exciting or wonderful at the time, but it finally comes to futility and frustration if death is the end of everything.

Not everyone shares this intuition. To the contrary, some argue that the belief death is final, rather than creating a problem for meaning, actually enhances the meaning of this life. The realization that life is fragile and finite underlines the fact that it is precious, and death not only brings this reality into focus but it also completes the narrative of our lives and brings them to a fitting conclusion. Moreover, there is the ancient argument that death poses no threat for us simply because when we are dead, we will not exist. While the process of dying may be something to be feared, death itself is nothing to dread, for when we are dead, we will no longer be subjects of experience, just as we were not before we were conceived. Our death should be no more troubling to us than our prenatal nonexistence.[33]

While these arguments have some superficial plausibility, I think they are profoundly unsatisfactory upon further reflection. There is something about the prospect of our death and future extinction that is troubling in a way that our prenatal nonexistence is not. The difference is that a man's death deprives him of life he could have enjoyed in the time beyond his demise. The same cannot be said about the time before his birth. As Thomas Nagel points out, anyone born substantially before he was would not be him but someone else. The window of time in which *he* can be born is relatively small. But while our lives have a distinct beginning, there is openness with respect to their end. The trouble, as Nagel goes on to observe, is that life introduces us to goods that death will eventually steal from us, and the very fact that life has this openended quality makes death such a terrible misfortune. "Viewed in this way, death, no matter how inevitable, is an abrupt cancellation of indefinitely extensive possible goods."[34]

To make this point more vivid, let us consider the thoughts of astronomer Carl Sagan as he faced his own imminent death from a rare disease. Sagan had looked death in the face six times before, and he reported that he had learned much about the value of life from those encounters. But one thing those encounters did not do was weaken his desire to continue to live. Rather, as he stood on the brink of death, Sagan movingly wrote of aspirations he saw as destined to go unfulfilled. He would have liked to grow old with his wife, whom he passionately loved. He wanted to see his younger children grow up and to contribute to their education and character development. He would have liked to meet grandchildren not yet conceived. Moreover, he longed to see the direction history would take, to witness scientific and technological advances and political resolutions. To miss out on all this is a poignant loss indeed.

Facing the prospect of his own demise that would later deprive him of all such experiences, Sagan readily admits, "I would love to believe that when I die I will live again, that some thinking, feeling, remembering part of me will continue." Such continued consciousness is obviously relevant to his unsatisfied aspirations, as he notes a page later. "If there were life after death, I might, no matter when I die, satisfy most of these deep curiosities and longings. But if death is nothing more than an endless dreamless sleep, this is a forlorn hope."[35]

Unfortunately for these aspirations, Sagan believed the hope of life after death is the product of wishful thinking that has little evidence in its favor, a belief he held to the end of his life. In the epilogue to his book, Sagan's wife, Ann Druyan, wrote with loving admiration of her husband's courage in the face of death. Contrary to the reports of some religious groups, there was no death-bed conversion. With unflinching consistency, he held fast to what he had believed true and refused to take refuge in the hope of heaven or an afterlife. Commitment to what he believed true took precedence over comfort, even if it cost him great emotional pain. Druyan writes, "As we looked deeply into each other's eyes, it was with a shared conviction that our wondrous life together was ending forever."[36]

The notion that a wondrous life is ending forever, terminating once and for all any prospect of further fulfillment and meaning, is a hard pill to swallow. Clearly, Sagan and his wife felt the pain of coming to grips with this grim conclusion. Their experience in this regard is not atypical. While not all naturalists express such regrets, it is hard to deny that the notion that death is the irrevocable end of life is a very difficult blow to absorb. Not surprisingly, naturalists have come up with a number of ways to soften this blow. What is particularly significant for our purposes is that some of these could be characterized as secular substitutes for heaven. Let us turn now to consider some of these.

V

The first of these views is represented by Richard Taylor, who takes the myth of Sisyphus as his point of departure. This tragic character was condemned by the gods to push a stone up a hill, which immediately rolled back down the hill, and to push it back up again, and so on, forever. Understandably, Sisyphus has been seen as the very epitome of meaninglessness, for nothing seems to be accomplished by his effort. He is locked into a cycle of endless futility. But Taylor ventures the further and more interesting claim that Sisyphus is also a striking image of human life and activity, for humans pursue goals that have only temporary significance and then move on to other such goals. The main difference between Sisyphus and us is that whereas he continues pushing the stone up the hill forever, we pass it on to our children. Civilizations come and go, and later ones take as their foundation the rubble of earlier ones. The cycle continues unabated.

Does this show that our lives are meaningless? Taylor does not think so. In order to make this point, Taylor suggests two ways the Sisyphus myth might be revised. Scenario one: Instead of Sisyphus rolling the same stone up the hill only to have it roll back down again, he is given different stones to roll up each time, and with these stones he constructs a temple at the top of the hill. In this case, his labor would have a point, and the specter of utter meaningless would be banished. Scenario two: The gods choose to have mercy on Sisyphus, albeit in a perverse way, by implanting in him the strange and irrational impulse to roll stones up a hill. They do this by putting in his veins a substance that alters his desires in such a way that he has an obsession with rolling stones. It does not bother him when the stone rolls back down the hill, for he takes delight in rolling it back up again.

In Taylor's view, the first of these scenarios, while it would provide some meaning to Sisyphus, would eventually consign him to hell, for he would quickly tire of contemplating his temple and boredom would set in. The second scenario, by contrast, holds promise of heavenly delight, for in it, Sisyphus has endless opportunity to indulge his ever present desire. Taylor sees this second scenario as a helpful image of meaning for human lives.

Taylor's argument here hinges on his observation that human beings are born with an instinctive will to live and that we no more question whether it will be worthwhile to live than do birds or other creatures. What matters is simply that there are tasks to be done and that we have a natural compulsion to do them. So it was for our parents and so it will be for our children. If philosophers are tempted to despair by this picture, this is because they seek a meaning that is not to be found. But in Taylor's view, it is a mercy that things are as they are, for otherwise we would be consigned to boredom. He concludes his essay with the following hopeful line: "The meaning of life is from within us, it is not bestowed from without, and it far exceeds in both its beauty and permanence any heaven of which men have ever dreamed or yearned for."[37]

The meaning that Taylor sees as preferable to that afforded by any traditional view of heaven is apparently just the satisfaction we experience from doing the things we instinctively desire doing. How or why we have the "inner compulsion" that moves us to pursue the tasks we do is apparently irrelevant. There seems, in fact, to be little difference between this compulsion and the "irrational" desire implanted in Sisyphus in Taylor's second scenario.[38] Presumably nature or evolution has put in our veins the desire to perform the tasks we instinctively pursue, perhaps because of their survival value. But it is pointless to look for further meaning beyond the fact that we instinctively desire to engage in such activity. Indeed, meaning would be most evident in those persons who never raised such questions but simply pursued their tasks without distraction.

There is something appealing about this account of meaning, uncomplicated as it is by questions and reflections about the ultimate point of it all. We just act out our inner compulsion to accomplish the tasks before us and then hand the baton off to our children as we approach the grave. Unfortunately for Taylor, it is not that simple. In the first place, one of the most distinctively human things we do is to reflect on the deeper meaning of our lives. While the crisis of meaning may be a particularly modern and postmodern phenomenon, it has been characteristic of human beings through the ages, as Charles Taylor points out, to understand their activities in terms of larger frameworks of meaning.

Moreover, it is a commonplace observation that human beings typically do not find happiness and satisfaction in pursuing and accomplishing the tasks of this life. Even those who construct the most magnificent castles and build the biggest empires often express disappointment at the end of the day and wonder about the point of it all. Unlike Sisyphus in Richard Taylor's second scenario, we simply do not take mindless delight in pushing our stones repeatedly up our hills, never pausing to ask why. While it is no doubt true that we are born with an instinctive will to live and naturally engage the various pursuits of life, the compulsion to do so has its limits and does not carry us through to the end, blissfully indifferent to questions of deeper meaning and satisfaction.

These observations undermine Taylor's claim that his account of meaning "far exceeds in both its beauty and permanence any heaven of which men have ever dreamed or yearned for." Indeed, his claim of greater permanence is downright mystifying. Even if we all performed our tasks with perfect contentment and energy throughout our days, our lives inevitably come to an end. And if naturalism is true, then some generation of the future will make one final trip to the top of the hill, and sometime later, after all of life has disappeared, the hill itself will be destroyed. The Christian vision of heaven holds out the hope of literally unending joy and fulfillment, a happiness that is both rational and ecstatic. Whether any such heaven exists is surely a matter of debate. But Taylor's claim that his account of meaning exceeds in both beauty and permanence the heaven for which Christians devoutly hope is nothing more than a bit of philosophical bravado. In fact, it is clear that his account pales in comparison with the Christian view of heaven in both of these respects.

A second position, somewhat similar to the first, is the atheistic existentialist notion that we can endow our lives with meaning in the face of death. E. D. Klemke defends this view against those who argue that life has no value if there is no transcendent being or other ground of objective meaning. Klemke says the whole notion of objective meaning leaves him cold. Human beings are much more glorious, in his view, if we are free to forge our own meaning. Life can be subjectively meaningful for individuals if they have the creative and appreciative capacities to endow events, persons, objects, and accomplishments with value. This view differs from Taylor's in emphasizing the element of freedom in bestowing value. Whereas Taylor sees meaning in simply doing what human beings instinctively do, Klemke stresses that we must choose meaning in the face of our eventual doom.

In the final section of his essay, Klemke tells an ancient story of a Syrian camel driver who was pushed into a pit by one of his camels. At the bottom of the pit was a dragon waiting to devour him, but fortunately, his clothes were caught by a rosebush. Unfortunately, however, two mice were chewing away the roots of the rosebush. But as he hung, he was thralled to the point of utter contentment by a single rose, whose fragrance wafted into his face. Klemke says that he himself is that Syrian and he knows his inevitable doom is swiftly approaching. If he can find no rose to respond to or has lost the ability to respond, then indeed his fate is to be cursed. But again, underlining his view that it is up to us to endow our lives with meaning, he concludes with this rhetorical flourish.

> But *if* I can, in these last moments, respond to a rose—or to a philosophical argument or a theory of physics, or even to a Scarlatti sonata, or to the touch of a human hand—I say, if I can so respond and can thereby transform an external and fatal event into a moment of conscious insight and significance, then I shall go down *without hope or appeal* yet *passionately triumphant and with joy*.[39]

Here the hard end of naturalism is softened by the power of human freedom to bestow value almost in defiance of encroaching doom. While we cannot finally defy death in the end, we can at least defy the specter of meaninglessness it threatens us with if we go down passionately and with joy. And we can do this if we choose to appreciate and be grateful for what life affords us.

It is noteworthy that Sagan took a stance reminiscent of this in response to a question that he says was often raised to him, namely, how he could face death without the certainty of an afterlife. Professing that it had not been a problem for him, he quoted with approval a passage from Einstein in which the famous physicist said that he could not believe in a God who punishes or rewards or who even has a will in any way like ours. Moreover, he could not conceive or wish that an individual might survive his physical death. Completing his thought, Einstein wrote, "I am satisfied with the mystery of the eternity of life and a glimpse of the marvelous structure of the existing world, together with the devoted striving to comprehend a portion, be it ever so tiny, of the Reason that manifests itself in nature."[40] In affirming this position, it is clear that Sagan holds essentially the same view as Klemke, although he does not express it with the same sort of existentialist panache. He chooses to be satisfied with the goods offered by this life, represented here by the pleasure of understanding something of the structure of our world.

I am prepared to grant that this account shows how life can be worth living, even in the face of eventual annihilation. However, it is not without serious difficulties. First, with respect to Klemke, it is not clear that there is any substantive sense in which one can go down to final extinction with triumph. One triumphs when one fully achieves one's goals. It is hard to see how this could be compatible with final extinction unless one wanted to be extinguished or saw it as a good thing. Likewise, it is not easy to see how Klemke could view extinction in this light, since he celebrates things such as people, philosophical arguments, and work, not to mention roses. If these things are truly good things to be cherished, it is odd to say that it would be a triumph to be forever cut off from experiencing them. Would it not be better to go on having such experiences, or even richer ones if this were possible? If not, it is hard to see how these sorts of experiences could transform the prospect of death into a positive experience. At best, this sort of transformation could be a relative triumph, as well as a rather short-lived one. It might be better than to allow the prospect of death to rob one of all joy, but it is hardly for that reason an unqualified triumph. Klemke would be more realistic if he said that his view allows him to go down with some sense of satisfaction but not with the sort of unalloyed joy and triumph he now claims.

Notice how this sort of tension, if not inconsistency, is evident in Sagan. He claims, following Einstein, to have no interest in an afterlife and to be satisfied with what this life offers. On the face of it, this seems to be at odds with the passage cited earlier in which he admits to having deeply felt aspirations that he believed must go unfulfilled. It is also inconsistent with his admission that he would love to believe that when he dies he will live again because this would allow these aspirations to be satisfied. Either Sagan was fully satisfied with just a glimpse of the structure of our world, or he desired to see more of how science will unfold and to understand even more. Either he was fully satisfied with what he experienced with his wife and children, or he longed for further development of those relationships.

Of course, Sagan believed life after death is a forlorn hope, whatever our aspirations. He remained firm in this belief even though it meant he had to resign some of his deeply felt desires to futility. But the point is not merely that Sagan's felt aspirations were at odds with his beliefs, which remained consistent, but also that he gives inconsistent accounts of his own aspirations. On the one hand, he admits to longing for more, but on the other, he says he is satisfied as things stand. In the end, it appears the sort of stance represented by Klemke and Sagan is at best an ambivalent attempt to soften the blow of final extinction.

A third option for coming to terms with naturalism is offered by Bertrand Russell. This option is of particular interest since it is developed in the same essay as the famous passage cited at the beginning of this chapter. In that passage, Russell recommends a strategy of "unyielding despair" in the face of the inevitable ruin of all that we love and care about. The title of the essay is "A Free Man's Worship," and throughout Russell borrows religious terminology as he expounds a naturalist account of a meaningful life.

Like the existentialists, he believes the world was not made for us, which means that many of the beautiful things we crave may be forbidden us. In recognition of this reality, Russell counsels that we forge a wisdom that includes elements of both resignation and imagination. We must renounce the worship of power while having the courage to submit to the ruin of our hopes that power will effect with irresistible force. Yet in the realm of imagination we must build a temple to worship our own ideals. In so doing, we can transform all the experiences of this life into things of beauty, and thereby we triumph. For Russell, this even includes a version of heaven.

Let us preserve our respect for truth, for beauty, for the ideal of perfection which life does not permit us to attain, though none of these things meet with the approval of the unconscious universe. If power is bad, as it seems to be, let us reject it from our hearts. In this lies man's true freedom: in determination to worship only the God created by our own love of the good, to respect only the heaven which inspires the insight of our best moments.[41]

The fundamental choice we face as Russell sees it is whether we shall worship force or goodness. In his view, the philosophy of Nietzsche and the creed of militarism are examples of the human failure to maintain our highest ideals against a hostile universe driven by unconscious power. What is striking here is that Russell's account of what makes our lives truly meaningful depends so heavily on strong moral evaluations. This observation takes us back to the beginning of this chapter where we noted, following Mavrodes, that morality is superficial in Russell's universe. Ultimate reality is at best amoral, and ultimate reality will in the end crush and destroy all the living beings who have moral concerns and values.

We will come back to this point in the next section, but for now it is enough to note that Russell's heaven that inspires the insights of our best moments is a rather precarious buffer against the onslaught of death and ultimate extinction. This vulnerability is only exacerbated by the observation that, in Russell's view, our hopes and fears, our loves and beliefs, "are but the outcome of accidental collocations of atoms." Neither freedom nor worship of our highest ideals makes much sense in Russell's universe. Perhaps evolution has wired us to worship these ideals, and many humans will naturally do so as tenaciously and enthusiastically as Sisyphus rolled stones in Taylor's second scenario, but whether those ideals are worthy of that worship in any meaningful sense is another matter altogether.

A fourth option for coming to terms with the sense of meaninglessness that threatens us is offered by Thomas Nagel. In his view, there is warrant for neither distress nor defiance in response to our situation. In preference to these, he recommends irony as a realistic alternative. Nagel compares our tendency to ask questions about the ultimate meaning of our lives and to seek transcendental justification for what we do with the similar sort of questioning that generates epistemological skepticism. In both cases, there is an attempt to step outside of our selves and our lives to gain some sort of transcendent vantage point. "Reference to our small size and short life span and to the fact that all of mankind will eventually vanish without a trace are metaphors for the backward step which permits us to regard ourselves from without and to find the particular form of our lives curious and slightly surprising."[42]

It is precisely the ability to step backward in this fashion that allows us to take a perspective from which our lives seem absurd. The question Nagel presses is whether this awareness of absurdity is something to be regretted or avoided, but in order to answer the question fairly, we need first to consider what we would have to give up to do so. The answer to this latter question is that we would have to give up that which makes us most distinctively human. As Nagel points out, mice have no sense of absurdity, but that is no reason to want to be a mouse. Indeed, it is precisely our most advanced and interesting characteristics that give rise to our sense of absurdity. "If a sense of the absurd is a way of perceiving our true situation (even though the situation is not absurd until the perception arises), then what reason can we have to resent or escape it?"[43]

In response to this, I have two observations. First, Nagel's analysis leaves us with a dilemma similar to those we observed in recent moral philosophy. We must choose between a clear-eyed grasp of the truth and a life that is not shadowed by a sense of the absurd. Second, it is not clear why, in a naturalistic universe, "perceiving our true situation" should be preferred to a more comfortable illusion when doing so exacts a significant existential cost.

A fifth way naturalists can minimize the finality of death is by stressing the continuing influence and impact of a life that was well lived. Indeed, a person who "makes a mark" that is still clearly visible after he has died can even be said to live in some sense long after he has been buried. Again, Ann Druyan expresses this idea in reference to her husband, Carl Sagan, with appealing restraint. She does so in the context of sharing the fact that Sagan had been invited by NASA to assemble a committee that would select the contents for a phonograph record that would be attached to the *Voyager* 1 and 2 spacecraft. The gold records, with a shelf life of one billion years, would contain greetings in numerous human languages, photographs of life on earth, musical selections, and so on. Once gravitationally expelled from the solar system, the spacecraft could potentially provide information and communication to other possible beings in our vast universe. In the final paragraph of the epilogue she penned in tribute to her husband, she connects this part of his potential legacy to the immediately felt impact of his life.

> The Voyager spacecraft, with their revelations of a tiny world graced by music and love, are beyond the outermost planets, making for the open sea of interstellar space. They are hurtling at a speed of forty thousand miles an hour toward the stars and a destiny about which we can only dream. I sit surrounded by cartons of mail from people all over the planet who mourn Carl's loss. Many of them credit him with their awakenings. Some of them say that Carl's example has inspired them to work for science and reason against the forces of superstition and fundamentalism. These thoughts comfort me and lift me out of my heartache. They allow me to feel, without resorting to the supernatural, that Carl lives.[44]

In the sense that Druyan means, there is no denying that her husband still lives. Indeed, he made a mark larger than most, and it is likely that his mark will be visible for some time to come. But suppose our planet will survive another ten thousand years. Will his mark still be discernible? Who can say whether the achievements of even the likes of Newton, Galileo, and Einstein will still be celebrated into the far future? Who knows what political or intellectual currents may arise in the future and affect how the past is remembered? At any rate, if naturalism is true, eventually there will be no intelligent life on our planet, and thus no one to remember or celebrate any of the love, music, or science produced by the human race. Indeed, the same fate ultimately awaits any other intelligent life that might exist in outer reaches of the universe, including any potential creatures who might, millions of years hence, receive the information in the *Voyager* spacecraft. Ultimately, no legacy is secure against the ravages of naturalism.

Sagan knew this well and so does Druyan. The modesty of her claims is admirable. She does not exaggerate the comfort in believing that her husband lives in the fashion she describes. He "lives" only in some metaphorical sense of the word, and that affords some measure of consolation. But the very naturalism Sagan subscribed to circumvents any further sort of hope or comfort.

Perhaps, however, Sagan's account of the final outcome of things is mistaken, and there is reason to hold out for more, even on naturalistic terms. This is the final option we will consider, and it is certainly the most optimistic one on offer for naturalists who are not comfortable with the prospect of ultimate oblivion. This option is represented by some contemporary physicists who propose a hopeful cosmology over against the cosmology of final futility espoused by most naturalistic scientists.

The best-known such account is probably that of Frank Tipler, whose ambitious project is to make theology a branch of physics. The scope of his ambition is evident from the fact that he does not shrink from including in his project what he recognizes as the heart of religious aspiration, namely, the human hunger for immortality. Indeed, he aims to go far beyond Galileo, who, following an eminent churchman, wrote, "The intention of the [Bible] is to teach us how to go to heaven, not how the heavens go." Staking out new territory for his discipline, Tipler writes, "Science now tells us how to go to Heaven."[45] In the same vein, in the preface to his book *The Physics of Immortality*, he announces that the time has come "to make Heaven as real as an electron."[46]

When claims like this are asserted, the reader is braced for something extraordinary. On this score, Tipler does not disappoint. His book is a fascinating trek through the regions of contemporary physics and astronomy, with several forays along the way into philosophical and theological territory. His vision of how science will bring the kingdom of heaven takes scientific ambition to places it has never gone before.

The main thrust of Tipler's book is that "eternal progress is not only possible but inevitable, and will result ultimately in our salvation."[47] This entails for Tipler the ineluctable forward march of technological progress until the arrival of the "Omega Point,"[48] at which time life will have engulfed the entire created universe and will have achieved omnipotence and omniscience along with omnipresence. While Tipler does not believe in a God who existed before the cosmos and brought it into existence, he does believe that something like God will eventually emerge from the cosmos. This is perhaps the ultimate reversal of the traditional theistic view that mind and will are prior to matter. Moreover, he postulates that a supercomputer will have been constructed by this time that will provide the hope for a future "resurrection" of all persons who have died. In Tipler's view, the essence of a human being is a complex digital pattern, and in principle there is no reason why such patterns could not be emulated by the future supercomputer. Thus, the resurrection to be hoped for is the computer simulation of all persons who have ever lived.

Tipler's hope for resurrection depends on the view that the universe will eventually collapse back on itself in the distant future rather than expand forever, as most naturalistic scientists believe. It is this which will provide the energy necessary for an infinite amount of information to be processed and thereby make it possible for the "resurrected" persons to experience eternal life in subjective time, even though objective time ends with the "big crunch."[49]

Of course, all of this depends on the possibility of interstellar space travel, the invention of self-reproducing machines that will colonize the outer reaches of space, and other such intermediate technological marvels. Moreover, it assumes that human beings will cooperate as necessary for exceedingly long-term goals and that the God-like Omega Point will be benevolent. None of this daunts Tipler. This is what must be the case for us to achieve immortality. For an instance of this line of thought, consider his rather visionary claim that first the entire solar system and ultimately the entire universe of matter must be taken apart and converted into a suitable habitat for the expanding biosphere. While this might seem like a rather large difficulty for his theory, Tipler assures us "that in the very long run life has no choice: it must take the natural structures apart if it is to survive. So I conclude that it will."[50]

This brief summary hardly does justice to the complexity, ingenuity, and intrigue of Tipler's proposal. But at the end of the day, it is apparent that it depends too much on contested scientific claims, dubious applications of scientific consensus, doubtful philosophical assumptions, particularly about the nature of persons, and perhaps most of all, sheer optimism. Physicist John Polkinghorne sums up just this sort of appraisal in his judgment that Tipler's whole scenario is one of "desperate implausibility"[51] and suggests that it "corresponds to a kind of cosmic tower of Babel, the fundamental error of confounding creation with its Creator."[52]

We have now considered several naturalistic options for salvaging meaning in the face of death, particularly emphasizing some secular substitutes for heaven, and have pointed to difficulties in each of them. The fact that naturalists offer secular alternatives to heaven is, I suggest, very telling. It shows that we cannot easily dispense with heaven, indeed, that it is an irreplaceable resource in our efforts to give our lives the meaning we crave. So let us turn now to state more directly how the traditional Christian doctrine of heaven fully resolves the problems for morality and meaning that plague naturalism.

VI

Recall that naturalism poses a series of dilemmas for both morality and meaning. If the only goods to be enjoyed are of the Russellian variety and extinction is our final destiny, we may have to make the hard choice between acting for the happiness of others and acting to secure our own well-being. Similarly, we have to choose between a life with transcendent meaning and a life of intellectual honesty, haunted by the specter of the absurd. Underlying these dilemmas is what Wilson terms the "coming century's version of the struggle for men's souls," namely, whether the ultimate origin of morality is empirical or transcendental.

I agree with Wilson about the high stakes of this issue and all that hinges on it. Unlike him, I think there are powerful reasons to prefer a transcendental account of the origin of morality. To be more specific, morality is best accounted for by deploying distinctively Christian resources, including the doctrine of heaven. When I speak of morality, I am including, as indicated at the beginning of this chapter, concerns about meaning and the good life, concerns that have been neglected in much recent moral philosophy. I will argue my case by advancing three claims, the first two of which are especially closely related.

First, naturalistic theories such as Wilson represents are hard-pressed to account for altruism in a way that does not undermine the profound respect we naturally feel for altruistic actions, the most admirable aspect of morality. Indeed, I would contend that the more clearly one understands and affirms such naturalistic accounts, the less motivation one has to act altruistically, whereas the more clearly one understands the Christian account of ultimate reality, the more motivation one has to do so. Second, and in the same vein, naturalism, as an antirealist position, is at a loss to provide a persuasive account of moral obligation. This is not to deny that it can explain why we have feelings of obligation, but it is another matter altogether to show we really are obligated to behave morally.

Recall the role that deception, including self-deception, plays in evolutionary and sociobiological explanations of altruism. The question this obviously raises is what is left to motivate altruism when one finally sees through the various layers of deception? Even more to the point, what is left of altruism itself when clarity descends and one understands with reflective awareness that his tendency toward self-sacrifice is actually due to evolutionary conditioning that serves the purpose of promoting the welfare of one's genetic material? If this or something essentially like it is the origin of altruism, it can hardly be thought of in the same way it was before.

The same analysis applies to the naturalistic accounts of our sense of moral obligation that we have been examining. This sense of obligation depends on what many naturalists take to be a false belief, namely, that there is an objective ground of morality. Our moral convictions are thus misguided insofar as they are generated by this illusion.

Thus, we can grant that sociobiology holds promise of providing an entirely naturalistic way of explaining why we have deeply felt moral tendencies and even act on those tendencies. However, it must also be acknowledged that it tends to unsettle, upon reflection, any natural sense of assurance that we ought to follow those tendencies or that we are under any real obligation to do so. As Peter Singer argues, the demonstration that a specific behavior is ultimately biological in origin may have the opposite effect than expected. "Far from justifying principles that are shown to be 'natural,' a biological explanation can be a way of debunking what seemed to be eternal moral axioms. When a widely accepted moral principle is given a convincing biological explanation, we need to think again about whether we should accept the principle."[53]

Of course, Wilson cheerfully concedes that evolution cannot justify morality although it can produce it. That is why he says it serves a powerful purpose like Macbeth's dagger, even though it does not exist in substance. But the question I am pressing is how the "dagger" can continue to serve its purpose once we have seen through the fact that it is an illusory deception. Can such a dagger serve to influence behavior in any positive way, or defend morality from critical assault, once its pretensions to reality have been clearly exposed? It seems unduly idealistic to think it can.

The broader implications of seeing through this pretension are far-reaching indeed. Arguably, even the very importance of being committed to truth, a primary value for many naturalists, is without adequate defense if morality is no more substantial than Macbeth's dagger. Recall that Russell's account of meaning depends on some rather strong moral judgments and that Nagel's counsel for being at peace with a sense of the absurd assumes that it is better to know the truth about our situation than not. Indeed, it is our highest capacities that allow us to know the truth in this way. Recall also that an important part of what provided meaning for Sagan is that he took a courageous stand for what he took to be the truth rather than to accept the consolation of false hope.

This sort of commitment to truth has been a moral source for naturalists for some time, as Charles Taylor has pointed out. Indeed, naturalists have assumed the moral high ground over against those who are perceived as taking refuge in hopes that are illusory and ungrounded. Human dignity is demonstrated in the ability to face uncowed and without consolation the implications of the reality that we live in an indifferent universe of immense proportions.[54]

The question I want to press is why this stance should still be viewed with respect, if not reverence, as it has in the past. History is full of examples of people who have made enormous sacrifices, including their very lives, for what they believed true. The naturalists' sacrifice of hope and emotional comfort for the sake of truth continues broadly in this same vein. Indeed, such sacrifices are akin to altruism insofar as they involve giving up something of great value for the sake of another. In this case, the "other" is truth itself. We instinctively admire such sacrifices for truth just as we do altruism in the more ordinary sense of the word.

Indeed, some may go further and maintain that a commitment to truth is one of our primary moral duties, if not our most basic one. Aligning himself with this sort of view, C. S. Lewis once remarked, "The true doctrine might be a doctrine which if we accept we die. No one who speaks from within the *Tao* could reject it on that account."[55] "The *Tao*" is Lewis's term for fundamental moral axioms, and his point here is that it is axiomatic that we owe allegiance to truth, even if it costs us our lives. Of course, Lewis was not a naturalist, but he expresses a commitment to truth that many naturalists, as well as theists, would gladly endorse.

The whole notion of truth has lost much of its currency in postmodern thought, where it is typically construed as a matter of social and cultural construction, often motivated by dubious desires for power and manipulation. So construed, it is hard to muster the will to maintain loyalty to truth when it is costly, or even uncomfortable or inconvenient, to do so. Truth is far too elusive and elastic on postmodern terms to warrant such sacrifice.

But even if truth is what modernist naturalists claim it to be, the question remains of why we have a moral obligation to honor it or to prefer it to a more comfortable illusion? The truth, on their account, is that for the vast majority of the history of our cosmos, there were no conscious beings who were even capable of holding beliefs, let alone honoring truth. Moreover, the cosmos will eventually expand and disintegrate to the point that all intelligent life will be destroyed, and with it, all concern about truth. In the relatively brief interim in which we live, evolution has produced in us a natural desire to honor truth. Given the way we are wired, acting on this natural desire does indeed give our lives meaning and helps us to survive and thrive in the meantime.

But are we on that account beholden to the sense of the importance of truth that evolution has produced in us? Consider a scenario that modern technology makes imaginable, the sort of scenario depicted sometimes in the movies.[56] Suppose one were confronted with the choice of living in a virtual world in which one experienced great pleasure and subjective satisfaction, or living in the real world, which was difficult, painful, and haunted by a sense of the absurd. To keep the case simple, suppose also that one had no family responsibilities or other such commitments that would factor into the decision. Suppose, moreover, that naturalism is true and that in the real world one faced the prospect of oblivion after a life of difficulty and pain. Is there any compelling reason to choose the real world in this case? Is there some moral obligation to do so?

I think the answer to both questions is no. One may certainly choose the real world if he prefers, but that is far from saying he is obligated to do so. After all, in such a world, part of what is true is that virtual reality is now an option. It would be "reality" that virtual reality could be chosen in favor of the difficult world of normal experience. Evolution may provide an explanation for why we honor truth, just as it does for why we engage in altruistic actions, but it justifies neither preference. The more clearly we perceive the implications of explaining morality in terms of biology, the less reason we have to challenge those who would opt for virtual reality, not to mention comfortable illusion, over truth. Macbeth's dagger is a particularly ill-suited weapon to fight the battle for truth.

Let us turn now to consider the Christian account of the origin of morality, particularly altruism, and even more fundamentally, the ground of obligation. According to Christianity, ultimate reality is God, a conscious personal being who has always existed, and he is the creator of all else that exists. Human beings were created in God's image and have a special place in God's purpose for creation. Consequently, it is not the case, as Russell alleged, that our hopes and fears, our loves and beliefs "are but the outcome of accidental collocations of atoms." We were intended to exist, and our hopes and loves were created for fulfillment, not "extinction in the vast death of the solar system." The God who created us is essentially a God of love whose nature is such that he desires the flourishing of all that he has made. Indeed, his very personality consists in the fact that he exists in three persons in an eternal relationship of perfect love. This is the ultimate explanation of altruism. Even though we are fallen and estranged from God apart from his grace, we were created in the image of one whose very nature is love. So we naturally resonate in the depths of our being with acts of sacrificial love.

Colin Gunton has observed that the notion of sacrifice appears to be deeply rooted in human nature and the way we respond to the world, so much so that we may plausibly take it as a nearly universal, if not altogether so, feature of our life in this world.[57] Interpreting this theologically, he ventures the suggestion that sacrifice is the concrete "expression and outworking of the inner-trinitarian relations of giving and receiving. The inner being of God is a *taxis*, a dynamic orderedness, of love construed in terms of mutual and reciprocal gift and reception."[58]

It is a God like this in whose image we were created, according to Christian theology. Moreover, God's purpose in creating us was that we would enjoy relationship with him. Indeed, our true happiness and fulfillment comes from being brought into fellowship with the Trinity. This is what explains our attraction to altruistic actions. Sacrifice is the form Trinitarian love takes in a fallen world. In God's eternal nature, the dynamic of "mutual and reciprocal gift and reception" is one of pure joy and pleasure. In a fallen world, such love sometimes requires costly and painful sacrifice. When we witness or receive such love, we are drawn to it because it is a foretaste of the eternal joy for which we were created. It is an image of the sacrificial love that God has for us and that he desires we receive for the sake of our deepest well-being. The eternal love of God is a matter of both gift and reception. The more clearly we understand this, the more motivated we are to respect altruism and to act accordingly when called upon to do so. Reflective awareness not only sustains but deepens our moral motivation in this case.

To put the point another way, these beliefs provide rational reinforcement for our instinctive moral feelings. This is a significant observation for the obvious reason that we also have feelings and desires that oppose moral action. If rational considerations do not support morality but even undermine its rational credentials, it is not implausible to think that moral commitments may be unsettled by reflective awareness.

This reality underscores the importance of my next point, namely, that Christian claims provide an intelligible and persuasive account of how moral obligation has an objective transcendent ground. We are obligated to be moral because morality is an expression of the will of a personal being to whom we owe our very existence. Because ultimate reality is personal and has such a will, morality is as deeply rooted as it could possibly be. Our sense of moral obligation is consequently not illusory in any way. To the contrary, it mirrors the reality that we are essentially related by creation to a personal God and are forever accountable to that relationship. Moral obligation is thus far more deeply grounded in the very nature of things than it could ever be if its ultimate sources are biological, social, or cultural.

Let us return for a moment to the scene from *Les Miserables* we considered at the outset of this chapter. Recall that the observers of the scene initially felt pity for Jean Valjean because they thought he was mad. Only after he assured them that he saw clearly what he was doing and was telling them the truth did their reaction change to profound admiration. Notice also his words, "What I do at this moment God beholds from on high and that is sufficient." Valjean's belief that he was accountable to God was at the heart of what motivated him to do as he did, and his clarity and self-awareness about the nature of his motivation is essential to the admiration we feel for his act of self-sacrifice.

Suppose Valjean had been a naturalist who had been convinced of sociobiological explanations of morality and had offered such an account of his action. Suppose he had said, "Evolution has built into me the desire to speak the truth even when it is costly and has reinforced this tendency with an illusory sense that morality has a transcendent authority behind it. This sense has been further hardened by powerful cultural and social factors over many generations, and that is sufficient." Would we continue to admire him, or would we feel a sense of bewilderment or even pity?

Accounting for morality in terms of Christian resources allows us to admire the Jean Valjeans of the world without suspecting they are mad or misguided in any way. We can do so because on this view, the gift of sacrifice is given ultimately to a God of love who delights in giving us more than we can ever give in return. This God takes pleasure in the obedient sacrifices of his children and openly promises to reward them in the life to come.[59]

In this connection, it is noteworthy that in his recent encyclical on moral theology, Pope John Paul II casts the whole discussion in light of the Christian hope of eternal life. He describes martyrs as those who have "obediently trusted and handed over their lives to the Father, the one who could free them from death."[60] This description highlights the fact that altruistic actions are not easy for Christians just because they believe God will reciprocate their gifts of love. Those who offer such gifts are still required to sacrifice genuine goods of this life, and it takes an act of profound trust in God on the part of those who do so to hand over their lives to God in this fashion. Such acts are costly and often painful, sometimes to the point of great suffering or even death. Still, it follows from what Christians believe about the very nature of God that such acts cannot ultimately go unrewarded. In the logic of eternal love, in exchanges with the ultimate giver of gifts, more is received than can ever be given.

This brings us to the third reason to prefer the Christian account of the origin of morality, namely, that it provides powerful resources to resolve the dilemmas that have plagued moral philosophy for the past two centuries. Sidgwick's "dualism of practical reason," which fossilized in the twentieth century as the conflict between egoism and altruism, is simply dissolved on Christian premises. Indeed, it is an impossible dilemma from a Christian standpoint. The fundamental reason for this is that the ultimate good for all persons is an eternal relationship with God. To enjoy this relationship, we must trust and obey God, even when it is costly and difficult.

At the heart of what God requires of us is that we love others selflessly, but paradoxically, our own self-interest is best served when we do so. We should distinguish then between self-interest and selfishness. One is acting selfishly when he promotes his interests at the unfair expense of others. Christian morality, like most secular morality, would reject this sort of behavior as wrong. But there is nothing wrong with acting out of self-interest, since all rational creatures naturally and inevitably desire their own happiness and well-being. To love another person is to promote his happiness and well-being. The same thing that makes it right to promote these for other persons makes it right to desire these for oneself as well. All human beings share essentially the same nature and are alike valuable to God as creatures he loves.

Learning to love selflessly is what transforms us and prepares us to enter the fellowship of the Trinity. As we love in this fashion, we are being prepared to experience our own highest joy and satisfaction. Consequently, the conflict between acting for our own ultimate good and that of others simply cannot arise. But this assumes that the highest goods are not those mentioned earlier in the *Time* article, namely, things like a top job, political power, sexual allure, a lakefront spread, and so on. Recall that the article suggests that we need a redefinition of our wants so that they will serve society as well as self. I am arguing that the only sorts of goods that will fit the bill in a convincing fashion are heavenly ones. If naturalism is true, the goods of this life are the only ones available, and it is a utopian dream to think that we can consistently act in such a way as to promote these goods both for ourselves and for others.

Recognition of this point reiterates the fact that selfless actions are not easy on the Christian account of things, for it requires profound faith in God to resist the seductive temptation to believe that the only goods, or the most desirable ones, are those of this life. To sacrifice such goods for the sake of others is to trust that Trinity is ultimate reality, that giving is reciprocal and mutual in the end.

Because Trinitarian love is the deepest reality, the notion of altruism as ultimate sacrifice with no expectation of compensation is at best a distortion of the aboriginal truth about reality. At worst, the notion that such utter disinterest represents a higher or more admirable standard is pagan hubris. As previously observed, this view is represented in current thought by such writers as Levinas and Derrida. Similar notions were expressed by the Stoics in antiquity, and in the modern period Kant is no doubt the high-water mark of philosophers who worried that morality would be contaminated by any element of self-interest. Kant's postulation of God and immortality, as noted above, does not sit well with his desire to protect morality from self-interest.

In Christian thought, resurrection and immortality are not afterthoughts, nor are they postulates to salvage morality from irrationality. They are integral to the grand claim that ultimate reality is reciprocal love. Christ's resurrection, no less than his giving his life as a sacrifice for our sins, is a picture for us of the eternal dynamic of divine love. It is life, not death—as Levinas and Derrida contend—that gives morality substance. As John Milbank puts it, "[R]esurrection, not death, is the ground of the ethical."[61]

Consider in this connection the book of Hebrews, which presents a theologically rich account of how Christ offered his life as a sacrifice to save us from our sins. In two passages particularly relevant to our current discussion, we are informed not only that Christ yielded obedience to the one who could save him from death but also that it was for the joy set before him that he endured the cross.[62] Thus, the consummate sacrifice that gives meaning to all others according to the book of Hebrews gives no credence whatever to the pagan notion that the finality of death is necessary for ultimate sacrifice. To the contrary, the ultimate sacrifice in human history, the sacrifice that saves the world, was given in faith that joy will triumph over death.

In commending Christ as a model in this regard, this passage encourages Christians who suffer for their faith to do so with confident hope that the God whose nature is love will reciprocate their costly obedience. Self-interest in this regard is a straightforward component of Christian moral motivation. Indeed, it is a rather obvious implication of the logic of Trinitarian belief, for we cannot harm our well-being by obedience to God, just as we cannot promote it by selfishness.

Indeed, there is no other way to be happy and to find the fulfillment we desire than by obedience to God. Thus, there is no parallel problem in the Christian view to the one posed for naturalism by those who choose, often successfully, to cheat the system. God cannot be deceived or cheated in any way, so moral parasites are completely out of the question in this view. It might make rational sense to think that cheating could successfully serve one's ultimate well-being on naturalistic assumptions, but that could never be the case given Christian beliefs. This observation further confirms the power of Christian theology to account not only for why morality is objectively binding upon us but also for why any reasonable person should want to obey it. It provides a rationally persuasive and winsome account of moral motivation that nothing in secular morality can emulate.

Before concluding this section, let us return for a moment to Sidgwick and recall that he rejected the notion of theistic sanctions for morality, confident that morality could stand on its own. As Alasdair MacIntyre puts it, he held that at the "foundation of moral thinking lie beliefs in statements for the truth of which no further reason can be given."[63] MacIntyre goes on to argue that it was this sort of intuitionist view that undermined any claim to objectivity and that prepared the way for the emotivism of twentieth-century moral philosophy. Subsequent moral philosophy, not to mention the moral confusion of our culture, has surely shown that Sidgwick's faith was not well founded and that morality needs a better grounding than he or his heirs have provided. I have been arguing that the theism he rejected, particularly in its orthodox Christian forms, along with its teleological account of human nature and happiness, remains the most viable resource for resolving the problems we have inherited from him.

To summarize, I have advanced three connected arguments for the claim that Christian theology, including the doctrine of heaven, makes better sense of morality than does naturalism. Not only can it account for altruism in a way that reinforces our instinctive admiration for it, unlike evolutionary theory, but it also has a ready explanation for why moral obligation has an objective ground. In the Christian account of things, morality is not tarnished with the sort of deception and illusion that naturalistic accounts rely upon at certain points. Moreover, the doctrine of heaven provides moral philosophy the resources to resolve one of the most difficult problems it has been plagued with for the past several generations, namely, the conflict between egoism and altruism. Each of these arguments has force in its own right, but taken together they provide strong reason to prefer a Christian account of morality to naturalistic ones.

Of course, these arguments do not prove that morality must have a theistic source. While it is relatively easy to show that there is correlation between Christian theology and morality, showing causation is another matter. Evolutionary theory offers its own explanation of morality, and there is much that it can plausibly explain, so it can also be correlated with morality to a significant degree. Both Christian theology and evolutionary theory offer causal accounts of morality, but they make starkly incompatible claims. The question, again, is which of the two makes better sense of the various dimensions of morality. My contention is that Christian theology does so because it accounts for morality more naturally and more fully than does naturalistic evolutionary theory, for reasons I just summarized. Consequently, these reasons support causation as well as correlation.

VII

So much for the moral dilemmas of modernity and postmodernity and the relevance of heaven to their resolution. Let us turn now to the larger issue of meaning that has been suppressed in much recent moral philosophy. The Christian resources we have been discussing allow us to face this issue squarely and to regain what Charles Taylor calls our "moral articulacy," for the Christian vision of what we were made for involves a good of such overwhelming value that the threat of meaninglessness that haunts modernity and postmodernity is altogether banished. This provides further reason to prefer the Christian explanation of morality.

It has often been pointed out that the fact of being created for a purpose is not enough by itself to ensure meaning for our lives. If God's purpose for us is not something positive as well as important, our lives would not be meaningful in any deep sense, even if we performed our purpose very well. Robert Nozick has put a humorous spin on this point: "If the cosmic role of human beings was to provide a negative lesson to some others ('don't act like them') or to provide needed food for passing intergalactic travelers who were important, this would not suit our aspirations—not even if afterwards the intergalactic travelers smacked their lips and said that we tasted good."[64]

The important point here is that a fully meaningful life must be one that suits our aspirations, one that answers to our deepest longings and desires. I argued in the first chapter of this book that some doctrine of heaven follows from the claim that God is good, for a good God would not create us with the aspirations we have and then leave them frustrated and unfulfilled. This argument is only enhanced and enriched by the Christian vision of Trinitarian love. A God whose eternal nature is "mutual and reciprocal gift and reception" could not but deeply love any creatures he made and would surely be committed to fulfilling the natures he had given them.

Since we are made in the very image of God, our nature is such that it cannot be fulfilled by trivial things. As rational beings, we desire to know and understand the truth. As social beings, we long for relationships of mutual love that are honest and intimate. As free moral beings, we aspire to righteousness and integrity. As creative beings, we wish to discern, produce, communicate, and appreciate beauty in its various dimensions. These are the activities and experiences that energize our lives and charge them with meaning and significance. These are the components of meaning cited by the naturalistic writers discussed earlier in this chapter.

But naturalistic accounts of meaning come up short at the end of the day, as I have already argued. In the first place, our experience of the things that bring joy and satisfaction is typically fleeting, fragmentary, and unfulfilling. Second, there is the obvious problem that death cuts our lives short while we still thirst to know and understand more, while we are still learning to love honestly and intimately, while we are underdeveloped morally, and while we are just beginning to appreciate beauty in its endless dimensions. Indeed, all that we have created and cherished in our quest for meaning will finally disintegrate without a trace in the final cremation of the cosmos.

Christianity tells a profoundly different story. It tells us that there is an eternal source behind all the things that give our lives meaning, a source infinitely deeper, richer, and more fascinating than any of the things he has created. Moreover, these things are intimations of the boundless joy that comes from being united with their Author in a relationship of perfect love. This prospect holds out hope for us that our lives can be completely fulfilling and fully meaningful, that they are not destined to end with a sense of incompleteness or frustration.

Consider a specific instance of this notion recently developed by Alvin Plantinga, namely, our experience of erotic love. Surely this is one of the highest of human pleasures, and also one of the most fragile and elusive. Plantinga's interpretation of eros turns on its head the Freudian view that religious desire is actually sublimated sexual desire. As he sees it, our sexual desire points to something much deeper than itself: "Sexual eros with its longing and yearning is a sign and foreshadowing of the longing and yearning for God that will characterize us in our healed and renewed state in heaven; and sexual satisfaction and union, with its transports of ecstasy, is a sign and foreshadowing of the deeper reality of union with God—a union that is at present for the most part obscure to us."[65]

Plantinga points to other experiences that cause us to have this same sort of desire for union. Among these are the haunting beauty of the prairie on a June morning, the glorious aspect of the Cathedral group in the Grand Tetons, the crash and roar of the ocean, a great piece of music magnificently performed, and a kickoff returned the length of the field for a touchdown. In each of these cases, there is a yearning, a sort of nostalgia or a longing for something elusive that seems to be a desire for union with the thing experienced. Plantinga suggests that all of these are "types of longing for God; and the brief but joyous partial fulfillments are a type and foretaste of the fulfillment enjoyed by those who 'glorify God and enjoy him forever.'"[66]

This union with God and enjoyment of him need not be construed in a fashion that excludes other pleasures and relationships. Recall that one of the central issues in the history of heaven is whether it should be thought of theocentrically or anthropocentrically. Given these options, we should certainly opt for the theocentric view. However, I would interpret this to mean that union with God is the central integrating pleasure of heaven and that all other things are enjoyed in such a way that God is recognized as their source and glorified thereby.

The New Testament picture of salvation includes the promise that all of creation will be delivered from the bondage of sin and restored to glory.[67] This would suggest that heaven will not be a timeless experience that is oblivious to the delights of other persons or the beauty of the created order.[68] Rather, we will perceive the presence of God pervading his creation with luminous clarity and will be ever conscious of his love and presence. Whereas in this life we experience only fleeting glimpses of God, glimpses that fill us with longing for an elusive union, in heaven that union will be realized in such a way that even the memories of our former longing will be transfused with the light of his presence. With the past so illumined and the future stretching forward with the prospect of endless joy and satisfaction, happiness will be utterly secure, and the meaning and value of life will be altogether beyond question.

Nothing short of this will suffice to give us what we most deeply crave. The fact that we seek happiness is axiomatic, but I want to sharpen this claim and insist that true happiness is by definition perfect or complete. Clearly, if some partial experience of happiness is desirable, perfect happiness is even more so. Either we have such happiness or we do not. If we do not, then it is something we want, and if we never get it, our lives will end in some degree of frustration. On the other hand, if we have it, we would not want it to end. If it did, then again, our lives would end in frustration. The only alternative to a frustrating end to our lives is perfect happiness, happiness without an end.

Such happiness is not merely a quantitative thing. It is not merely a matter of having the opportunity to enjoy more finite goods for a longer time. Rather, it is a matter of knowing complete satisfaction by achieving union with the boundless source of happiness who lies behind all finite goods. With complete satisfaction comes a corresponding sense that our lives are fully meaningful, as opposed to partially or largely so.

As wonderful as this may sound, some are put off by the very idea of end-less life and even doubt whether eternal happiness is a coherent notion. These critics are haunted by the specter of tedium and charge that any sort of expe-riences we could have, no matter how delightful, would eventually lose their charm. Strictly speaking, therefore, eternal happiness is impossible.[69] In one sense, this is a rather ironic concern and one peculiar to our age. As Carol Zaleski has remarked, "Our ancestors were afraid of Hell; we are afraid of Heaven. We think it will be boring."[70]

Zaleski is little worried about the prospect of boredom, noting that in heaven we will be gazing on the face of the Beloved, an inexhaustible source of fasci-nation. Moreover, she suggests that we have a hard time imagining happiness flowing from a condition of perfection, since that notion has become alien to us. We prefer things open ended, ever changing and developing. But this is to pose a false dilemma as she sees it, for "*true* perfection is evergreen and alive, including within itself everything that we value about change."[71]

Another response to the boredom challenge is similar to Zaleski's sugges-tion about the inexhaustible face of the Beloved, namely, to point to God's infinite nature. Richard Swinburne, a contemporary representative of this view, argues that the only sort of life worth living forever would be one in which continued progress was valuable in its own right but that required an infinite time to complete. Swinburne believes these conditions are met by a relation-ship with God, who "has ever new aspects of himself to reveal, and the bring-ing of others into an ever-developing relationship with God, would provide a life worth living forever."[72] Notice that Swinburne includes a human social dimension to this traditional idea that exploring God's nature will be sufficient to make eternity fascinating for us. That is, the joy of growing in the knowl-edge of God will be enhanced by sharing the experience with other persons who assist each other in the quest to understand and appreciate the endless riches of the divine nature.

An idea worth pondering here is whether the notion of mathematical in-finity may illumine this conception of heaven. It is not insignificant in this regard that Georg Cantor, the mathematician who made revolutionary discoveries about mathematical infinities, was convinced of the soundness of his discover-ies partly because of his beliefs about God's infinite nature.[73] Perhaps mathe-matical infinity is an image of God's infinity and gives us at least some faint idea how the delights of heaven have no end. An interesting twist on this notion is the suggestion that heaven will afford us the opportunity to grow ever closer to God, indeed, as close to God as it is possible to do while remaining finite creatures. We might, in other words, grow infinitely close to God.

Another response to Williams's boredom challenge has been offered by John Martin Fischer. He draws a distinction between self-exhausting pleasures and repeatable ones. An example of the former would be doing something just to prove to oneself that one could do it, such as, for instance, climbing a moun-tain to overcome fear of height. Once the fear is overcome, that sort of plea-sure is exhausted. But other pleasures are intrinsically satisfying and are capable of enjoyment over and over again. Examples here would include listening to a beautiful piece of music, sex, eating fine food, and so on. Fischer's suggestion is that if such pleasures are distributed in appropriate patterns, there is no reason to think they would ever become boring.[74] Fischer's scenario gains plausibility when considered in conjunction with the points just made. That is, a God of infinite creativity could be expected to produce an endless array of patterns of pleasurable activity for the enjoyment of his beloved creatures.

Other arguments could no doubt be mustered, but I suspect they would be powerless to dispel altogether the fear of boredom for those who feel it. Like a dark cloud, it hovers over the hope of eternal joy and threatens to overwhelm it like a storm. One thing is clear. Perfect happiness could not include fear of boredom, for such fear by definition would cast a shadow over joy and compromise it. So if perfect happiness is a reality, it will banish forever the specter of tedium. The fact that we fear the prospect of boredom, even in heaven, shows how far we are from such happiness.

Perhaps at the end of the day, the issue comes down to whether we can believe in God, for the Christian view of God is that he is a being whose very nature is to be ecstatically happy. He has been joyous from eternity and will forever be so.

If such a being exists, perfect happiness is not only a possibility but also a reality. Perhaps our boredom and our fear that it is even more powerful than joy is a symptom of how far we have fallen from God. G. K. Chesterton once observed that children, because they have abundant vitality, want things repeated over and over. They invoke adults to "do it again" until adults are worn out, for adults are no longer able to exult in monotony: "But perhaps God is strong enough to exult in monotony. It is possible that God says every morning, 'Do it again' to the sun; and every evening, 'Do it again' to the moon. . . . It may be that He has the eternal appetite of infancy; for we have sinned and grown old, and our Father is younger than we."[75] Heaven holds out the hope that vitality can be restored and that the weariness that so often accompanies boredom will displaced with boundless energy. Time will not be the measure of growing old but of growing ever more deeply in love with the source of life and vitality.

The question of whether we believe in God is another form of the question of whether the fleeting glimpses of joy we experience in this life are intimations of a deeper wellspring of happiness, or whether they are tantalizing illusions, shadowy hints of a satisfaction that does not really exist. To believe in God is to believe happiness is stronger than boredom. It is to believe that our transient delights in this life are invitations to enter eternal happiness and that the author of the invitations is fully worthy of our trust.

CONCLUSION

Pascal, who was not given to moderation when stating his religious convictions, made the following claim about the crucial significance of the issue of eternal life.

> The immortality of the soul is something of such vital importance to us, affecting us so deeply that one must have lost all feeling not to care about knowing the facts of the matter. All our actions and thoughts must follow such different paths, according to whether there is hope of eternal blessing or not, that the only possible way of acting with sense and judgment is to decide our course in the light of this point, which ought to be our ultimate objective.[1]

As Pascal saw it, everything rides on whether we believe in heaven or not. The choice we face on this matter is a Frostian path that diverges in the woods, and which direction we take will make all the difference.

The argument of this book supports Pascal's claim. It is no exaggeration to say that our path will vary in more ways than we can imagine depending on "whether there is hope of eternal blessing or not." Indeed, we can hardly overstate the importance of the issue of what we can rationally hope for. Who we are, the very essence of our humanity, is defined by our hopes. While human beings seem instinctively prone to soaring aspirations, our hopes in the West have, ever since the onset of modernity, been brought down to earth. Although the "Enlightenment" was a predominantly optimistic movement, it nevertheless lowered the ceiling on our hopes. The kingdom of heaven was replaced by various dreams of earthly utopias. But however splendid these dreams, the ultimate pessimism of naturalism could not be evaded. Russell's final scenario, cited in chapter 7, makes transparent the severe limits of naturalistic optimism.

Postmodernism represents the further erosion of hope. Indeed, one insightful way to characterize the ever elusive notion of postmodernism is to see it as the extension and ascendancy of the nihilistic impulses that were present in modernity from the beginning.[2] With the utopian dreams of modernity shattered and the cultural capital generated by Christianity largely spent, naturalism has been left to its own resources. The result has been a deeply diminished sense of hope.

Consider the path taken by the postmodern traveler. First of all, the traveler himself lacks a clear sense of identity and wonders whether there is any substantive content to the very notion of a self. The moral landscape is uncertain and littered with the remains of various theories and accounts of the good life. But he is dubious of all such truth claims and suspects that they are deceptive attempts to control and manipulate him, for in his view, conflict and the will to power are deeper and more real than love and truth. He can respond to his situation with either despair or playful irony, but his long-term prospects are not good. At the end of his path lies disintegration and oblivion.

What I have defended in this book is a vision of reality that is profoundly more hopeful than secular accounts, whether modern or postmodern. My focus has been on heaven, but as I have pointed out, this doctrine is an integral part of a larger web of beliefs, and it can only be fairly assessed in that setting. Although a full-scale defense of these beliefs is beyond the scope of this book, the arguments I have advanced are an important part of the overall case that can be marshaled in their behalf.

At the center of this larger web is the belief that we, as well as our world, were created by a God who is perfectly good. Whether it is rational to believe in heaven hinges crucially on whether it is rational to believe in such a God. The distinctively Christian account of this claim is the richly suggestive doctrine that God has forever existed as a Trinity of persons in a relationship of mutual love, of reciprocal giving and receiving. He is our true good, and the fact that the One who is perfect love is also supremely powerful is a frontal challenge to the notion that all truth claims are disguised bids for power by self-deceived persons scheming for control.

Consider what it is like to take the path illumined by these truths. To do so is to proceed with a sense of identity and/selfhood rooted in a relationship to one whose eternal nature is personal love. Truth and love are thus immeasurably deeper and more real than deception, conflict, and the will to power. There is an objective truth about how we ought to live and what is good for us. Since the God of truth is also a God of love, we can follow this truth with confidence and trust that to do so will serve our ultimate well-being. Our long-term prospects are as good as they could possibly be since the end we are promised is complete happiness in a perfected relationship with God and other believers that will never end.

I have argued, moreover, that since this relationship is the ultimate fulfillment for all persons, nothing that happens in this life, no matter how terrible, can prevent us from arriving at this end. God's creative grace is such that he can defeat even horrendous evils and make of any life a thing of beauty and joy. Furthermore, given God's perfect goodness and optimal grace, all persons who have ever lived, regardless of when and where they were born, will have every opportunity to achieve the happiness for which they were created. Joy and meaning are not restricted to the fortunate few who have access to the goods and resources of this life. Rather, the true good that brings satisfaction to human beings is available to all persons, and only the persistent refusal of grace can preclude anyone from final joy.

The picture I have described then is not one of merely individualistic hope but one that allows us to maintain hope for other persons and the rest of creation. In the same vein, it does more than provide motivation for personal morality. The belief that God loves all his creatures and desires their ultimate well-being does not give us reason to ignore their present plight. Rather, it gives us power-ful motivation even now to treat others with the love and justice of God. In-deed, this transforms us and prepares us for the life to come in which such love will be perfected. It is no accident that many of those who have taken the hope of eternal life as their paramount concern have also worked diligently to re-form society and bring a foretaste of heaven to life on earth.[3]

In the introduction to this book, I suggested that the transmutation of be-lief in heaven from a vitally positive spiritual and moral source into a decidedly negative one represents a religious and cultural shift of cosmic proportions. I would now add that the shift has had a markedly negative impact. Our attempts to make moral and spiritual sense of our lives without the hope of heaven have left us empty and adrift. The fact that modernity has conjured various secular substitutes for heaven is reluctant testimony to our need for transcendent hope, and the obvious spiritual hunger of postmodernism is further witness to the same reality. We profoundly need to quiet the suspicious suggestions that the desire for eternal life is a morally pernicious notion and to give thoughtful attention to the longing for perfect happiness that persists in our hearts, de-spite our attempts to stifle it.

I want to emphasize that what I am urging here is that this question de-serves the best thinking we can muster. I do not mean to suggest that we should believe in heaven just because it answers to deeply felt needs, but at the same time I would insist that we should not dismiss it out of hand because it does so. Rather, the fact that it answers to our deepest longings deserves respectful attention as we weigh the various factors involved in assessing the Christian vision of reality. Not the least of these factors is the necessity of an adequate account of who we are in the depths of our being.

To recover heaven as a positive moral source is to recover our very humanity. To believe that ultimate reality is Trinitarian love grounds our deepest convictions and warrants our highest aspirations. It enables us to sustain morale with reflective awareness. It allows us to hope that the worst things that happen can yet come to a good end rather than to dread the pros-pect that the best things will come to a bad end. And if it is indeed the Holy Spirit who inspires this hope, it is a hope that will not be disappointed.[4]

NOTES

Introduction

1. St. Augustine, *Confessions*, Trans. R. S. Pine-Coffin (London: Penguin, 1961), 9:10.
2. Ibid., 9:13.
3. Gordon D. Kaufman, *Systematic Theology: A Historicist Perspective* (New York: Scribner, 1968), 471.
4. Rosemary Radford Ruether, *Sexism and God-Talk* (Boston: Beacon Press, 1983), 257.
5. Ibid., 258.
6. G. W. Leibniz, *Theodicy,* ed. Austin Farrer, trans. E. M. Huggard (London: Routledge & Kegan Paul, 1951), 442.
7. John Wesley, *Works* (Nashville: Abingdon, 1985), 1:104–105.
8. John Locke, *The Reasonableness of Christianity*, ed. I. T. Ramsey (Stanford, Calif.: Stanford University Press, 1958), 70.
9. See Charles Taylor, *Sources of the Self: The Making of the Modern Identity* (Cambridge: Harvard University Press, 1989), 235, 241.
10. Colleen McDannell and Bernhard Lang, *Heaven: A History* (New York: Vintage, 1990), 228, 265.
11. Cited by Kenneth L. Woodward, "Heaven," *Newsweek*, March 27, 1989, 53.
12. B. A. Robinson, "Religious Beliefs in the U.S.," www.religioustolerance.org.
13. Woodward, "Heaven," 54.
14. McDannell and Lang, *Heaven: A History*, 336.
15. Ibid., 351–352.
16. Westminster Confession of Faith, 33:2 (*The Book of Confessions,* the United Presbyterian Church in the United States of America, New York, 1967).

17. *The Book of Common Prayer* (Kingsport, Tenn.: Kingsport Press, 1977), 862.

18. McDannell and Lang, *Heaven: A History*, 178.

19. Kenneth Grayston, "Heaven and Hell," *Epworth Review* 19 (1992): 19.

20. W. V. Quine, *The Time of My Life* (Cambridge: MIT Press, 1985), 14.

21. Kaufman, *Systematic Theology*, 468.

22. Taylor, *Sources of the Self*, 313.

23. Ibid., 311.

24. Immanuel Kant, *Critique of Practical Reason*, trans. Lewis White Beck (Indianapolis: Bobbs-Merrill, 1956), 134.

25. Ludwig Feuerbach, *The Essence of Christianity*, trans. George Eliot (New York: Harper Torchbooks, 1957), 174.

26. Sigmund Freud, *The Future of an Illusion*, trans. W. D. Robson-Scott, rev. and ed. James Strachey (Garden City, N.Y.: Doubleday Anchor, 1964), 52–53.

27. Kaufman, *Systematic Theology*, 469–470.

28. See Jerry L. Walls, *Hell: The Logic of Damnation* (Notre Dame, Ind.: University of Notre Dame Press, 1992); Alan E. Bernstein, *The Formation of Hell* (Ithaca, N.Y.: Cornell University Press, 1993), and Jonathan L. Kvanvig, *The Problem of Hell* (New York: Oxford University Press, 1993).

1. Heaven and God's Goodness

1. James Boswell, "An Account of My Last Interview with David Hume, Esq.," appendix A in David Hume, *Dialogues Concerning Natural Religion*, ed. Norman Kemp Smith (Indianapolis: Bobbs-Merrill, 1977), 76.

2. Ibid., 78.

3. David Hume, "My Own Life," supplement to *Dialogues Concerning Natural Religion*, 239.

4. Hume, *Dialogues Concerning Natural Religion*, 215; cf. 202, 214.

5. Ibid., 227.

6. Ibid., 218.

7. Cf. David Hume, *An Inquiry Concerning Human Understanding*, ed. Eric Steinberg (Indianapolis: Hackett, 1977), 98.

8. Hume, *Dialogues*, 193.

9. Ibid., 198.

10. Ibid., 199.

11. Hume, *Inquiry Concerning Human Understanding*, 97.

12. Ibid., 98.

13. Ibid., 99.

14. Hume, *Dialogues Concerning Natural Religion*, 205.

15. Ibid., 211; cf. 204.

16. Ibid., 212.

17. Ibid., 205.

18. David Hume, *An Inquiry Concerning the Principles of Morals*, ed. J. B. Schneewind (Indianapolis: Hackett, 1983), 87. My emphasis.

19. Ibid., 83.

20. Ibid., 88.

21. Robert Merrihew Adams, "Moral Arguments for Theistic Belief," in *Rationality and Religious Belief*, ed. C. F. Delaney (Notre Dame, Ind.: University of Notre Dame Press, 1979), 135.

22. Steven M. Cahn, "Cacodaemony," *Analysis* 37 (1977): 72.

23. Ibid., 73.

24. John King-Farlow, "Cacodaemony and Devilish Isomorphism," *Analysis* 38 (1978): 60–61.

25. Paul Davies, "Physics and the Mind of God," *First Things* 55 (1995): 34.

26. Ibid., 35.

27. Paul Davies, *God and the New Physics* (New York: Simon & Schuster, 1983), 191–197.

28. Ibid., 213.

29. Ibid., 98–99.

30. Richard Swinburne, *Revelation: From Metaphor to Analogy* (Oxford: Clarendon, 1992), 72–74.

31. Cf. Richard Swinburne, *Responsibility and Atonement* (Oxford: Clarendon, 1989), 4–5.

32. Cf. Thomas F. Torrance, *Space, Time, and Resurrection* (Grand Rapids: Eerdmans, 1976).

33. John Wesley, *Works* (Nashville: Abingdon, 1985), 2:510.

2. Heaven, the Nature of Salvation, and Purgatory

1. John Calvin, *Institutes of the Christian Religion*, ed. John T. McNeill, trans. Ford Lewis Battles (Philadelphia: Westminster, 1961), 3.25.11.

2. So named because the central question is whether one can have Jesus as Savior without also having him as Lord. For a concise statement of the issues, see Millard Erickson, "Lordship Theology: The Current Controversy," *Southwestern Journal of Theology* 33 (1991): 5–15.

3. Immanuel Kant, *Religion within the Limits of Reason Alone*, trans. Theodore M. Greene and Hoyt H. Hudson (New York: Harper, 1968), 162.

4. John 8:24, NIV.

5. Richard Robinson, *An Atheist's Values* (Oxford: Clarendon, 1964), 151.

6. Augustine, *The City of God*, trans. Marcus Dods, in *Nicene and Post-Nicene Fathers*, vol 2 (Grand Rapids: Eerdmans, 1977), 22.30.

7. Ibid., 21.15. The quote in the previous paragraph is also from 21.15.

8. Ibid., 19.5.

9. Ibid., 22.30.

10. Thomas Aquinas, *Summa Contra Gentiles*, trans. Vernon J. Bourke (Notre Dame, Ind.: University of Notre Dame Press, 1975), 3.51.6; cf. 3.52.7.

11. Ibid., 3.151.4.

12. Ibid., 3.151.3.

13. Jonathan Edwards, *Works* (New Haven, Conn.: Yale University Press, 1992), 10:475.

14. John Wesley, *Works* (Grand Rapids: Baker, 1979; reprint of the 1872 edition), 10:364.

15. C. S. Lewis, *Mere Christianity* (New York: Macmillan, 1943), 86.

16. John MacArthur, *The Glory of Heaven* (Wheaton, Ill.: Crossway, 1996), 118.

17. Jeffrey Burton Russell, *A History of Heaven* (Princeton, N.J.: Princeton University Press), 6.

18. Alister McGrath, *Iustitia Dei; A History of the Christian Doctrine of Justification* (Cambridge: Cambridge University Press, 1986), 1:184.

19. Ibid., 1:185.

20. Ibid., 2:11.

21. Ibid., 2:37.

22. "The Gift of Salvation," *First Things* 79 (January 1998): 21. The authors of this document also produced earlier the much-discussed statement "Evangelicals and Catholics Together: The Christian Mission in the Third Millennium." A number of conservative evangelicals, particularly in the Reformed tradition, have been critical of these ecumenical initiatives.

23. Philip L. Quinn, "Swinburne on Guilt, Atonement, and Christian Redemption," in *Reason and the Christian Religion*, ed. Alan G. Padgett (Oxford: Clarendon, 1994), 300.

24. Marilyn M. Adams, "Redemptive Suffering: A Christian Solution to the Problem of Evil," in *The Problem of Evil*, ed. Michael L. Peterson (Notre Dame, Ind.: University of Notre Press, 1992), 174.

25. Ibid., 178.

26. Blaise Pascal, *Pensees*, trans. A. J. Krailsheimer (London: Penguin, 1966), no. 192.

27. Ibid., no. 212.

28. Eleonore Stump, "Atonement and Justification," in *Trinity, Incarnation, and Atonement*, ed. Ronald J. Feenstra and Cornelius Plantinga, Jr. (Notre Dame, Ind.: University of Notre Dame Press, 1989), 201.

29. Philip L. Quinn, "Abelard on Atonement: 'Nothing Unintelligible, Arbitrary, Illogical, or Immoral about It,'" in *Reasoned Faith*, ed. Eleonore Stump (Ithaca, N.Y.: Cornell University Press, 1993), 291.

30. Ibid., 295.

31. Ibid., 296.

32. Ibid., 300.

33. Colin Gunton, "The Sacrifice and the Sacrifices: From Metaphor to Transcendental?" in Feenstra and Planting, eds., *Trinity, Incarnation, and Atonement*, 221.

34. Ibid., 223.

35. Richard Swinburne, *Responsibility and Atonement* (Oxford: Clarendon, 1989), 153.

36. Quinn, "Swinburne on Guilt," 292.

37. John E. Hare, *The Moral Gap* (Oxford: Clarendon, 1996), 247.

38. Ibid., 249.

39. Ibid., 213.

40. Pascal, *Pensees*, no. 835.

41. Ibid., no. 840.

42. Cf. New Testament scholar Joel Green's comment that "although Paul's notion of atonement takes sin with utmost seriousness, it is concerned above all with the restoration of the divine-human relationship, not with the mollification of a God angered by masses of misdeeds." Joel B. Green and John T. Carroll, *The Death of Jesus in Early Christianity* (Peabody, Mass.: Hendrickson, 1995), 264. It should be noted that Green does not think penal substitution is taught in the New Testament.

43. John Wesley, *Works* (Nashville: Abingdon, 1986), 3:89–90.

44. Philip Nobile, "The Final Resting Place of Princess Diana," *Chicago Tribune*, August 27, 1998, section 1, p. 13.

45. Zachary J. Hayes, "The Purgatorial View," in *Four Views on Hell*, ed. William Crockett (Grand Rapids: Zondervan, 1992), 95–99.

46. Calvin, *Institutes of the Christian Religion*, 3.5.6.

47. Charles Hodge, *Systematic Theology* (New York: Scribner, 1909), 3:751.

48. Edwards, *Works*, 10:586.

49. John Wesley, *Letters*, ed. John Telford (London: Epworth Press, 1931), 5:39.

For an excellent account of Wesley's soteriology, see Kenneth J. Collins, *The Scripture Way of Salvation, The Heart of John Wesley's Theology* (Nashville: Abingdon, 1997). On Wesley's view of when sanctification occurs, see pp. 177–180.

50. Hayes, "Purgatorial View," 117.

51. David Brown, "No Heaven without Purgatory," *Religious Studies* 21 (1985): 477.

52. Ibid., 450–451.

53. See Jerry L. Walls, *Hell: The Logic of Damnation* (Notre Dame, Ind.: University of Notre Press, 1992), 57–111; Walls, "The Free Will Defense, Calvinism, and the Goodness of God," *Christian Scholar's Review* 13 (1983): 19–33; Walls, "Why Plantinga Must Move from Defense to Theodicy," *Philosophy and Phenomenological Research* 51 (1991): 375–378.

54. Stump, "Atonement and Justification," 191–192.

55. Ibid., 194.

56. Swinburne, *Responsibility and Atonement*, 131.

57. Hayes, "Purgatorial View," 116.

58. Ibid.

59. Peter Kreeft, *Everything You Ever Wanted to Know about Heaven* (San Francisco: Ignatius, 1990), 56–57.

60. Edwards, *Works*, 10:323.

61. Millard J. Erickson, *Christian Theology* (Grand Rapids: Baker, 1985), 3:1184.

62. William J. Crockett, response to Zachary J. Hayes," in Crockett, ed., *Four Views on Hell*, 125.

63. MacArthur, *Glory of Heaven*, 74.

64. Cited in MacArthur, *Glory of Heaven*, 124.

65. MacArthur *Glory of Heaven*, 125.

66. See Hayes, "Purgatorial View," 101–108.

67. Thomas Oden, *Systematic Theology* (San Francisco: Harper, 1992), 3:374.

68. Ironically, MacArthur is a major participant in the Lordship Controversy on the side of those who oppose cheap grace.

69. Gregory of Nyssa, *Ascetical Works*, vol. 58 of *The Fathers of the Church*, trans. Virginia Woods Callahan (Washington, D.C.: Catholic University of America Press, 1967), 241.

70. C. S. Lewis, *The Great Divorce* (New York: Macmillan, 1946), 42; cf. 31.

71. Richard Purtill, *Thinking about Religion* (Englewood Cliffs, N.J.: Prentice-Hall, 1978), 141–143.

72. Ibid., 148.

73. Ibid., 143.

74. Ibid., 152.

75. Kreeft, *Everything You Ever Wanted to Know*, 68–70.

76. These are, of course, the famous words from the answer to question 1 of the *Westminster Shorter Catechism*. The question is: "What is the chief end of man?"

77. I addressed related issues earlier in *Hell: The Logic of Damnation*, 124–133. The position I have taken agrees essentially with James Sennett, "Is There Freedom in Heaven?" *Faith and Philosophy* 16 1999), 69–82.

3. Heaven and Its Inhabitants

1. Timothy C. Morgan, "SBC Targets Clinton, Disney, Jews," *Christianity Today*, July 15, 1996, 66.

2. The issue of Jewish evangelism is complicated by the fact that Judaism has a relationship to Christianity not shared by the other world religions. The common phrase "the Judeo-Christian tradition" is one indication of this fact. It would take us too far afield to engage these complex issues, but I would simply note that the Christian belief that Jesus is the fulfillment of the Old Testament is a parting of the ways of enormous proportions.

3. J. A. DiNoia, "Jesus and the World Religions," *First Things* (June–July, 1995): 25.

4. Ibid., 26.

5. For more on these points, see Jerry L. Walls, "Must the Truth Offend?" *First Things* 84 (1998): 34–37.

6. While some theologians have argued that universalism is the only position that is even possibly true, more often unversalism is defended as a probability or a possibility for which we should hope. On the range of positions on this question, see Jerry L. Walls, *Hell: The Logic of Damnation* (Notre Dame, Ind.: University of Notre Dame Press, 1992), 8–14.

7. For further defense of these assumptions, see Walls, *Hell*.

8. Carl F. H. Henry, "Is It Fair?" in *Through No Fault of Their Own? The Fate of Those Who Have Never Heard*, ed. William V. Crockett and James V. Sigountos (Grand Rapids: Baker, 1991), 254.

9. Roger Nicole, as cited in W. Gary Phillips and R. Douglas Geivett, "Response to Clark H. Pinnock," *Four Views of Salvation in a Pluralistic World*, ed. Dennis L. Ockholm and Timothy R. Phillips (Grand Rapids: Zondervan, 1995), 139.

10. For more on the notion of optimal grace and its relation to the notion of a decisive choice, see Walls, *Hell*, 88–104.

11. Cited in John Hick, "Response to R. Douglas Geivett and W. Gary Phillips," in Phillips and Geivett, eds., *Four Views of Salvation*, 250.

12. Henry, "Is It Fair?" 253.

13. W. Gary Phillips and R. Douglas Geivett, "Conclusion," *Four Views of Salvation*, 260.

14. "A Particularist View: An Evidentialist Approach," *Four Views of Salvation*, 214.

15. Cited in Harold A. Netland, *Dissonant Voices: Religious Pluralism and the Question of Truth* (Grand Rapids: Eerdmans, 1991), 269.

16. See Luis de Molina, *On Divine Foreknowledge*, Part 4 of *The Concordia*, trans. Alfred J. Freddoso (Ithaca, N.Y.: Cornell University Press, 1988).

17. William L. Craig, *The Only Wise God* (Grand Rapids: Baker, 1987), 150–151.

18. Geivett and Phillips also suggest this. See "Conclusion," *Four Views of Salvation*, 270.

19. Willim Hasker, "Middle Knowledge and the Damnation of the Heathen," *Faith and Philosophy* 8 (1991): 382.

20. "Response to Alister E. McGrath," *Four Views of Salvation*, 196.

21. "Response to Clark H. Pinnock," *Four Views of Salvation*, 135.

22. John Wesley, *Works* (Grand Rapids: Baker, 1979; reprint of the 1872 edition), 7:48.

23. Richard Swinburne, *Faith and Reason* (Oxford: Clarendon, 1981), 156.

24. "A Particularist View: A Post-Enlightment Approach," *Four Views of Salvation*, 178.

25. "Response to Clark H. Pinnock," *Four Views of Salvation*, 135.

26. For a fuller defense of these claims, see Walls, *Hell*, 83–138.

27. "A Pluralist View," *Four Views of Salvation*, 43.

28. John Hick, *Disputed Questions in Theology and the Philosophy of Religon* (New Haven, Conn.: Yale University Press, 1993), 171; see also 158–159.

29. John Hick, "Religious Pluralism and Salvation," *Faith and Philosophy* 5 (1988): 371.

30. Kelly James Clark, "Perils of Pluralism," *Faith and Philosophy* 14 (1997): 316.

31. "A Pluralist View," *Four Views of Salvation*, 51.

32. "A Pluralist View," *Four Views of Salvation*, 53.

33. See John Hick, *The Metaphor of God Incarnate* (Louisville, KY: Westminster/ John Knox; 1993).

34. George I. Mavrodes, "A Response to John Hick," *Faith and Philosophy* 14 (1997): 291.

35. Clark, "Perils of Pluralism," 318.

36. "An Inclusivist View," *Four Views of Salvation*, 101.

37. "An Inclusivist View," *Four Views of Salvation*, 107. For a discussion of Lewis's views on this issue and how they compare with traditional evangelical orthodoxy, see Scott R. Burson and Jerry L. Walls, *C. S. Lewis and Francis Schaeffer* (Downers Grove, Ill.: InterVarsity Press, 1998), 226–234.

38. "Conclusion," *Four Views of Salvation*, 82.

39. For a discussion of some of the historical precedents of inclusivism, see John Sanders, *No Other Name: An Investigation into the Destiny of the Unevangelized* (Grand Rapids: Eerdmans, 1992), 131–280.

40. Richard Swinburne, *Responsibility and Atonement* (Oxford: Clarendon, 1989), 176; see also 181.

41. Ibid., 181.

42. See Sanders, *No Other Name*, 181–188. It is worth noting that Sanders labels only the last of these positions "inclusivism." I am using the term more broadly to include any view which allows that persons not evangelized in this life may be saved.

43. Ibid., 164.

44. Paul J. Griffiths, "The Properly Christian Response to Religious Plurality," *Anglican Theological Review* 79 (1997): 24.

45. John 8:42, NIV.

46. Olin Alfred Curtis, *The Christian Faith* (Grand Rapids: Kregel, 1905), 402.

47. E. Stanley Jones, *Gandhi: Portrayal of a Friend* (Nashville: Abingdon, 1948), 8.

48. Ibid., 59.

49. Ibid., 54–55.

50. Alvin Plantinga, "Pluralism: A Defense of Religious Exclusivism," in *The Rationality of Belief and the Plurality of Faith*, ed. Thomas D. Senor (Ithaca, N.Y.: Cornell University Press, 1995), 205.

51. Benjamin Breckinridge Warfield, "The Development of the Doctrine of Infant Salvation," in *Studies in Theology* (New York: Oxford University Press, 1932), 411–446. For a more recent discussion of infant salvation and damnation, see Sanders, *No Other Name*, 287–305.

52. Warfield, "Doctrine of Infant Salvation," 441.

53. Ibid., 433. Warfield is citing Spanheim in this argument.

54. David K. Clark, "Warfield, Infant Salvation, and the Logic of Salvation," *Journal of the Evangelical Theological Society* 27 (1984): 462.

55. Wesley defends animal redemption in his sermon "The General Deliverance," in *Works* (Nashville: Abingdon, 1985), 2:436–450.

56. Rom. 8:18–25.

57. C. S. Lewis, *The Problem of Pain* (New York: Macmillan, 1962), 140.

58. For a contemporary defense of animal souls, see Richard Swinburne, *The Evolution of the Soul* (Oxford: Clarendon, 1986), esp. 180–196.

59. See Stephen H. Webb, *On God and Dogs: A Christian Theology of Compassion for Animals* (Oxford: Oxford University Press, 1998), 167–184.

4.   Heaven, Trinity, and Personal Identity

1. The full text of this song can be found in many popular songbooks and hymnals.

2. Thomas V. Morris, *The Logic of God Incarnate* (Ithaca, N.Y.: Cornell University Press, 1986), 64. For a similar methodological argument that gives epistemic priority to belief in the Trinity, see Bruce D. Marshall, *Trinity and Truth* (Cambridge: Cambridge University Press, 2000).

3. Vladimir Lossky, *The Mystical Theology of the Eastern Church* (London: James Clarke & Co., 1957), 65.

4. See Wolfhart Pannenberg, *Basic Questions in Theology*, trans. George H. Kehm (Philadelphia: Fortress, 1971), 2:228-231.

5. Cornelius Plantinga, Jr., "Social Trinity and Tritheism," in *Trinity, Incarnation, and Atonement*, ed. Ronald J. Feenstra and Cornelius Plantinga, Jr. (Notre Dame, Ind.: University of Notre Dame Press, 1989), 29.

6. See Alvin Plantinga, *Warrant and Proper Function* (Oxford: Oxford University Press, 1993), 19.

7. Plantinga, *Warrant and Proper Function*, 55.

8. See Morris, *Logic of God Incarnate*, 111–120.

9. Plantinga, *Warrant and Proper Function*, 61.

10. Antony Flew, "Locke and the Problem of Personal Identity," in *Readings in the Philosophy of Religion: An Analytic Approach*, ed. Baruch A. Brody (Englewood Cliffs, N.J.: Prentice-Hall, 1974), 640.

11. Blaise Pascal, *Pensees*, trans. A. J. Krailsheimer (London: Penguin, 1966), no. 651.

12. Richard Swinburne, *The Evolution of the Soul* (Oxford: Clarendon, 1986), 166.

13. For a description and assessment of traditional accounts of dualism, as well as more recent versions of dualism that attempt to avoid the problems of those traditional accounts, see William Hasker, *The Emergent Self* (Ithaca, N.Y.: Cornell University Press, 1999).

14. Luke 23:43, NIV.

15. For a Christian materialist interpretation of this text and other dualist "proof texts," see Peter van Inwagen, "Dualism and Materialism: Athens and Jerusalem?" *Faith and Philosophy* 12 (1995): 480–485. This issue of *Faith and Philosophy* is devoted to the mind-body problem and includes excellent articles defending both dualism and materialism.

16. Joel B. Green, "'Bodies—That Is, Human Lives': A Re-examination of Human Nature in the Bible," *Whatever Happened to the Soul? Scientific and Theological Portraits of Human Nature*, ed. Warren S. Brown, Nancey Murphy, and A. Newton Malony (Minneapolis: Fortress, 1998), 153–154.

17. Ben Witherington III, *Conflict and Community in Corinth: A Socio-Rhetorical Commentary on 1 and 2 Corinthians* (Grand Rapids: Eerdmans, 1995), 391.

18. John Perry, *A Dialogue on Personal Identity and Immortality* (Indianapolis: Hackett, 1978), 16–17.

19. Joshua Hoffman and Gary Rosenkrantz, "Are Souls Unintelligible?" in *Philosophical Perspectives, 5, Philosophy of Religion, 1991*, ed. James E. Tomberlin (Atascadero, Calif.: Ridgeview, 1991), 193.

20. See Swinburne, *Evolution of the Soul*, 161.

21. John Searle, *Minds, Brains, and Science* (Cambridge: Harvard University Press, 1984), 92. See also Keith Campbell, *Body and Mind* (Notre Dame, Ind.: University of Notre Dame Press, 1980), 90.

22. Stephen T. Davis, *Risen Indeed: Making Sense of the Resurrection* (Grand Rapids: Eerdmans, 1993), 136.

23. Ibid., 119–123.

24. Another option I have not dealt with is the fascinating, but somewhat idiosyncratic, view of Peter van Inwagen concerning how God maintains personal identity. Van Inwagen has suggested that at death, God preserves our corpses, contrary to all appearances, and then replaces them with a simulacrum that then rots or is otherwise destroyed. Or perhaps he preserves only the brain and central nervous system in this fashion. For discussion and critique of this view, see Hasker, *The Emergent Self*, 222–231.

25. I have not addressed the issue of what constitutes spatiotemporal continuity in a human body. For an excellent treatment of this issue, see Philip L. Quinn, "Personal Identity, Bodily Continuity, and Resurrection," *International Journal for Philosophy of Religion* 9 (1978): 101–113.

26. Alvin Plantinga, "Self-Profile," in *Alvin Plantinga: Profiles 5*, ed. James E. Tomberlin and Peter van Inwagen (Dordrecht: D. Reidel, 1985), 92.

27. Nicholas Wolterstorff, *Lament for a Son* (Grand Rapids: Eerdmans, 1987), 33.

28. Alasdair MacIntyre, *Three Rival Versions of Moral Inquiry* (Notre Dame, Ind.: University of Notre Dame Press, 1990), 199.

29. Ibid., 199.

30. Flew, "Locke and the Problem," 623.

31. Colin Gunton, *The One, the Three, and the Many* (Cambridge: Cambridge University Press, 1993), 207.

32. Ibid., 191.

33. Green, "Bodies—That Is, Human Lives," 9.

34. Gal. 1:23, NIV.

35. Gal. 2:20, NIV.

36. Gal. 6:17, NIV.

37. John 17:21, NIV.

38. John Hick, *Death and Eternal Life* (Louisville, Ky.: Westminster John Knox, 1994), 462.

39. Ibid., 410–411.

40. Here I follow Aquinas. See his discussion in *Summa Theologica*, supplement to the Third Part, Q 86, Art. 1. Aquinas also distinguishes between scars that are due to defect and scars that are received for the sake of the faith or for justice and argues that the latter will increase their own joy as well as that of others in heaven. He cites Augustine, who held that such scars would make their recipients more glorious. "A certain beauty will shine in them, a beauty though in the body, yet not of the body but of virtue" (supplement to Third Part, Q 82, Art. 1). The passage from Augustine appears in *City of God*, 22. 19.

41. Friedrich Nietzsche, *Beyond Good and Evil*, trans. Marianne Cowan (Chicago: Henry Regnery, 1955), no. 68.

5. Heaven and the Problem of "Irredeemable" Evil

1. G. Richard Hoard, *Alone among the Living* (Athens, Ga.: University of Georgia Press, 1994), 60.

2. Ibid., 158.

3. David Hume, *Dialogues Concerning Natural Religion*, ed. Norman Kemp Smith (Indianapolis: Bobbs-Merrill, 1977), 199.

4. Fyodor Dostoyevsky, *The Brothers Karamazov*, trans. Constance Garnett (New York: Modern Library), 254.

5. Marilyn McCord Adams, *Horrendous Evils and the Goodness of God* (Ithaca, N.Y.: Cornell University Press, 1999), 27–28.

6. Cited in Martin Tady and John Railey, "A Test of Faith," *Winston-Salem (N.C.) Journal*, January 18, 1998, A10.

7. Nicholas Wolterstorff, *Lament for a Son* (Grand Rapids: Eerdmans, 1987), 46–47.

8. This reminds us that the role of theodicy is not the same as that of pastoral support. Faith does not depend on our making sense of evil or showing how it is compatible with God's goodness. For many people, faith is sustained by the practices of the believing community, including particularly the practice of lament. This is not to deny, however, that theodicy can also play a role in sustaining faith for many persons.

9. John Wesley, *Works* (Nashville: Abingdon, 1986), 3:101.

10. Ibid., 3:104–105.

11. Lewis explores these themes in *The Four Loves* (New York: Harcourt Brace Jovanovich, 1960).

12. See Romans 8.

13. Wolterstorff, *Lament for a Son*, 86.

14. Adams, *Horrendous Evils*, 147. In an earlier essay, Adams made the same point by saying that "strictly speaking, there will be no *balance* to be struck." See her "Redemptive Suffering: A Christian Solution to the Problem of Evil," in *The Problem of Evil: Selected Readings*, ed. Michael L. Peterson (Notre Dame, Ind.: University of Notre Dame Press, 1992), 183.

15. Adams writes that she eschews "justification of horrors for the double reason that (as Ivan Karamazov contends) horrors are 'too big' to be rectified by justice . . . and God is 'too big' to be networked into our systems of rights and obligations." *Horrendous Evils*, 188; cf. 157–158.

16. Adams understands this to mean that all persons will be saved and will in fact come to see their lives as good things. She argues that God will override freedom if necessary to save all persons. See *Horrendous Evils*, 49, 103–104, 191. I disagree with Adams about God's willingness to override freedom, and I would accordingly argue that all that is necessary for God's perfect goodness is that God will make it possible for all persons to view their lives as great goods. Some may refuse the grace that makes it possible to own their lives as great goods.

17. Rom. 8:18, RSV.

18. 2 Cor. 4:17, NIV.

19. 2 Cor. 11:22–33.

20. Adams, "Redemptive Suffering," 185.

21. Wolterstorff, *Lament for a Son*, 81.

22. Ibid., 97.

23. Ibid., 73.

24. C. S. Lewis, *A Grief Observed* (New York: Bantam, 1976), 61. For discussion of this point, see Scott R. Burson and Jerry L. Walls, *C. S. Lewis and Francis Schaeffer: Lessons for a New Century from the Most Influential Apologists of Our Time* (Downers Grove, Ill.: InterVarsity Press, 1998), 222–224.

25. As Alfred J. Freddoso puts it, "[S]ome metaphysically contingent states of affairs become necessary simply by virtue of being fixed unalterably as part of the history of

the world, regardless of their causal ancestry." For further discussion of these issues, see Freddoso's introduction to his translation of Luis de Molina, *On Divine Foreknowledge* (Ithaca, N.Y.: Cornell University Press, 1988). The quote here is on p. 13.

26. Elizabeth Templeton, "On Undoing the Past," in *The Strangeness of God* (London: Arthur James, 1993), 43.

27. Patrick Sherry, "Redeeming the Past," *Religious Studies* 34 (1998): 166.

28. Cited in Sherry, "Redeeming the Past," 172.

29. Adams, *Horrendous Evils*, 149.

30. Sherry, "Redeeming the Past," 170.

31. Hoard, *Alone among the Living*, 131.

32. Ibid., 180.

33. See Hoard, *Alone among the Living*, 124–125.

34. C. S. Lewis, *Mere Christianity* (New York: Macmillan, 1943), 87.

35. Hoard, *Alone among the Living*, 207.

36. Ibid., 213.

37. Ibid., 215.

38. John Hick, *Death and Eternal Life* (Louisville, Ky.: Westminster John Knox Press, 1994), 165.

39. Tady and Railey, "Test of Faith," A10.

40. For the record, I am glad both for the tournament and for all of Indiana's victories over Carolina.

41. William Hasker, "On Regretting the Evils of This World," in Peterson, ed., *Problem of Evil*, 156.

42. Ibid., 159.

43. Ibid., 162.

44. Rev. 21:4.

6. Heaven and Visions of Life after Life

1. John Littlejohn, "Journal of John Littlejohn," transcribed by Annie L. Winstead. The transcript is from Kentucky Wesleyan College, where the original and a microfilm version are kept. During the war of 1812, President James Madison—who had to flee Washington—gave Littlejohn the original Declaration of Independence and other priceless documents for safekeeping.

2. Cited in Raymond A. Moody, Jr., M.D., *Life After Life* (New York: Bantam, 1976), 63–64.

3. Betty Malz, *My Glimpse of Eternity* (Carmel, N.Y.: Guideposts, 1977), 88.

4. Allan Kellehear, *Experiences near Death* (New York: Oxford University Press, 1996), 76.

5. Ibid., 91.

6. Carol Zaleski, *Otherworld Journeys: Accounts of Near Death Experience in Medieval and Modern Times* (New York: Oxford University Press, 1987), 99.

7. Susan Blackmore, *Dying to Live* (Buffalo, N.Y.: Prometheus, 1993), 4–5.

8. Moody, *Life after Life*, xii.

9. Bruce Greyson, "The Near Death Experience Scale: Construction, Reliability, and Validity," *Journal of Nervous and Mental Disease* 171 (1983): 369–375.

10. Bruce Greyson, "Near-Death Encounters with and without Near-Death Experiences: Comparitive NDE Scale Profiles," *Journal of Near-Death Studies* 8 (1990): 151–161.

11. Zaleski, *Otherworld Journeys*, 189.

12. Moody, *Life after Life*, 107.

13. Richard John Neuhaus, "Born toward Dying," *First Things* 100 (February 2000): 19.

14. See William M. Alnor, *Heaven Can't Wait* (Grand Rapids: Baker Books, 1996).

15. Zaleski, *Otherworld Journeys*, 190.

16. Ibid., 187.

17. Ibid., 184.

18. Ibid., 191–192.

19. Ibid., 192.

20. Ibid., 198.

21. Ibid., 199.

22. Carol Zaleski, *The Life of the World to Come: Near Death Experience and Christian Hope* (New York: Oxford University Press, 1996), 34.

23. Ibid., 33.

24. Ibid., 35.

25. Blackmore, *Dying to Live*, 138.

26. See Blackmore, *Dying to Live*, 150–164.

27. It is worth noting that Zaleski has defended life after death more strongly in her recent Ingersoll Lecture on Immortality at Harvard Divinity School. See her "In Defense of Immortality," *First Things* 105 (September 2000): 36–42.

28. Alvin Plantinga, *Warrant and Proper Function* (New York: Oxford University Press, 1993), 19.

29. Alvin Plantinga, "Reason and Belief in God," in *Faith and Rationality*, ed. Alvin Plantinga and Nicholas Wolterstorff (Notre Dame, Ind.: University of Notre Dame Press, 1983), 78–82.

30. Plantinga, *Warrant and Proper Function*, 23.

31. William P. Alston, *Perceiving God: The Epistemology of Religious Experience* (Ithaca, N.Y.: Cornell University Press, 1991), 1.

32. Ibid., 223.

33. Ibid., 177.

34. Ibid., 171.

35. Ibid., 55.

36. Ibid., 232.

37. Ibid., 274.

38. Ibid., 304.

39. Ibid., 17–20.

40. For data on this issue, see Blackmore, *Dying to Live*, 32–33.

41. Alston, *Perceiving God*, 59.

42. Ibid., *Perceiving God*, 66.

43. See 2 Cor. 12:1–4. The account of his stoning appears in Acts 14:19–20.

44. Alston, *Perceiving God*, 98.

45. See, for example, Maurice Rawlings, *Beyond Death's Door* (Nashville: Thomas Nelson, 1978).

46. J. P. Moreland and Gary R. Habermas, *Immortality: The Other Side of Death* (Nashville: Thomas Nelson, 1992), 92–93.

47. Alston, *Perceiving God*, 270. It is also worth noting that Alston suggests this strategy in response to John Hick's charge that his position is afflicted with arbitrariness. See his "Response to Hick" in *Faith and Philosophy* 14 (1997): 287–288.

48. Alston, *Perceiving God*, 94.

49. Blackmore, *Dying to Live*, 175.

50. According to William J. Serdahely, Blackmore's bird's-eye hypothesis is based on very tenuous evidence. He advances this criticism along with others in his article "Questions for the 'Dying Brain Hypothesis,'" *Journal of Near-Death Studies* 15 (1996): 41–53.

51. Blackmore, *Dying to Live*, 182.

52. Ibid., 213–235.

53. For criticism of Blackmore on this point, see Patrick Glynn, *God: The Evidence* (Rocklin, Calif.: Forum, 1997), 113–120.

54. Blackmore, *Dying to Live*, 182

55. Ibid., 48.

56. Ibid., 253–254.

7. Heaven, Morality, and the Meaning of Life

1. Victor Hugo, *Les Miserables* (London: Standard Book Co., n.d.), 1:263.

2. Ibid.

3. Ibid., 1:265.

4. Bertrand Russell, *Why I Am Not a Christian* (New York: Simon & Schuster, 1957), 107.

5. Charles Taylor, *Sources of the Self: The Making of the Modern Identity* (Cambridge: Harvard University Press, 1989), 89.

6. James Rachels, *Created from Animals: The Moral Implications of Darwinism* (Oxford: Oxford University Press, 1990), 205.

7. George Mavrodes, "Religion and the Queerness of Morality," in *Rationality, Religious Belief, and Moral Commitment,* ed. Robert Audi and William Wainwright (Ithaca, N.Y.: Cornell University Press, 1986), 216.

8. Ibid., 218.

9. Ibid., 220.

10. John E. Hare, *The Moral Gap* (Oxford: Clarendon, 1996), 23.

11. See Hare, *The Moral Gap*, 91–96.

12. For helpful historical analysis, see David W. Lutz, "The Emergence of the Dualism of Practical Reason in Post-Hobbesian British Moral Philosophy" (Ph.D. diss. University of Notre Dame, 1994).

13. Henry Sidgwick, *The Methods of Ethics* (Chicago: University of Chicago Press, 1962), 404, n. 1.

14. Ibid., 405.

15. Ibid., 507–508.

16. John Rawls, *A Theory of Justice* (Cambridge: Harvard University Press, 1971), 136.

17. Lutz, "Emergence of the Dualism," 8.

18. Walter Shapiro, "What's Wrong," *Time*, May 25, 1987, 17.

19. Ezra Bowen, "Looking to Its Roots," *Time*, May 25, 1987, 29.

20. John Milbank, "The Ethics of Self-Sacrifice," *First Things* 91 (March 1999): 34.

21. For a helpful discussion of these theories, see Jeffrey P. Schloss, "Evolutionary Accounts of Altruism and the Problem of Goodness by Design," in *Mere Creation*, ed. William B. Dembski (Downers Grove, Ill.: InterVarsity Press, 1999), 236–261.

22. Michael Ruse and Edward O. Wilson, "The Evolution of Ethics," in *Religion and the Natural Sciences: The Range of Engagement*, ed. James E. Huchingson (Fort Worth, Tex.: Harcourt Brace Jovanovich, 1993), 310.

23. Ibid.

24. See Hare, *Moral Gap*, 170–174.

25. Edward O. Wilson, "The Biological Basis of Morality," *Atlantic Monthly*, April 1998, 54.

26. Ibid., 70.

27. For a discussion of these points, see Taylor, *Sources of the Self*, 14–32.

28. Robert W. Jensen, "How the World Lost Its Story," *First Things* 36 (October 1993): 21.

29. Ibid.

30. Cited in John Polkinghorne, "Eschatology: Some Questions and Some Insights from Science," in *The End of the World and the Ends of God*, ed. John Polkinghorne and Michael Welker (Harrisburg, Pa.: Trinity Press International, 2000), 32.

31. A minority position that has been held by some naturalistic scientists is that the universe will end in a "big crunch" in which the universe will collapse upon itself. The most important cosmological discovery of 1998 was that the rate of expansion of the universe is accelerating, which supports a forever expanding universe rather than an eventual collapse. For an account of this discovery and some of the theories and speculations surrounding it, see Jeremiah P. Ostriker and Paul J. Steinhardt, "The Quintessential Universe," *Scientific American* 284, no. 1 (January 2001): 46–53.

32. *Lexington (Ky.) Herald-Leader*, May 3, 1997.

33. For essays on both sides of these debates, see John Martin Fischer, ed., *The Metaphysics of Death* (Stanford, Calif.: Stanford University Press, 1993).

34. Thomas Nagel, "Death," in Fischer, ed., *Metaphysics of Death*, 69.

35. Carl Sagan, *Billions and Billions* (New York: Random House, 1997), 215.

36. Ann Druyan, epilogue to Sagan, *Billions and Billions*, 225.

37. Richard Taylor, "The Meaning of Life," in *The Meaning of Life*, 2d ed., ed. E. D. Klemke (Oxford: Oxford University Press, 2000), 175.

38. See Taylor, "Meaning of Life," 173–174.

39. E. D. Klemke, "Living without Appeal: An Affirmative Philosophy of Life," in Klemke, ed., *Meaning of Life*, 197.

40. Cited in Sagan, *Billions and Billions*, 221.

41. Russel, *Why I Am not a Christian*, 109.

42. Thomas Nagel, "The Absurd," in Klemke, ed., *Meaning of Life*, 183.

43. Ibid., 185.

44. Druyan, epilogue to Sagan, *Billions and Billions*, 228.

45. Frank J. Tipler, *The Physics of Immortality* (New York: Anchor Books, 1994), 8.

46. Ibid., xv.

47. Ibid., 104.

48. Tipler has borrowed this phrase from Pierre Teilhard de Chardin.

49. Recall that the "big crunch" theory is a minority position that has been dealt an apparently fatal blow by recent discoveries. See note 31 above.

50. Tipler, *Physics of Immortality*, 57.

51. John Polkinghorne, *Belief in God in an Age of Science* (New Haven, Conn.: Yale University Press, 1998), 20–21.

52. John Polkinghorne, *The Faith of a Physicist* (Princeton, N.J.: Princeton University Press, 1994), 165. For a detailed and telling critique of Tipler, see also M. A. Corey, *The Natural History of Creation* (Lanham, Md.: University Press of America, 1995), 204–272. See also Ted Peters, "The Physical Body of Immortality," *CTNS Bulletin* 15, no. 2 (Spring 1995), 1–20.

53. Peter Singer, "Ethics and Sociobiology," in Huchingson, ed., *Religion and the Natural Sciences*, 321.

54. Taylor, *Sources of the Self*, 94.

55. C. S. Lewis, *The Abolition of Man* (New York: Macmillan, 1947), 39.

56. I have in mind here *The Matrix*. The hero of this movie, of course, chooses truth over life in the matrix, and his choice is depicted as an admirable although difficult one. But the point remains that such a choice may not be preferable, let alone obligatory, in a naturalistic world.

57. Colin Gunton, "The Sacrifice and the Sacrifices," in *Trinity, Incarnation, and Atonement*, ed. Ronald J. Feenstra and Cornelius Plantinga, Jr. (Notre Dame, Ind.: University of Notre Dame Press, 1989), 215.

58. Ibid., 221.

59. The New Testament is unabashed in teaching that obedience and sacrifice will not go unrewarded. For just one example, see Matt. 19:27–30.

60. Pope John Paul II, *The Splendor of Truth* (Boston: St. Paul Books and Media), 114.

61. Milbank, "Ethics of Self-Sacrifice," 38.

62. Heb. 5:7; 12:1–3.

63. Alasdair MacIntyre, *After Virtue*, 2d ed. (Notre Dame, Ind.: University of Notre Dame Press, 1984), 65.

64. Robert Nozick, *Philosophical Explanations* (Cambridge, Mass.: Belknap Press, 1981), 586.

65. Alvin Plantinga, *Warranted Christian Belief* (Oxford: Oxford University Press, 2000), 317.

66. Ibid., 318. Plantinga's quote is, of course, from the Westminster Shorter Catechism.

67. Rom. 8:18–25.

68. Polkinghorne points out that resurrected bodies will be not only located in "space" but also immersed in "time." In view of this, we should conceive our future as everlasting rather than as timeless eternity. See Polkinghorne, "Eschatology," 39–40. For further theological arguments for temporality in heaven, see in the same volume Miroslav Volf, "Enter into Joy! Sin, Death, and the Life of the World to Come," 265–278.

69. Probably the most famous such argument is that of Bernard Williams in his article "The Makropulos Case: Reflections on the Tedium of Immortality." This article is reprinted in Fischer, ed., *Metaphysics of Death*, 73–92.

70. Carol Zaleski, "In Defense of Immortality," *First Things* 105 (September 2000): 42. This essay is adapted from her Ingersoll Lecture on Immortality, given at Harvard Divinity School.

71. Ibid.

72. Richard Swinburne, *Faith and Reason* (Oxford: Clarendon, 1981), 135. See also Swinburne's *Responsibility and Atonement* (Oxford: Clarendon, 1989), 188–190.

73. See Timothy J. Pennings, "Infinity and the Absolute: Insights into Our World, Our Faith, and Ourselves," *Christian Scholar's Review* 23, no. 2 (December 1993): 159–180.

74. John Martin Fischer, "Why Immortality Is Not So Bad," *International Journal of Philosophical Studies* 2, no. 2, 262–267. Fischer offers other arguments against Williams in the remainder of this essay.

75. Gilbert K. Chesterton, *Heretics/Orthodoxy* (Nashville: Thomas Nelson, 2000), 218. This quote is from *Orthodoxy*.

Conclusion

1. Blaise Pascal, *Pensees*, trans. A. J. Krailsheimer (London: Penguin, 1966), no. 427. Of course, the Christian hope of immortality includes resurrection of the body, not merely survival of the soul. Pascal's comment should be read in that light.

2. See Lloyd Spencer, "Postmodernism, Modernity, and the Tradition of Dissent," in *The Routledge Critical Dictionary of Postmodern Thought*, ed. Stuart Sim (New York: Routledge, 1999), 161–162.

3. For a classic defense of this claim, see Timothy L. Smith, *Revivalism and Social Reform* (New York: Harper & Row, 1957). By contrast, it is worth noting that sociobiology tends to undermine motivation for social reform. It offers a genetic explanation for various human behavior and practices, including ones that are unjust. All such behaviors "were selected for" in the course of evolution and are thus hardwired into our nature. See Tom Bethell, "Against Sociobiology," *First Things* 109 (January 2001): 18–24.

4. See Rom. 5:1–5.

INDEX